After the EAGLES Came

A Farmer's Journey

GEORGIA BARG

ARNICA PRESS

Published by ARNICA PRESS
www.ArnicaPress.com

Copyright © 2022 Georgia Barg
On the Cover: Éowyn and the Red Poll Cattle
Photo by Georgia Barg

www.LearnToFarm.ca
www.GeorgiaBarg.com

This work is a memoir. It reflects the author's present recollections of her experiences over a period of years. Certain names, locations, and identifying characteristics may have been changed, and certain individuals are composites. Dialogue and events have been recreated from memory and, in some cases, have been compressed to convey the substance of what was said or what occurred.

ISBN: 978-1-955354-30-1

For Clayton
I'm the shadows, you're the stars...

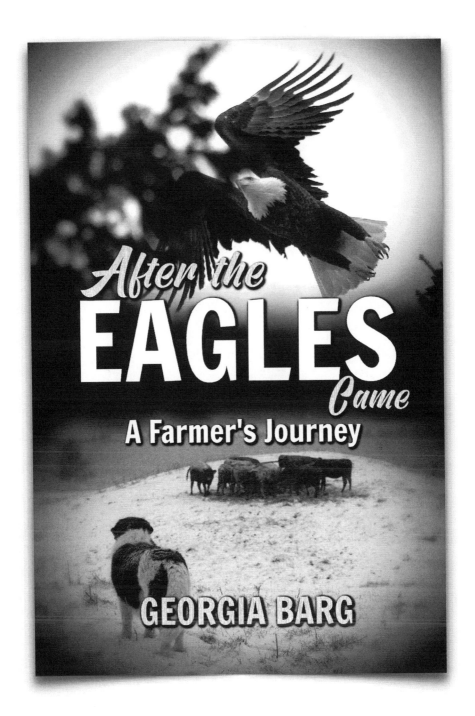

TABLE OF CONTENTS

Introduction.. 11

Don't Move!...13
Born in a Concrete Jungle 19
First Flight..27
Best Christmas Present, Ever 33
You Win Some, You Lose Some 39
Digger, My Trusty Steed...45
BBs, My Royal Sheep 57
Hohl in One..61
That is a Mouthful!...69
Once Burned, Two Die...75
Hanz & Franz Fly the Coop 79
Wyatt, The Comedian 83
Strait to Texas...89
The Adventures of Wyatt & Harley 95
Nobody's Grandma, Ivy 105
When the Clock Struck Midnight 109
Spiritual Awakening Notwithstanding Devastation.............111
Learning To Fly...121
For Whom the Belle Told..127
A Match Made in Heaven..133
Seeing God..137
Worth the Wait..143

Manifesting My Vision 149
Welcome, Precious Child 161
Oreos with Butter? 165
The Death of Comedy 171
In Search of Protection 179
Tails of Fancy 183
Éowyn, The Shieldmaiden 189
Gandalf, The Wizard 195
Araglas, My Champion 201
The Art of Letting Go 209
No Rain in Spain, Only Snow 213
Seeing Double 221
Éowyn's Dystocia 225
Brandy Waves 231
The Trouble with Goats 237
Thorin Embraces His New Identity 249
Saving My Shieldmaiden 255
The Miracle Sixteen 265
The Eagles Arrive 277
The Red Polls of North Carolina 283
A Light in my Dark World 293
Alive? Yes. Living? No 299
Donnamira's Devastation 305
"One side is good enough for me!" 313
Writing the Road to Recovery 321
The Life I'd Known Was Over 327
In the Fog with Thorin 333
It was the Best and Worst of Times 341
The Season of Darkness 355
It was the Spring of Hope 359
Change of Fortune 365
The Jumping Spider 371

Becoming Georgia 377
First Champion Argibel 385
Trek to the Tree 389
Tensions Were Running High 395
Angels Among Us..401
Digger, My Best Mate 407
Not a Happy Camper 415
Going Home...427
Home of the Eagles 433
Learn to Farm with Georgia 439

Acknowledgments...451
About the Author...457

INTRODUCTION

This book is written for those who dream of getting back-to-the-land and wish to reconnect with the natural world. I wrote this book for all of you, who desire to become more self-sufficient, grow your own food and raise animals. My goal is to help boost the confidence of all aspiring farmers and homesteaders, so they never give up on their dreams!

In 2018, my life as a farmer and breeder of Pyrenean Mastiffs was abruptly halted, when my son and I were in a tragic accident. Life as we knew it, became like a jigsaw puzzle tossed onto the floor. It was through the process of writing this book, that I was able to put the puzzle back together again. The pieces no longer fit the way they once did, but I found a way to create a new picture – a new life. By not giving up, I was able to stay true to my dreams and find healing for my mind, body and spirit.

If you dream of farming, glean what you can from the knowledge and stories shared upon these pages. I invite you to fly high like the Eagles and never give up on your dreams!

Don't Move!

T he sun rose in the morning like it always did; the beautiful spring day was off to a good start. My day began unremarkably, doing my farm chores and taking care of my homeschooled son. I would never have guessed that April 12, 2018 would become a day that I would never forget. We were driving home from town, along the river road, when I noticed a large figure, above and off to my right. Quite close to the road, perched in a leafless tree, was a very large, juvenile Bald Eagle. Its white plume was mottled with brown on its head, I suspected it to be about three years old. The bird was alert and it watched my every move; I slowed down as I drove past. It felt like it was looking straight into me. My eight-year-old son, Clayton, was quietly reading a new book that he had just picked out at the library. He was startled when I yelled "Eagle!" while pointing into the tree. I thought about that Eagle for the rest of the short journey to our farm.

After a brief stop at home to hook-up the hay wagon, we left on our journey to pick up raw dog food at the butcher's and planned to get bales of straw on the way back. As we started driving, I was going to listen to one of my audiobooks, but my son had other ideas.

"No noise," he had said. "I'm trying to read!"

As we drove along in complete silence, we passed through a small native community town, about seven minutes from our place. I was paying extra attention as I was driving through town, because I was hauling an empty sixteen-foot flat rack wooden wagon behind my truck. It was about four o'clock in the afternoon when we were exiting the community.

I was looking way down the road, because there was no one in front of me. I noticed a black car approaching in the oncoming lane. The car started drifting over the middle line, barreling towards us at high speed. My mind immediately started whirling; what are the options? I glanced briefly to my right and saw a small shoulder and a very deep ditch. With precious cargo onboard and a long wagon following behind; the ditch was not an option. I couldn't go into the opposing lane, could I? Well, first off it is illegal and second, I'd be in the way when the driver quickly made their course correction! I've seen many cars cross a tire over the line and they abruptly go back. Why would this be any different? I slowed down and gave them more space to get back on their side.

The oncoming Chevy Malibu never wavered in its speed or direction. It all happened so fast! The car was already completely in our lane, directly in front of us when I alerted Clayton. "We are going to be hit!"

He looked up from his book to see the car directly ahead, only a few feet from us.

In an unconscious effort to protect my little boy, Clayton says that I cranked the wheel to the right. I received the full brunt of the car in the driver's side front corner. I heard the loud crunch of the metal as the two vehicles collided. The front corner buckled and Clayton says the floor under my feet exploded. We were pushed at high speed over into the ditch and the wagon followed close behind, landing on the back of the truck. Everything went black.

When the truck had settled in the ditch, part way over on her side – Clayton unbuckled and sprang up with the velocity of a jack-in-the-box. He wanted out. It was the most welcomed sight ever! We had survived!

"I'm hurt!" I exclaimed. I was unaware to what extent. This was my very first accident – I had no idea even what to expect.

Growing up, I watched *Dukes of Hazzard* and knew smoke means you are about to blow up! I smelled and saw smoke! Clayton was right - we had to get out!

People were on the scene very quickly. No sooner had we figured that the doors would not open, there was a rap on the window and a man said, "Help is on the way!"

I called out to him, "Get us out of here!"

The man got the door to open and helped me out. I was in great pain but climbed out of the truck and made my way up the ditch bank. It was very steep and with the pain in my leg and neck, I could barely manage. I basically crawled onto the shoulder of the road and laid down. They said there is too much glass to lay down there; I didn't care. A woman held her hands under my head to protect it from the glass and gravel. As she started to move her hands around to get more comfortable, I asked her just to put my head on the ground, as the pain was unbearable when she moved.

Clayton soon followed out of the truck, carrying a snowbrush and my brand new, unwrapped, Audiobook by Rhonda Byrne – *The Power*. He handed it to me as he clutched the snowbrush. It fell from my hand onto my chest and from there I never saw it again. I couldn't hold on to it and couldn't understand what had just happened? If my thoughts and words create my reality, what about all the great things I had been manifesting? I had never dreamed of such an event – now this??

It was not long before the fire department was on the scene. They asked me to rate my pain. I said my leg hurt and my neck pain was 10/10 – really off the charts. They looked at the layers of clothing that I was wearing and said; "We are going to have to cut off your sweater."

I said, "No! Not the sweater!"

It was the one piece of clothing that I cared about. There are not many pictures of me in the world and of the few I have of my son and I through the years, is with that sweater on. No, not the sweater. I always had wished that it was a zip up, but it was pullover with a ¼ zipper. The fire fighters talked amongst themselves for a moment and then one knelt down with a pair of scissors, using them to slice through the purple polar fleece in a ragged zigzag fashion. Yes, the pain in my body was bad, but the pain of losing my favourite sweater tipped me over the edge. I cried out in anguish as my tears flowed. I could hear Clayton sobbing as he watched the firefighter seemingly cut his mother in half. I felt bare and exposed. The control of my life was slipping away, although I had no idea that this was just the beginning.

When the paramedics arrived, they put a large hard collar on my neck before placing me haphazardly on the flat board. As they were setting the board on the stretcher in the ambulance, I said, "What about my son?"

They said, "Is he a patient?"

How the hell should I know? I wondered internally.

"If he is a patient, he will have to wait at the roadside for another ambulance to come for him. If he is not, he can ride along with you."

I said, "He is coming with me."

Clayton grabbed his snowbrush, climbed into the ambulance and off we went.

A couple of hours later, my husband had stopped by the hospital for a moment, but had already taken Clayton home by the time the CT scan and X-ray results had come back. I was alone in a crowded room in the Emergency area, when the nurse came to my bedside and said, "You have broken your neck."

What does that even mean? How could someone break their neck and survive? I couldn't wrap my head around it and had no one there to support me.

Next, she said, "You are being transferred to Hamilton General Hospital to the trauma unit as we are not equipped to deal with your injuries here."

What? What is going on here? How can I be alive? I asked the nurse if she would please call my sister Sue, and she went to make the call. When she came back, she said that my sister was already en route and informed her of the change of venue. I was placed back on the hard board, with my head strapped to it and the ill-fitted collar on my neck. I was loaded into an ambulance and the paramedics asked the nurse if this was a case for lights and sirens, or if it was a walk in the park. She responded that they told her it was "Life and Limb." This meant I had a serious bodily injury and may not make it.

As the driver pulled out of the parking lot onto the road, the siren pierced the night air. I did my best to get into "the zone" and focus on what I wanted, instead of what I didn't want. I had peaceful thoughts and imagined being in a serene environment. It was frequently interrupted by the nurse asking how I was doing. I wanted her to leave me alone. It was hard to get back to that peaceful place, especially as we neared the General Hospital. I remember every bump as the ambulance sailed over each pothole and crack in the worn-out streets.

When we arrived, I felt like I had been dropped into a scene from some movie or emergency room drama TV show. I remember seeing the lights passing by overhead and feeling each bump as we passed over the lines between each section of floor. When I was finally placed on a table, I again felt like it was some script playing out and not my life. The bright light shone directly on me. About a dozen faces surrounded me, filling the space from all directions, each one telling me their name and what they were going to be doing. Every test and X-ray from the previous hospital was repeated and more were added. I was surprised I wasn't glowing from all the X-rays. I was poked and prodded from head to toe and then they topped it off with a full body CT scan.

When the dust settled, every one of those people left the large Emergency room. Suddenly, I was all alone. After an unknown period of time, my sister Sue arrived at the door, a welcome sight. She had come straight from work and although it was probably quite late by that time, I was glad for the company.

A short time later, my husband showed up. He informed us that he had left Clayton with our neighbours John and Lois's for the night. He then talked to Sue for a few minutes before they said their brief good-byes to me and left. As the door swung shut and latched, I drifted out of consciousness into a fitful state of sleep.

I ended up in the Intensive Care Unit and although they had installed a catheter, I thankfully have no memory of that. I was on an IV and had some air contraption on my leg that was squeezing it to keep me from getting blood clots.

A nurse came and tucked me in for the night. She said, "You can be fitted for a collar after the store across the road opens at 8 o'clock tomorrow morning. It is important that you do not move. This is not a joke. You have an IV and a catheter, there is no reason for you to make a move. Don't make any movements, your life depends on it."

Born in a Concrete Jungle

I almost wasn't born. My parents had wanted a family with four children and took great effort to plan and space them out accordingly, to get three years in between each one. After Brenda, Gerry and Susan were born, they had decided that helping a child in need would be the best, so they adopted my brother Brian at six months of age, and their family was complete. Dad had a vasectomy to ensure that. I still needed to be born, but I was not deterred and I did not give up.

In the spring of 1973, my mother became ill. She had a busy family and like many women, didn't take the rest that she needed. Mom thought she had the flu and was just pressing on, but ended up dehydrated and in the hospital. That is when she found out that she was miraculously pregnant! She hadn't even considered the possibility since my father had already had his operation… and no, I don't look like the milkman.

With my mother in hospital and quite ill, five dominant males started talking about her options. Conversations took place between my father, our minister, my Dad's uncle who was a doctor, our family doctor and the specialist that had performed the botched operation. They concluded that since this pregnancy was in error, for the reasons to follow, an abortion would be in order; Mom and Dad were poor, they already had the four children they planned for, the doctor had made an error, and Mom was now sick. These men made this decision, but did not consult with my mother on it.

At that time, the Reverend's wife came to visit my mother and asked her how she felt about all this talk of abortion. My Mom promptly told her that she wanted to run away and keep the baby! My Dad overheard the conversation and that was the end of the abortion talk. I'd made it through my first hurdle; my mother didn't give up on me, and Dad came on board as well!

I was born in Scarborough General Hospital, as Elizabeth Ann Barg on September 20, 1973. I was named after a relative Elizabeth that died in a car accident not long before my birth, but they chose to call me "Beth".

My father's parents came to Canada as part of the mass emigration of persecuted Mennonites from Russia. They were considered to be Russian Mennonite although not Russian at all, and originally from Prussia. My father was the oldest of eight children, and was raised on a farm in Alberta. My mother's side of the family were considered to be Swiss Mennonite, because they emigrated from Switzerland to Pennsylvania, United States and then eventually to Ontario. My mother's family was in construction and buildings. As per her religion, my mother wore a dress, a covering on her head and did not cut her hair until well after they were married. My siblings and I were raised in the city as what I always called "modern" Mennonites. But that is not entirely accurate. I just thought that, because we didn't have those strict rules like my mother had growing up.

We were raised in the true expression of what being Mennonite was about. My parents were on the ground, making things happen for less fortunate people on a daily basis. They shared the Mennonite philosophy of non-violence with a dedication to peacemaking, restorative and social justice, while living in a community of faith. In essence, they *lived* the teachings of Jesus, didn't just talk about them. They most certainly, walked the walk.

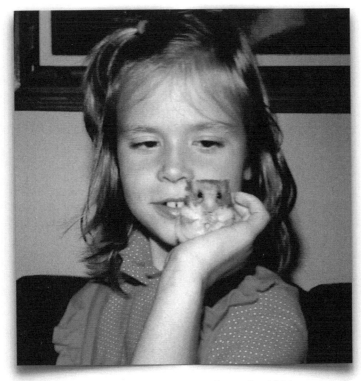

With my hamster Hammy, September 1981

All I ever wanted was to have a pet. For Christmas when I was five years old, my father hid my present in his suit coat little side pocket. After several attempts and getting my tiny hand stuck, I thrust in with all the force I could muster…and my present bit me!

I did not have a great experience with my first pet – a gerbil, and was then terrified to hold her for the rest of her life. I had hurt her, and she had bit me – we both remembered! My brother Brian had threatened me, telling me that I must name it George. But she was a girl, so the best I could come up with on short notice was Georgina.

After Georgina passed away, I moved on to pet number two and then three. Hammy, the hamster was a much more amenable friend. I used to watch the fun old show, *Hammy the Hamster*, where the rodents drove little toy cars, boats and airplanes around; my Hammy looked exactly like the Hammy from the show. After he passed away, Yi came along – another wonderful hamster. I named him that because he was white with brown patches with a "Y" shape on one side and an "i" on the other! The biggest problem with my little pets was that they didn't have a long lifespan and it was terribly upsetting to have my friends keep on dying.

In the summertime, I used to have tent caterpillars for pets. Freddie was my favourite. I often raced them with friends. One day, my friend accidentally sat on Freddie. I took this as a clear affirmation that I was barking up the wrong tree with this kind of pet.

Before I was born, my father had been a science teacher. My mother was an elementary school teacher until she retired, but my Dad had several careers. When I was growing up he, was doing church-work and running a community centre in a low-income neighbourhood near the suburbs where we lived. It was before I was born that I'd imagine he was much more fun and interesting! He started out teaching in a one-room schoolhouse and eventually became a science teacher, head of the Scarborough School Board Science Department.

My father had been blessed with some unusual animals he kept for his science classes. Why I wasn't born earlier to enjoy these creatures is beyond my knowledge. I remember hearing the story about a small owl that stayed in our house for a time. It used to sleep by day, perched somewhere amongst Mom's beautiful collection of houseplants. One evening, my parents had a small group of church ladies over for a visit. There was a lovely basket of flowers in the living room on a small table. The owl sat, unmoving, while sleeping on top of the basket handle – looking much like a unique life-like decoration.

As the evening wore on, the ladies were drinking their tea and having a lively discussion when the nocturnal owl woke up. At this time there was a very loud scream of terror heard throughout the house! The owl, which they had thought was plastic, had blinked at the light and turned its head, glaring at the women! One lady reacted with a loud scream which was immediately followed by silence in the room.

When nothing worse happened, everyone laughed! Mom did not use the opportunity to tell the ladies that my father used to feed the owl live mice in the basement. The mouse was placed in a box and the door to the room was shut to keep the owl in. The next day, Mom was less than impressed to find all the bits the owl couldn't digest, vomited up on the floor!

I don't know where my Dad got the baby raccoon from, but apparently it lived in our house for at least a few weeks. It was in the late 1960s, my oldest siblings Brenda and Gerry took the raccoon to school for show-and-tell and fed the little guy eggs and porridge! I am certain I would have liked a baby raccoon! There may have been others, but the most important pet my Dad had before I was born, was a bat named Herbie. I spent a lot of time with Herbie the bat. In Grade 2, I even took him to school for show-and-tell. How could I have taken to school a bat that lived before I was born? Well, it was because he wasn't alive - he was dead. He died many years before I was born. Weird, I know.

The story was that a wild bat somehow ended up in Dad's classroom at school and he shut the door – keeping the bat in his class. My sister remembers Dad bringing Herbie home and letting him fly around in the house! First thing Brenda did was hit the floor and crawl under the bed! My brother Gerry made a beeline for the closet and slammed the door! Welcome Herbie. Anyway, at some point, Herbie met his maker in the science room where an African Clawed Frog lived. Herbie flew into the tank and drowned in the water. I guess Dad was very sad and wanted to keep his friend, so he preserved him in a jar of formaldehyde and kept him for many years later. I have to admit that Herbie didn't look so great when I knew him! Since I gravitated to any animal I could find, or various stories of animals, or even as evidenced here a dead one in a jar, maybe you are beginning to understand that I needed to be around animals.

What I really wanted was a dog, but we lived in the suburbs of a city, and my parents were dead set against it.

When my mother was growing up, she had a beloved little Rat Terrier named Tiny. I remember her telling me the story about the dog having lumps and needing to be "put down". I assume this happened before my parents were married, because my grandfather instructed my father to take the dog to the vets to be euthanized. Dad followed the instructions, but it was done without my mother's knowledge! Mom was devastated. Her best friend and companion of fourteen years, was basically ripped from her life by the men that she loved. Due to Mom's reaction, Dad didn't want Mom to have to go through the pain of losing a dog again – so he didn't allow her to have another one. That is until my sister Sue was two years old and Dad brought home a Labrador puppy. They only had it for two weeks and decided they couldn't handle it and sent it back. After that, no other dog was allowed – ever.

I felt in my heart that I needed to be with dogs. I was determined that I would have my own dog one day although I didn't know how or when, but I would not give up on my dream!

People were always commenting to my parents and I, that with such a love for animals I should become a vet. How many times did I hear that? I never had aspirations to work with sick and dying animals. I had known on some level that an alternative way to work with animals was in my future, I just didn't know what.

In the summertime, when Mom and my siblings were not in school, Dad would take his vacation time from work and we would travel for about a month to visit family. One year we would travel west to the Prairie Provinces to visit my father's side and the next year, east to the Atlantic Provinces to visit my mother's relatives. My parents had made an agreement that family was important and they would split their visits that way. We would all pile into the station wagon that was pulling a tent trailer and off we'd go!

I loved to get away from the city at any chance I could. I enjoyed watching for wildlife as the trees and rocks zipped by my window while we headed to the East. The big sky and endless farmland kept my attention until I would fall asleep somewhere in Saskatchewan when we headed to the West. I never slept when we drove up through the mountains! The chance to spot a bear, elk, mountain sheep or even a moose made it very exciting. We often went to National Parks and I loved every moment I could get seeing God's wonderful creations of plants and animals, except I did not appreciate the giant-sized slugs they had in British Columbia!

My father's four brothers and their families all lived in Alberta and his three sisters in Manitoba. He had relatives all the way across to British Columbia. I remember being at my cousin's place in Alberta and supposedly petted their German Shepherd "the wrong way" and she bit me! She was laying on her side and I petted her back. Maybe she didn't see me coming from that angle. It sure made me wary of dogs after that, but I didn't give up my dream. The next summer, I was chased by a black Scottish terrier at a campground. I jumped up on a swing to try and get away from it, which was clearly not the best defense, but it was a small dog! The vicious little terrier had grabbed me by the ankle before I was finally rescued! From that little interlude with danger, I decided that I still liked big dogs much better and my dream of dog ownership continued.

FIRST FLIGHT

I never felt like I fit in, living the city life. My father looked after his large garden and some fruit trees in our backyard so that was nice, but it was surrounded by buildings and people. Being the youngest in the family was challenging for me. My closest brother used to torment me, but it was more than that - I felt like an outsider. It wasn't until I was eight years old, when my sister Brenda married Shane – a sheep farmer, when I realized why city life wasn't working for me. I was a natural born farmer, who was being raised in the city and it was time for me to go home.

As many weekends, holidays and summers as I could, I was there on their farm. What a glorious place to be! Wide open spaces, animals and birds everywhere! It was a lot of work and even as a child, if you were there, you had to be working! Best of all though, they had a dog! Bandit was a beautiful and very intelligent, working Border Collie. I spent every moment I could with him!

In the early years, Brenda worked away from home for a week at a time and that left Shane and I to look after the farm. I was young but I was keen to learn and like a sponge, soaked in any information Shane shared with me.

Although Shane was about average in height, he always seemed tall and strong to me, looking up at him as a young girl. Every memory I have of Shane is of him wearing a light green, button down shirt, with the sleeves sawed off at the shoulders. He had well-muscled arms that protruded like Popeye's after eating a can of spinach in the old cartoons. He had the epitome of a farmer's tan.

His face and arms were darkened by the sun while the rest of him was shock white, which I noted when we sometimes went swimming at Big Bay on a Sunday afternoon.

Shane taught me how to work-hard, think for myself, be responsible, and about natural remedies and alternative ways of farming. He also shared with me his vast knowledge of wild birds. He taught me to scan the skies and local environment for birds, while continuing to work of course!

How a bird flies, its habits and time of year all make a difference in bird identification. Shane taught me to listen to the different calls, so that I was able to identify many birds – without being able to see them. I remember going bird watching in the winter with the gentle snow falling all around, as we walked in a forest. My young ears listened to each different and beautiful song while my eyes searched in the direction of the sounds. I am forever in Shane's debt as my life would not be what it is today, without his early influences.

Although I liked all the birds, my favourite were the birds of prey. The majestic hunters that could soar through the air seemingly suspended by magic itself. When I was outdoors I kept one eye on the sky or the treetops, so that I would not miss seeing an interesting species. It was wonderful to see different kinds of hawks, owls and occasionally a falcon. I was delighted to one day spot a very rare, Pileated Woodpecker, almost twenty inches high, hanging off a tree at Big Bay! But the big bird that I really wanted to see wasn't yellow and on TV... I longed to see an Eagle!

When I was ten years old, Brenda and Shane taught me to drive the tractor. They had an old "H" row tractor, with the skinny close-together wheels at the front. They did what parents do to children when riding a bicycle. One minute they were riding on the back and the next they were gone! Yikes! No one told me how to stop!! I made a big circle back to them as they stood there laughing and luckily they instructed me in braking, before I broke something! It was quite a while before I was willing to try backing up though – I was too scared. They placated me for a while, but then had enough! "Do it!" I faced my fears and backed up the tractor! It wasn't too many years before I could back up to the wagons perfectly, almost every time! It was something I ended up being good at, but if I hadn't gotten over my fear, I wouldn't have known.

Knowing how to drive the tractor was very useful on the farm, so I could haul hay and grain wagons between the fields and the barn. At times I remember driving the tractor, pulling the small square baler, which in turn pulled a flat wagon. On that wagon one or more poor souls had to take each bale from the baler and stack it high on the flat deck. I was too slight to be able to help with that task until I was bigger, so I drove the tractor slowly down the rows of hay while Shane, Brenda or a local teenager sweated the day away, stacking hay.

At age eleven I had a memorable year of firsts. In July, I had my first flight! My Dad took me to a flight school in Arthur, where he bought me a ride in a glider. I climbed in the aircraft with the pilot and a small plane pulled us high into the sky! When we unhooked, everything was quiet. We flew around looking for thermals and sailed free like a bird for over half an hour! It was an experience to be remembered!

I was too shy to strike up a conversation, so my mind wandered as the pilot remained extremely quiet throughout most of the ride. I had wished at the time that I could have stuck my head out of the top of the glider to feel the wind rush past on my face and breathe-in the cool fresh air from so high in the sky. I didn't know why we were suddenly climbing higher into the sky. The pilot had found a thermal and we were going round and round in a big circle. He was using the same updraft that my beloved big birds like hawks, Eagles and vultures use to "ride" effortlessly up into the sky. For the rest of the time, I continued to watch the skies around me hoping that maybe if I went right to the clouds, I would finally see an Eagle.

That summer, my new best friend was born – Midnight. Actually her full name would be Midnight Moonlight Barg. She was born in the barn at Brenda and Shane's farm. Looking back now, maybe she was the plainest kitten in the bunch, but I thought she was the most beautiful feline I had ever seen. Her coat was dark and black as the night with only a small circle of white fur like the moon, at the front of her neck. I wanted a dog very badly but there was no way; yet my parents finally gave in and let me have this kitten.

I was the first child in my family to have a pet that wasn't a fish, reptile, or rodent! I spent every waking moment that I could with my cat and she slept on my bed every night; my constant companion and friend. What a character she was! She loved to sit on the piano bench and tap out a tune with her paw. She was very tolerant and even allowed me to dress her up in the little clothes my mother had made for my favourite doll. I used to walk her on a harness to school sometimes, next to the curb to keep her going in a straight line, like a dog on a leash. She didn't get to come home to live with me in Scarborough until November, but I was so happy when Mom and Dad finally agreed! I finally had a friend in place for life, well at least the next sixteen years!

My father didn't like to show his softer side. One day I got home from school for lunch ahead of him and I hid in my bedroom closet. When he arrived, his assumption was that I hadn't gotten home yet and I heard him chatting away to Midnight. "Don't worry, your Master will be home soon!" I jumped out of the closet and said, "Ha! I caught you talking to Middy!" Um, well... you could say he wasn't impressed. I got scolded and was told in no uncertain terms, never to do that again!

With my cat Midnight and Grumpy

For Christmas that year, my sister Sue tried her hand with sewing and made me my very own Care Bear – my favourite Grumpy, a blue bear with a cloud and rain on his belly. This proved to be my most long-lasting gift ever. The gift that just keeps on giving!

Who knew that I would still be sleeping with this Grumpy Bear every night and he's still going strong. Well, he's not that robust anymore, but looking pretty good for his age! He also went on all trips with me and I have pictures of him all over the world!

I guess if I had to be honest, Midnight was an awesome friend, but that didn't change the fact that I still wanted a dog. I decided that my dear new blue friend Grumpy would be like my shadow dog… bear, dog – ah, close enough! I didn't necessarily play with Grumpy all day because I had Middy, but I did snuggle him up against me each night, the way I figured a dog would lay its head on my chest… if I had a dog.

BEST CHRISTMAS PRESENT, EVER

When I was twelve years old, Brenda and Shane had to go away for the weekend and needed someone to do chores for them. Who do you think they asked? ME! I was left in charge to take care of, feed and water 300 ewes, which are female sheep. Many of them had lambs and some even gave birth to new babies while Brenda and Shane were away.

There was one instance I remember in particular. I went out to the barn to do the chores and check on the sheep like usual. There was one ewe, standing away from the others. I snuck around behind her and saw some placenta hanging down her back end. I had helped deliver lambs in the past, but this would be my first time doing it all by myself! Instead of the usual appearance of a nose and two little feet, there was just one hoof! Oh no! I hung around and did some chores while I waited for mama-sheep to lay down.

When the sheep finally laid down to push, I pulled off my sweater and hung it on the feeder. I crept up behind her and sat down on the straw. This was before the age of plastic gloves so I slowly ran my bare hand along the baby lamb's leg to see where the rest of the lamb was hiding! It was very warm inside the sheep and the pressure of the small space made it hard to maneuver. The baby lamb's other leg was folded back. The mother was pushing and pressing very hard on to my hand, so I had to take it out and regroup. What to do? What did they tell me!?

I tried my best to pull on the leg that was sticking out, but the baby lamb would not budge. Since I could not get the leg to come out, I would have to push the baby lamb back inside in order to have room to get the other leg unfolded. Let me tell you – that baby lamb did *not* want to go back in. Neither did the mama want the lamb returning to the womb after she'd worked so hard to get it out! It took every ounce of my strength to go against nature, the lamb and the Mama. Once the leg and head were back inside, I was working blind. I had to use my imagination to picture what my hand was feeling.

At this point I am laying on the ground and my arm is three quarters of the way up inside the sheep, trying to re-arrange the trouble causing leg. Finally I got both legs together and lined up with the baby lamb's head, so that the nose was between the legs. "Okay girl – time to push!" I gently said to the mother sheep. The ewe seemed to feel the shift and took up pushing again. The all-black lamb was soon delivered and I wiped the placenta from its nose with a handful of clean straw. The delivery had been a long one and I was worried, because it hadn't started breathing yet. I picked the lamb up by the back legs and held it high in the air, swinging it back and forth to try and clear out any fluid from its lungs. Still nothing. I swung it again and this time I tapped its nose on the ground each time as it swung past the floor - I was beginning to freak out! I laid the little lamb on the ground again and was tapping its chest as it finally started to sputter. It was alive!! I laid the lamb in front of the mother's nose and she started to lick life into the little guy.

While she was still laying down, I used the opportunity to go back in and look for more lambs! I reached in as far as my arm could go and managed to find three legs. What? THREE?? Which two do I pull on? I carefully felt each leg, which way it bent, where the joints were and picked the two that were the same and pulled! They were the back legs this time, it was a breech birth. The mother helped with a big push and out came lamb number two – this one was completely white! After ensuring the lamb's airway was clear and she was breathing, I laid her with the other in front of the mother. I gently pulled on each of the mother's two teats and removed the wax plugs, making sure that the colostrum was available from both sides. I picked up the two lambs and held them low and walked slowly backwards. The mother jumped up and followed me, bleating to her babies. I placed them gently in a 4' x 4' lambing pen and closed the gate after the mother followed me in. I gave the mother a bucket of water, some hay and ensured that the two new little ones were able to have their first drink. Later that day, I recorded the ewe's ear tag number as well as the sex and colour of the lambs. I put an elastic ring on each tail, placed a small metal tag in one ear of each lamb and recorded the information. I also had to give each newborn Vitamin E and Selenium as a subcutaneous injection. That was a lot of responsibility for a twelve-year-old, but I did not give up and managed to help two beautiful beings into this world.

I had always been shy and uncertain of myself, but after having so much responsibility and persevering through the struggles that weekend, it helped to boost my confidence! I had proved to my sister and to myself, that I could do it!

It was shortly after this, that a fun fair came to my Public School in Scarborough. The principal asked for a volunteer to help with the outdoor pony rides. My usually shy-self could not turn down an opportunity to work with animals and my hand shot up! I was the only one chosen from all of the grade 6, 7, 8 classes. I alone was asked to help with the outdoor pony rides, as I was the only child in the entire school with previous farming experience. I was very happy and proud to be around the beautiful equines in the schoolyard and to be entrusted with leading the children around.

That Christmas, Brenda and Shane gave me the best live Christmas present ever! I was given a gift certificate that said that I could pick out any female sheep from their entire flock! I was so excited! I believe, on that day, I became the only twelve-year-old in Scarborough to be a sheep owner!

The gift certificate had stated: "Good for one ewe or ewe lamb picked from the flock." Any one that I wanted from 300 sheep or their babies. At first I picked a black lamb with a white spot on her head sort of like Midnight, but Brenda thought that I might not be happy with it having the white spot. My gaze turned to the left when I caught sight of the most stunning lamb I'd ever seen, completely black from head to hooves. I knew instantly and without question, that she was the one.

Georgian had been born on October 13, 1985. She was comprised of at least three breeds – Dorset, Suffolk and Karakul. I loved her then and still have her descendants to this day! She was almost three months old at Christmastime when she suddenly became the object of my affections; she was not as thrilled as I was, to say the least!

I didn't get to spend much time with her until the following summer, as I was at the farm only a few week-ends and holidays during the school season. But by the summer, I had her eating out of my hand, literally! It took food and lots of it to win her heart, but then she was my buddy. I would yell "Georgie" out to the flock of 300. From the back somewhere, pushing her way to the front of the line, she would come for a handful of whole corn. Shane was less than impressed to find corn stalks growing up all over the farm where corn had fallen from my hand onto the ground! Oops! To me, they were just signs of how much I appreciated my Christmas present!

Georgian wore a leather collar. On occasion, I would attach a leash and walk her on the trails or down the lane leading to the back of the farm. Once again, if no one would give me a dog, I would make do with what I had!

With Georgian, 1986

YOU WIN SOME, YOU LOSE SOME

On Saturday, February 6, 1987, Georgian gave birth to her first-born baby, who I aptly named "Little George." I called her LG for short. Unfortunately, I missed the birth, but it wouldn't be long before I had that little one in my arms!

As it happened, my parents were against working on Sunday, so I knew they could be free! As far as I was concerned, any social engagement they might have had, wouldn't be as important as where I needed to be! I suggested that they take this wonderful opportunity to visit their first born ... while I visit mine! I guess my argument was strong enough because they gladly complied with the six-hour round trip the following day. Even though we lived in the city, they must have realized how important it was, to allow me to be who I was born to be: a farmer.

LG was a gem; a bright shining light in my soul. As soon as we met, I knew I needed to keep her. She was completely black with the long ears of her Suffolk breed sire. Brenda and Shane reluctantly agreed, as how could they say no? She was so cute! It would not be long before there were two sheep coming from the flock when I called. Brenda and Shane were always amazed that I could go away for a long time and come back, call to them and they would come, every time. At some point it was mentioned that I could not keep more than one lamb a year no matter how many lambs were born because otherwise, before long, all the sheep would be mine!!

That year I also joined the 4-H Beef Club and tried my hand with showing cattle. Brenda and Shane only had one cow at the time, so choices were limited with only one calf to choose from! I didn't realize that my calf was about a year too small, so it didn't go so well. Leading around a calf by the halter and making it stand square wasn't as easy as some of the more experienced show people made it look! I was carrying a Cattle Show Stick that was used to tickle the animal under the belly in order to make it put its back straight. It was also used to encourage the proper placement of the feet without wrestling the animal or putting my head down by the legs that can kick!

There were two days of shows, so the cattle were all cooped up overnight and were quite frisky on the morning of day two. My calf had been castrated, but I hadn't been aware that if not done properly, I would still have a bull on my hands. The heifer in front of my so-called steer was apparently in heat. My small steer jumped ahead and mounted the heifer in front of us. That started a chain reaction and all the cattle began mounting each other; it was quite an embarrassing scene! Needless to say, I never showed cattle again, but it was a good experience even just to find out that it wasn't my thing!

The next year, I joined the sheep 4-H Club and that was a better fit for me. Sheep have always occurred as easier to handle than cattle. I can, at any time, throw my entire body weight on a sheep and have a hope of wrestling it to the ground or at least to a standstill. With cattle? Not so much.

I had my own beautiful sheep that I wanted to show off and it was nice to have a reason to work with them during the summer in preparation for the fall show. I always showed my black sheep so I never had to shear, scrub and prepare them, like the other contestants had to with their white sheep! Black sheep are shown in full fleece so I only had to trim off the dirty bits. Black sheep were easier and definitely didn't show manure or urine stains like the white ones did!

Bandit and I, 1981

At the fall fair, I showed LG and her younger sisters Yiorgus and Spaz, winning Best Pair of Fall-born ewe lambs as well as Get of Sire! I guess I sort of lied to the judges to win Get of Sire – because as it states in the title, it is supposed to be a group of sheep out of one father – siblings in essence. I had no idea who the father might be, so to my young self, all my girls with the same mother should be good enough to go for the gold! It was a conformation class for them as individuals and then together they were assessed on how similar they were to each other. Each group was then compared to the next group and judged on the best conformation and best similarities overall. I was so happy when we won!

In March of 1991, disaster struck the farm. Bandit – the Border Collie, had gotten hurt so he was in the house when he normally would have been outdoors. Brenda came home from grocery shopping with their one-and-a-half-year-old son, Jordan and smoke was pouring from the eaves! Brenda ran to the front door and opened it, creating a backdraft and subsequent explosion! The house was on fire!

When Shane was alerted, he ran to every door of the house, opening it and calling in vain for Bandit to come out. Every time he shut a door, a window would break and the fire would spread. Bandit never made it out and was found later, lying dead under the table, from smoke inhalation. Losing the house was a tragedy for them, while losing Bandit was unbearable for me.

My parents and I had been leaving for a trip to Florida when we got the call about the house and Bandit. We drove directly to Brenda and Shane's farm to see how we could be of service, before we departed for our trip. Digging through the rubble, I found the door knob and the bedspring that had fallen from my second story bedroom. They lost everything in their home and their treasured working sheep dog – but they never gave up.

Bandit was the first dog that I had been given the opportunity to spend a lot of time with in my life, beyond the neighbourhood dogs in the city. I had a lot of time to think about him as I looked out the window during the 3150 km drive to Florida.

Bandit was so incredibly intelligent. We had a connection that I couldn't really put my finger on. He knew me so well and he was so responsive to the things I asked of him. Shane had been very clear from the time that I was young, that I shalt never say the word "Come" to him, unless he was working the sheep. If I wanted him to "Come" I needed to say "Here," I was never to say "Come here!" Why? Because with Bandit's keen ability to work the hundreds of sheep, Shane needed him to stay very clear on his commands. "Come-Bye" meant that Bandit should run clockwise around the sheep, and if instructed "Away-to-me" he would run counter-clockwise! If that ability was hindered, it could mean trouble for both: the shepherd, the dog and me, if it was my fault!

I remembered fondly the time that I had lost my bicycle in the tall pasture grass in one of the back fields. I had been moving the sheep and had dropped it on the ground and ran off to do something in a hurry, not paying attention to the bike. When I was done with the sheep, I was left scratching my head in wonder about where my bike was!? I looked over at Bandit and said, "Where is my bike Bandit?" As though he was a Lassie incarnate, he gave a couple barks to get my attention and went running to the next field. I could do nothing but follow with interest. A short time later he stood, barking and wagging his tail. I ran through the grass to his side and lo and behold – there was my bike! "Good boy, Bandit!!"

Another story that crossed my mind was the day I had Bandit "watch the sheep" for me. He was to watch that the sheep didn't get out while I moved the electric fences. When I was done with the fence that morning, I went back to the house to get a drink. Later in the day, Shane asked me if I had seen Bandit recently. Hmm. He had been with me when I moved the sheep and the last command I remember giving him was "Watch the sheep!" We drove to the back of the farm in the truck and there was Bandit – doing just as I had asked. He was sitting by the gate, still watching the sheep!

DIGGER, MY TRUSTY STEED

At age sixteen, during the school year, I worked at a gas station, as that was the closest I could get for outdoor work in the city. For a while, my mother took me out in the country for riding lessons each week. She paid for the gas, but I had to pay for the lessons. The nearest riding stable was very far and expensive, so my riding lessons were short-lived. Oh, how I longed for my own horse…someday.

My mother understood how important it was to me to be connected with animals. Maybe she instinctively knew that I didn't belong in the city where I was stationed for far too many of my earlier years. She was very supportive of my intentions to be around animals at every opportunity.

In the summer, in addition to doing chores and helping on the farm, I got a job at a nearby General Store in Big Bay, scooping ice cream. The following year in addition to farm work, I tried my hand in the motel business, but only lasted three days. After that, I got a job in a restaurant, first peeling potatoes for a few days until all three waitresses who were sisters quit and suddenly, I became a waitress. In addition to all that, after work I would bike to a horse farm and do hard labour in exchange for riding lessons.

In Spring of 1991, I graduated high school and enrolled into Humber College, in Equine Studies that started in the fall. I was excited to be starting college at seventeen, finally something I was interested in! I did really well with my courses. They seemed very easy and I made it on the honour roll without much effort!

Part of my course was book learning, while the other part of the course was riding and hands-on. I spent the year in the city, with horses. When they originally built the college it was in the country, but since the city grew up around it, I was now walking my "project horse" Northern around in Etobicoke, in my spare time. Northern was an Appendix Quarter Horse, meaning a cross between a Thoroughbred and a Quarter Horse. He was a beautiful chestnut colour with a striking snip of white on his nose! I loved taking care of him and as part of my schooling I had to muck out his stall, water, feed, groom and hand-walk him.

That year, my brother Brian offered my siblings and me plane tickets to anywhere in the world, as he worked for American Airlines - all we had to do was to pay the tax on the ticket. Of anywhere in the world we could have gone, for my sisters and myself I picked the San Diego Zoo. Where else could I see all the animals I wanted, while remaining in a safe environment?

When I graduated the year-long program in the Spring of 1992, I had the unfortunate experience of not being able to find a job "in my field" so to speak. I sent out over thirty resumes to horse farms all over the Province and I didn't even get one reply. Then, my good friend and fellow classmate Denise, suggested I apply at Millar Brooke Farm in Perth, Ontario. How could I? After what had happened when we had gone to the Royal Agricultural Winter Fair in November? Denise and I had lined up to meet a true Canadian icon – Ian Millar, the owner of Millar Brooke Farm and the rider of the famous horse Big Ben. Ian had been nicknamed "Captain Canada" for his brilliant role with the Canadian Equestrian team. Ian and Big Ben were virtually unbeatable in show jumping competitions for years. Ian currently holds the record for completing the most Olympic Games in history. Between 1972 and 2012, he competed in ten Olympic games! As we got closer to him, he seemed larger than life. He was quite tall, standing over six feet, with thinning hair and glasses. He was wearing the standard attire for a member of the Canadian Equestrian Team - white britches, red show jacket and tall black leather riding boots. As Denise and I approached him, I had been my usual shy self, but instead of just remaining silent, I had burst into tears! I had been so happy to finally meet him, but had felt completely embarrassed from my outpouring of emotion that day. But here I was with no job, so I penned a letter to Millar Brooke Farm… what could it hurt?

A couple weeks later I noticed my answering machine flashing. I rewound the tape and listened to a woman named Lynn Millar telling me that I had secured a position on the Millar Brooke team! WOW!! I remember my joy and excitement as I jumped around in my living room! It was a memorable moment!

I put my belongings and my cat Midnight into the car and moved five hours away from home, into an apartment above the barn with several other show grooms. If I didn't know what it felt like to *be* dirt – I was about to find out.

It was certainly a learning experience, but not all that fun. It was long hours, lots of work and no room for error. These were top of the line, expensive, show jumping horses and they needed top notch care.

I didn't go near Big Ben and that was okay, I admired him from afar. The special thing for me was that I got to look after Lonesome Dove. She was a beautiful, liver chestnut, Oldenburg mare who had some temperament issues and I loved her dearly. She had a problem with banging her head on things, like low-hanging doorways and so on. I taught her to bow her head like I did, when walking under something low. She would walk anywhere with me, even under flapping, low hanging plastic, blowing in the wind at an outdoor show. I spent so much time with that horse that I could tell her temperature without taking it and I could tell Ian before he went in the ring, if she was going to win or not. They had even gotten her spayed in an attempt to level out her moods, but they never did figure her out. Still, she was a wonderful horse. I looked after some of the others too, but she was the one that had stolen my heart.

The year I was there, we travelled around to many shows in Ontario and I got to visit Halifax, Nova Scotia as well. The furthest I went was Washington, with Winchester, the black stallion. He was being retired, it was to be his last show and I was so proud when he won! Being on the road was interesting, but lots of work. The strangest bit was the fact that the grooms had to ride *in* the horse trailer *with* the horses, to make sure the horses were okay! Those were some long trips and it was not the safest way to journey across the country.

Some of my fellow grooms had travelled out to Spruce Meadows in Alberta that year. An unhinged driver intentionally drove into the big truck filled with horses and grooms, somewhere along the Trans-Canada Highway. The grooms made it out alive, but not all the horses did. There were many injuries to deal with when they returned home.

I stayed on at Millar Brooke until early 1993 when I had to come home. I was incredibly sad to be leaving my Dovie. I was Lonesome for Dove. I ended up going back to high school for one semester to finish my three Grade 13 courses, so I could go to university in the fall. That summer I got a job as the Horse & Pony Director at Fraser Lake Mennonite Camp in Bancroft, Ontario. It was a bit of a step down from Show Groom. The pay was only $115 a week and I had to stay there the entire summer, but nevertheless, I was surrounded by horses!

It was that summer, that I met the best friend a girl could ever have. Of all the horses to arrive at the camp, one stood out as special to me. He looked exactly like the horse from my favourite books from childhood – he was a dead ringer for Blaze.

Digger with a baby lamb

As a child I had read every Billy & Blaze adventure ever written and here stood Blaze – well almost. This horse had only three white feet and Blaze had four, but from my viewpoint, that was the only difference!

The people who dropped off the horses, told me his name was Gravedigger. As I said, I was working at a Mennonite Camp, and I hardly thought that the name Gravedigger was suitable for a children's horse, so I shortened it to Digger. After the summer was over, I found out his real name was Bones!

Even with the change of name, this horse was not suitable for children. He seemed to have no patience and no training! I had to start over and train him from scratch, just so I could use him to lead the trails! I had never trained a horse before and Digger did not make it easy for me. He thought himself very funny, dumping me off on the ground with a thud - more times than I could count, during the first six weeks of being there. He had very upright pasterns, which made sitting his trot next to impossible as it was extremely bumpy. It was sort of like riding a jack-hammer. He knew I could not stay on without a saddle, so if I was riding bareback, I always avoided trotting by having him walk or run! But he picked up a bad habit and learned he could run back to the barn… and really, I couldn't stop him!

After six weeks, I took the bit out of his mouth and purchased a mechanical hackamore. I finally had a little bit of control over my wild horse! Even though he was kind of a jerk, I loved him to bits. I would go out to the edge of the pasture and call him:"Dig, Dig, Dig, Dig, Dig, Dig, DIGGEEERRR!" and he always came running!

My assistant for the summer was a teenager with the camp name of Cajuna. I was called Quinn – as in Dr. Quinn Medicine Woman. I had helped out with a couple of injuries with staff the week before the children had come and the name had stuck. I had a lot of experience with horses, from my brother-in-laws horses on the farm, riding lessons, my College program, working as a show groom and so on. I managed to teach this young punk a whole lot of stuff about horses. He had gotten stationed with me, because he had more experience with horses than the other people at camp – I think his uncle owned a few horses. Anyway, I was older and wiser than him, but he thought he knew everything, especially as it got later in the summer.

I couldn't let anyone else ride Digger, because he wasn't very safe. Cajuna was always bugging me to have a turn riding him. One day I finally gave in to his request, with the warning that I didn't think it was a good idea. As we were leading a trail of children through the forest, Cajuna got messing around with Digger, trying to prove his superiority. That didn't fly, but the rider sure did! As Digger reared up, I called out to Cajuna to lean forward and let the reins loose. As usual, he knew better and kept pulling on Digger's mouth. This action held Digger's head so he had to rise higher and higher to get relief. The biggest relief was when Cajuna was dumped onto the ground in a heap! Luckily, Digger did not fall on him. There were no injuries, except for Cajuna's pride. Atta boy Dig!

When the end of summer came it was time for the horses to go back to their owner, a horse dealer. I knew they had to go; they just hadn't told me when. One day, while the staff were eating lunch in the cafeteria, I felt that something was wrong and I stepped outside. The horse section was the furthest point of the camp. I closed the door to block out the noise from the cafeteria and had a listen. I could hear commotion and a horse screaming in the distance! I took off at a run.

When I got to the field by the horses, there was a large furniture truck and several men loading the horses and ponies into it. Most alarming was what they were doing to Pistol. She was a beautiful, grey speckled, Welsh-cross horse with the gentlest disposition. I had thought she was too young at age two to be in the Pony Program at all, but I guess they figured children were light. The men had a pulley hooked to the truck and a long rope attached to it. They had the rope around her head and in her mouth, pulled tight - dragging her towards the truck! There was blood streaming from her lips and she was covered in white lather from sweat. I was furious! I ran over to the man and pushed him to the side, immediately taking the bloodied rope from her mouth. I told them to stay away from her while I hand-walked her around until she had calmed down. When Cajuna came along after he'd finished his lunch, I had him get some towels and we dried her off.

When the time came for Pistol to be loaded – I didn't want to. A staff member's daughter had been interested in a horse and so I offered to buy her right then. I still had to load her up, but I did so without issue as she trusted me. Digger had to go on this truck too. I didn't know how I was going to do it, but this wasn't over for me.

The following week I went with the family to purchase Pistol at a cheap price – especially for the ill treatment that they had done to her. I was relieved to know that she would be taken care of in her new home.

I moved into residence at the University of Guelph and Pistol was only about half an hour away, so I worked out a deal with the family. I would give the daughter riding lessons on Pistol in exchange for something really important to me – a home-cooked meal! And that is what I did that year, I would drive out to see Pistol, train the girl and fill my belly. It worked out well for all of us!

Summer was over and I started my two-year program at the University of Guelph, taking Farm Operations and Management. For this first year, I lived in residence. All winter, I was plotting and scheming how I could afford to buy and where I could keep a horse. Finally in February of 1994, my mother drove with me out to the horse dealer's property north of Toronto. I had to find Digger.

I stood by the fence, next to a big pasture covered in snow and gazed out at more than two hundred horses. How would I ever find Digger in that bunch? They had long hair to keep them warm from the cold winter winds, which was good as I saw no shelter for them. Many of the horses had their heads down low, while eating hay. How would I even know if he was out there??

I watched the horses for a few minutes while pondering the options. I wasn't going to go in there with that many unknown horses, so there was really only one thing that I could do. I stood by the fence and yelled at the top of my lungs, like I did so many times the previous summer, "Dig, Dig, Dig, Dig, Dig, Dig, DIGGEEERRR!" With that, Digger's head popped up above the crowd! He backed out of the bunch and ran straight towards me! My Mom just stood there with her mouth hanging open! I would have hardly recognized him had I been out searching. He was very furry and his winter coat was much lighter, almost orange compared to his usual dark liver chestnut colouring. There was no mistaking him now! There stood my most beloved friend that I had missed so much. We drove back to talk to the owner. He commented that I had already bought a horse!? I explained that one wasn't for me, I needed this one. The purchase price was $800, which turned out to be money well spent. At that point, I had no idea that he would be my best friend for more than the next twenty-seven years.

I felt joy in my heart and had a spring in my step when Mom and I went home that day. As we were about to leave, I whispered to Digger, "Don't worry Dig – everything will be alright now. I love you!" But what I should've explained to him was that he wasn't actually going to be with me. I still lived in the city and it was again thanks to Brenda and Shane that I could buy him, as his first stop was to be their farm. I wasn't along when he was picked up, nor when he was dropped off at their place. Perhaps Digger didn't realize that he was actually "with me" even though I wasn't there. It was a few weeks before I could get up to see him and he had managed to get himself into some trouble.

Apparently, he had a hard time adjusting to being in with the sheep and occasionally beat them up. He was young and I was far away. Eventually, I had to move him to a neighbour's place down the road that had horses. I spent all holidays, some week-ends and the entire summer with Digger, while working on the farm. We went on daily adventures as my time off work permitted.

My beautiful friend and first sheep Georgian, died in April at almost nine years of age, due to pregnancy toxemia. I was not with her when she died, but I was heartbroken all the same. That summer, I worked on the farm again, but this time as farm manager. During the summer, I saved up enough money to pay for Digger's boarding fees and supplies for the whole year. I put the money in a separate account that I would not touch for any other purpose. Digger was extremely important to me and I wanted to be sure he would always be safe, well cared for and secure! Failing was not an option; I would never give up on him.

In June of that year, my parents moved from our long-time family home in Scarborough to a house in Kitchener, where I lived with them for my second year at Guelph. I was then able to move Digger to a place just north of Waterloo, where I could visit and ride him every day.

I used to ride Digger in the forest and along the river. It took quite a lot of encouragement to get him to cross the water, but on rare occasions he did. One time we were riding across a field, when we were surprised by three angry Rottweilers! We were scared and took off at a run with the three dogs hot on our heels! When we got to the end of the field, I realized that we were fenced in! What could I do? When we could no longer flee, I chose to fight.

With the loud scream of a banshee, I turned Digger around and we ran straight at the dogs! It didn't take too long and they were off and running away from us! We chased them right out of that field! It was exhilarating! As I always say - never give up!

One time I was riding Digger on a newly made, two-lane gravel road, in the north end of Waterloo. It was built up to be much higher than the field that it was cutting through, with very steep, deep ditches on either side. Due to the road construction, not one but two huge gravel trucks passed each other, one in each direction at the exact same time at the precise point in the road that Digger and I were. We were right at the edge of the road next to the ditch, less than 18 inches from being in contact with the closest truck! The wind from the trucks whipped dust into our faces. Digger put his head down to try to protect himself. I closed my eyes, hung on and prayed that we would be okay! To his credit, Digger did not spook or misstep – he marched forward as if our life depended on it, and it did. He was a dependable and true friend.

Digger was so brave – most of the time. If we came across a coyote or a fox when out in the country fields or forest, he wouldn't bat an eyelash and could even stand up to gravel trucks! Big things were no big deal to him, but boy could that horse spook at something little, like a frog!! Boo! A frog jumps in his path and without much further ado, I am sitting on my butt in the puddle, next to the frog, while Digger runs away! He was not like the well-trained horses in the movies; he was never one to hang around and wait for me to get back on. You are probably saying that I'm supposed to hold on to the reins when falling off – but who plans for that anyway?

Once, I needed to pick up something at Conestogo Mall, so I took my favourite transportation! I rode Digger to the mall and tied the reins onto the last glass door handle on the main entrance. I was actually worried about leaving him unattended, so only made a quick trip to the bathroom before going back out to see him. He had his face pressed flat on the glass looking in, trying to find me. It was priceless to watch the mindless shoppers exiting the mall, to look up and see a horse in their face!

Another time, I rode him all the way to Breslau to visit my brother Gerry's used car lot, Barg Automotive. While I was there, a Police car pulled in and an Officer came and asked me where I was going. I told him that I had already reached my destination! I said that I was a Mennonite and Digger was my transportation! It was quite a hike to get there too; 40 km round trip!

I trusted Digger and he trusted me. We had a connection that was so deep and strong, that I can hardly find words for it – he was "part" of me.

BBs, My Royal Sheep

In April of 1995, just before graduating from Guelph, I bought my first truck. It was a 1991 Ford Ranger, dark blue, with almost black tinted windows. Maybe it wasn't my dream truck, but I did get it for a reasonable price through my brother's car lot. You have to start somewhere and at least I finally had a truck!

Knowing that it was time to set foot into the real world, I had applied to many different farming operations looking for a job following the end of school. I had several farming career opportunities available to me, but during our graduation party, I unexpectedly found myself two-stepping the night away with a fella from my program. Although we'd known each other for two years, we decided to start dating on the last day of school. He was planning on going home to work on his family farm so he had a confirmed destination, but I had not committed to any place just yet. I only knew I would not be returning to the city! As sometimes is the case, I was blinded by young love and I gave up the opportunities to farm, in order to be near to him. Maybe it was love or maybe it was lack of confidence? It was surely a step backwards, but I moved to Kettleby, north of Toronto, to work on a race horse breeding farm for the next five months. I had some co-op experience working at the racetrack during the year I was at Humber College. This job was mostly working with mares and babies so it was much more interesting. I couldn't bring Middy because the other staff member already had cats in the living quarters, so she had to stay with my parents. I was glad to be able to board Digger nearby though.

The property I worked at was very beautiful with miles of white fences. It was so picturesque that occasionally movies were filmed on the property. Part of the movie that was being shot while I was there was called "It Takes Two." This movie starred the Olsen Twins in their first major motion picture, along with Steve Guttenburg and Kristy Ally. I have a great picture of myself with the young twins!

After leaving that job, I moved in with my boyfriend on one of his parent's farms. My new employment was still in the horse industry, but this time working at a horse tack shop in Newmarket. After too long apart, I was able to bring my cat Midnight to be with me again, and also moved Digger close by. After ten years of sheep ownership, this was my first opportunity to move my sheep from Brenda and Shane's farm to be with me. Finally, I was farming on my own! Even with the loss of my original sheep Georgian, I still managed to have kept five of her relatives - LG, Belle, BB, Royal-Tea and Q. Georgian had many daughters, but LG was her first and Q was her last one.

My boyfriend became extremely jealous of my relationship with Digger and hated him for it. He believed that I loved Digger more than I loved him – which was quite possibly true. I can't quite believe that I did it, but by October, I had sent Digger to live far away - back up near Brenda and Shane's farm.

My parents were not pleased about me moving in with this guy and told me I needed to take all my stuff out of their house. The relationship with my boyfriend was not good, but I was young and it was hard to see that from up close.

In November of that year, I trailered my beloved sheep BB – Baby Belle, daughter of Belle – to Toronto to attend a class at the Royal Agricultural Winter Fair. Normally I could not show sheep at the Royal, because I didn't have registered purebreds. This time it was different, as it was a specialty called the *Ladies Lead and Wool Class*. Participants could be no more than twenty-two years old, so it was my last year to be in it. Each participant had to show a sheep, wear clothes made out of wool and make a public speech advertising the benefits of wool.

BB had never been to a show before and although I had worked with her a little, she'd never been off the farm. Now there we were, smack dab in the middle of Toronto, inside of a big building. I remember vividly standing next to a staircase in a hallway, waiting for our turn in the ring. BB was running around me in circles at top speed and she wouldn't stop! I was beginning to freak out!

I knelt down next to BB and whispered into her long black ear, "If you will please walk quietly and stand in the ring like we've practiced, I promise to never take you to a show again!"

BB proceeded to run rings around me. Then it was finally our turn and the door opened. I led her into the center of the ring. With the bleachers filled with people looking on; I held my breath.

She did not let me down. She was an absolute dream! The other sheep pulled around at their people, but my BB, she walked strong and steady. She stopped and stood when asked. She didn't put a foot out of line and hands down was the most well behaved sheep in the show! To be sure, all the other competitors had nicer wool clothes, purebred sheep and had family in the sheep shows…so no, we didn't win – but I couldn't have been prouder of my girl that day! To me, she was the winner! I kept my promise to her not to show her anymore, except once years later, I did take her to be in a live nativity and I remember hearing her question in the back of my mind, "Isn't this a show?" I assured her that it was different, but I made her a new promise, in future she could just be a sheep…and so she was!

HOHL IN ONE

O n Groundhog Day in 1996, my boyfriend proposed! We were engaged to be married on October 19, of that year. Maybe things were not great, but perhaps my judgement was clouded, because in addition to my other animals, I had high hopes of getting my first dog!!

I had been missing Bandit since losing him in the fire, so when I had the opportunity – I bought a six-month-old Border Collie female, who I named Kes!

Sadly, by April, things went from bad to worse and after returning from a visit to my parents, my fiancé met me outside of the barn and said, he wished to break off our engagement. Although it turned out to be one of the best events that occurred in my life, at the time I felt like I'd been ripped in half.

My sister Sue and her husband Al were kind enough to invite me to stay with them at their rental home in the country near Wellesley. Although they let me bring Kes to live outdoors, I very soon got a job where I would be living on a farm near Brussels and couldn't take her with me. I had to let her go to a friend of Brenda and Shane's that had a sheep farm. Within two weeks of arriving to her new home, she had been struck by a car on the road and killed... another heartbreak! From May through July, I lived on the farm where I worked. There were hundreds of pigs and thousands of acres of crops to look after. The family ran into some personal problems soon after I arrived and the whole situation quickly went downhill.

By mid-July, I found out that my father's mother, Grandma Barg was dying in Winnipeg and I decided to quit my job and take a road trip out to see her. She had always lived out of province so I didn't know her very well and this was to be my only opportunity. I was so grateful for the four days that I spent with her in Winnipeg that year. She died the day after I left for Ontario.

Since I had abruptly left my job which included a place to live, my sister Sue, once again, allowed Midnight and I to move back in with them. They lived in the farmhouse on an 80-acre pig farm, commonly referred to in the neighbourhood as "The Hohl Place." The previous owner, Elmer Hohl, (pronounced hōl, hole, whole), was a well-known exotic World Champion Horseshoe Player! The current owners were Ohmer and Esther, a lovely Amish-Mennonite couple that lived on their "Home" farm nearby.

It was August of 1996, when I moved back to the Hohl Place. One of Ohmer's sons was managing the 85 sow, farrow to finish barn. A farrow-to-finish operation includes all stages of pig production from breeding, gestation, farrowing, lactation and weaning through to market weight hogs. To "farrow" means for a female pig to give birth to a litter of piglets. To "Finish" is to raise pigs for meat, to a live weight of 225-300 pounds.

The present manager, upon hearing that I had moved in and was looking for work, promptly asked me if I wanted to take over the operation, so he could follow his dream of driving a truck instead. I thought about it. Approximately one minute later, I said, "Sure, why not?" No commute! I asked him when I should start and he said, "Right away!" I was trained intensively for about one week before he started his long-distance hauling in a big rig. With a smile on his face, he waved good-bye, drove away and left me to it. I rarely ever saw him again!

After I took over as manager, I soon realized that there wasn't anything natural about the conventionally run pig barn. The pigs were all kept on cement or slatted floors, with no bedding of any kind, as it was a liquid manure system. There were very few windows in the concrete jungle that became my second home for more than the next decade. I was always wanting to blow a hole in the wall and let the sows out into the sunshine and fresh air. I really didn't feel right that the growing pigs were fed antibiotics, while the sows were given regular vaccines and other medications. There were many activities that I was now suddenly responsible for that I didn't agree with and didn't want to do.

There were so many things I had to do with the baby piglets! I was supposed to cut off their sharp little teeth with a side-cutter – crunch – so they wouldn't damage their mother's udder or each other. Next job with the side cutter was to chop off their tail, so that another bored pig would not be tempted to play with the curly tail and possibly chew it off later. It was topped off with giving them a shot of iron in the neck, to avoid anemia in the piglets. The young females, called gilts, had to have their ears notched out to identify them according to their lineage. It was an interesting number system that correlated to the notches, but I hated punching out parts of their ears to do it! Ear tags didn't stay in and having to wrestle grown pigs to check their ear tattoos wasn't really an option.

For the young boars – males, I had to slice out their testicles with a scalpel, which I did when they were as young as a few days old, as it was much worse for everyone involved if I waited until three weeks, like my predecessor had. All of that was terrible work. I hated giving needles for routine vaccinations to 600 pound sows, while obviously chopping off God-given parts of the babies was in no way fun either. The vet seemed to have to come out on a regular basis to do herd-health stuff and deal with a ream of problems. I did have several strange diseases come through the barn, but with following the recommendations from the vets, the animals were not getting any healthier. It wasn't long before I was asking Ohmer if he minded, if I did things a little differently.

Over the next five years, I saved Ohmer between $7,000 and $20,000 a year by moving to a more natural direction with the help of a company called Bio-Ag Consultants and Distributors. Shane had told me about them years earlier, so I knew that they would be able to help. The medications in the feed were replaced with probiotics and supplements. I gave the sows some hay to eat, which helped to give their dull lives a little texture. After increasing the nutrition, I stopped vaccinating the sows and used inexpensive homeopathic remedies to prevent and treat problems. I put various toys and objects in the growing pigs' pens, which gave them something to do other than eating each other! This meant I could stop cutting off tails of the babies! I also stopped the horrific teeth clipping and they managed just fine!

Soon after I started working with the pigs, I felt the aching in my heart, missing my horse Digger so much. It was time for us to be reunited and I asked Ohmer, if I could bring Digger to live with me. My original idea for Digger was to have him on a nearby farm of Ohmer's, where he could live with the beef cattle and have a big field to run in. Ohmer had said no to the beef farm, but had agreed to allow Digger to live on the lawn. To start, he would live in a very old building, right next to the house. It wasn't long before he had sourced an old tin building that one of his neighbours had wanted to get rid of. He had brought it over for Digger to live in; it still stands there to this day.

That summer, Ohmer pointed out how glad I was, to have not moved Digger over to the beef farm. More than just that, I loved having him right with me, but the fact was that most of the animals in that field had been killed with one strike from the heavens. There was an old Elm tree in the center of the field where the animals often stood below the wide branches, for shade and shelter. On that particular day, thirteen cows, three calves and the bull were all killed instantly when lightning struck the tree! It was the only time that I have ever seen Ohmer cry.

I had to admit that he was right though. It was the best decision ever to have Digger right with me where I could keep him close by and safe.

After Digger's future was secured, I had then mentioned to Ohmer, if I was going to stay, I also needed a place to keep my sheep! He owned several farms and happened to have a small barn that I could rent, only 4 km away. I drove there to look after them at least twice a day for the next fourteen years.

With Ohmer's help to ensure that I could have my beloved animals nearby, I was extremely grateful. In return, I did my very best work for him. This may have been the first time that Ohmer came to my rescue, but it would not be the last. A true friendship was born that has continued throughout the years.

We did not always see eye to eye, still don't – but we found a way to be able to say what needs to be said, whether the other one likes it or not. Sure, there were the grumpy times, but somehow, we always came back to seeing reason and worked through our problems.

I listened to his stories, his not-so-funny ever repeated sayings and named them "Ohmerisms."

For example, "You tell 'em cabbage – you've got the head!" or "Two heads are better than one – even if one is a cabbage head!"

If you were to say, "Do you think it is going to rain today?"

He'd say, "It all depends on the weather."

And I could fill up the whole book with Ohmerisms, but you get the point! I did what he asked me to do, even if I thought it was "below my station." If I had words to say about it, he would hear me out and listen to my side, if not in the heat of the moment, then later. Occasionally, I would get my way too – if not right away, but eventually! It helped to live by the motto "Never give up!"

Ohmer's wife, Esther was a modest and humble woman, but we were both horrified at our first meal together. This first memory of her is forever etched into my mind. It was a day where I was working with "the boys" in the field, instead of alone in the pig barn. One son Harold, had kindly invited me to eat "dinner" with them, to save me driving home for lunch. I don't even know how to describe how I was feeling on that day; it was my first meal with the family. I was already nervous and feeling out of place with at least eight family members at the table. I also felt bad, knowing that I was invited last minute, without the cook's prior knowledge.

How do you think I felt when the main dish available to eat was *pig tails*!?

The platter of giant pig tails was passed around. I was hungry, but more so, I wanted to fit in and not make a fuss. I took one of the pink tails and put it on my plate. I have no idea what else was served that day, but I definitely remember the pig tail. It looked like someone had walked up to one of my sows, cut a chunk out of its ass and pulled the tail off, skin and all. The image I had in my mind? I could imagine every pig in the barn and someone pulling their tails off. I thought I was going to be sick. How could anyone eat that? I couldn't even *look* at the others devouring their meals. I picked away at the pork butt plug thing on my plate and attempted to eat a little of the meat. I was *not* cutting through that skin. I wanted to be polite, but there was just no way was I *that* hungry!

Esther had been embarrassed that she had served pig tails for my first meal. I had been embarrassed that I couldn't eat my first meal with the family. For the next twelve years, I ate delicious meals at their kitchen table on the home farm at least six days a week. Every day, my dessert included the special "black" cookies that were my favourite and baked especially for me! They were double chocolate chip. Another staple at dinner was homemade cabbage salad. I've never been able to recreate it at home, but it was cabbage, cream and sugar and I loved mixing it with her potatoes and canned meats. In all the years to follow, Esther kindly never served me pig tails again!

At the house on the farm of my new sheep barn lived Ohmer's nine-year-old granddaughter, Rachel. We immediately hit it off as forever friends. When Rachel got older, in addition to teaching her about sheep and lambs, I taught her how to take care of the pigs. Sometimes she helped to pressure wash the pens which seemed to be at least a weekly, if not daily job that got old for me, after a while.

The pig barn was over-run with rats and mice. I worked all alone and often talked to the animals that were in earshot. Occasionally, a mouse would fall into the feed cart. I would explain to them that I was here to help! The mouse would just have to trust me and follow my directions.

"Get onto my hand and I will lift you out..." I would tell them. Sometimes they would frantically try and get out by other means jumping up and down or running crazily around. In those instances, I would build them a bridge to give them something to climb out by themselves. Other times, they complied and just climbed on my hand! I was originally concerned that they would take a run up my sleeve so I usually put gloves on and tucked my coverall sleeve into the gloves, just to avoid me doing a freaky dance with a mouse loose somewhere in my clothing layers!

One time Rachel came in the barn as I was helping a mouse to safety. It was sitting on my hand and I was lifting it out. She had a smile on her face when she said, "Now that is not something that you see every day!"

THAT IS A MOUTHFUL!

By April of 1997, I was feeling secure in my surroundings and it was finally time for me to fulfill my dream of having my very own dog. I didn't do any research on breeds, but thought a registered Border Collie would be perfect. I also assumed that it would be healthy, simply because it was registered! I learned that is not the case!

Ohmer drove with me to pick out my first puppy, Chakotay. He was so cute and perfectly marked for a Border Collie; wide white collar, white stripe down his muzzle, with four white feet and a white tip on his tail. I paid my $150 and we drove away. While Ohmer was driving, I was holding Chakotay on my lap. All was well until he rolled on his back and I saw that he had the biggest overbite imaginable! I hadn't even considered checking the bite – especially not of a registered puppy!! I had wanted to do breeding, but already only fifteen minutes in, my hopes were dashed. I couldn't return him – he was my first puppy and I already loved him dearly.

In addition to my puppy, it was another year of firsts. I bought my first calf and named her Texarkana. Her breed was Holstein, which is a dairy breed crossed with a Limousin, a beef breed. I found her as a cute little anomaly in Ohmer's dairy barn. The other calves were all white with black patches. This sweet little calf appeared solid black, but when in bright sunshine, her hair sported beautiful golden-red undertones, which she had inherited from her Limousin sire. I paid Ohmer boarding fees to keep her at the dairy barn until she was bigger.

In the summer, Digger and I started taking roping lessons. I'd load him up in a trailer and drive about thirty minutes to the farm, where we'd learn the finer details of roping. I was apparently a born natural at throwing a rope from the ground, so now we just needed to get Digger and I to figure out how to do it at a run!

At the last roping lesson I ever went to, Digger was getting very jumpy in "the box". The box is where the horse and rider wait for the calf to be released. I believe the instructors should have had me just spend some time in the box without releasing the calf, but there were other students waiting their turn, so they kept running us through as quickly as possible. Digger had been acting up with excitement in the box, but somehow we still managed to rope the first eight steers they had released for us.

Another issue I had with Digger, maybe he was hard of hearing or something, I am sure I told him to CHASE the steer, but I believe he heard RACE the steer. Digger would run so fast he would blow right by the calf. The purpose of breakaway roping is that once the rope is around the calf's neck, the rider is supposed to stop the horse and the rope will become taut and then breakaway. The moment the rope breaks, the time is up. Perhaps you remember where I said earlier that I had some trouble stopping Digger? Well in this case, the rope was breaking after we were still running past the other side of the calf!

The ninth run we were going to make was my last for the day and for my hopes of ever riding in the rodeo. I should've quit while I was ahead, but I didn't know better. Digger reared up in the box as they opened the chute and out ran the calf. He started running so fast I had to try to slow him down. I "checked" the reins giving a sharp tug on the hackamore and he stopped suddenly! From a dead run, he stopped and reared up! My body was still going full speed when my horse's head showed up in front of my face. As my teeth were shoved through my lips, I felt like I was eating the back of

Digger's head. As they drove me to the hospital, I curiously wondered what had possessed me to think I ever wanted to be in the rodeo!

The lower part of my face was only black and blue for a week or two and the bite marks thankfully healed up without leaving a scar. The only scar was on my heart, as I had to come up with a new pastime. Maybe we would try barrel racing? I did get some big blue barrels and set up a course and gave it a go, but I ended up with the same problem again! Digger was fast enough, but he didn't want to slow down to go around the barrels, same as he didn't want to slow down to let me rope the calf! I would never give up on Digger, but sporting events were not to be in our future!

A few months later, my sister Sue had a visit from her friend with three young children. They wanted to have their picture taken on Digger, so the mother lined them up on his back and I held him steady. I had one arm up to make sure no one fell off. Little did I know that the woman had the flash on for an outdoor picture!! One giant flash of light later, Digger spooked and all three children came tumbling down at once! I managed to break their fall with my outstretched arm and although no child was injured, my arm did hurt for several days! Digger never did like cameras after that. He would always "head for the hills" if he saw someone attempt to get a photograph of him! He was forever more to be the epitome of camera shy!

That fall I bought my first brand-new pickup truck! It was a forest green, GMC Sierra, regular cab, long box, standard transmission with "roll by hand" windows. I was so proud of my accomplishment! I loved that truck and kept her for ten years before I sold her to Ohmer, so I could buy an extended cab truck the next time!

That fall for my birthday, Ohmer gave me a sow, which I named "PIG," since I loved the movie Babe! "PIG" had become extremely lame with an abscessed leg, so she was unable to be shipped for meat. I had fallen in love with her, so Ohmer let me keep her instead of "doing away with her."

"PIG" was a uniquely coloured sow. The majority of her body was covered in leathery gray skin that had black hairs coming out of it. The rest was pink which sported white hair in creative, star-shaped patches. I loved how she would grunt at me and gaze into my soul with her amber-coloured eyes. She had a cheery yet regal presence, she might as well have been wearing a top hat and using a walking stick!

I loved that sow and brought her out of the concrete jungle to live out her remaining days in the natural world. She lived with Digger in his house on the lawn. Before she came out, she gave birth to her second litter of piglets including six males and six females that I named; Kara, Tequila, Fiesta, Wilma, Black Pebbles and Red Pebbles. I kept all six females and it brought the barn sow total to ninety-two sows.

"PIG" lived out with Digger all through the winter. She didn't have much hair at first since she had lived in the hot pig barn, so I often covered her with a blanket when she was resting. I have the cutest picture of my nephew Jacob sitting with the 600 pound "pig in a blanket!" To overcome boredom, "PIG" managed to chew off Digger's mane and tail hair while he slept, so he looked pretty ridiculous!

My brother-in-law Al, used to marvel at how strange his life had become since I moved in with them. Occasionally, a giant limping black pig with white stars, would hop past the kitchen door as he drank his coffee in the morning!

PIG and Digger

ONCE BURNED, TWO DIE

One day, Ohmer's son Harold had some extra time and was helping me out by pressure washing in the farrowing room. When he was finished, he let me know that I could turn off the pressure washer. I promptly went upstairs and switched off the power to the propane heated pressure washer as directed. Without thinking, I closed up the chimney to keep the cold air from freezing the machine – like I always did. This involved taking plastic feed bags and shoving them up into the chimney. The thing was, usually I clean up the area I am washing in, put the hose and other items away BEFORE putting the bags up there.

This time was different, because I did it immediately after turning off the heat, without giving the chimney time to cool down. As I pushed the feed bags up into the chimney, the hot plastic melted instantly and fell down onto my bare hands. The plastic burned into my skin and stuck there. I screamed so loudly, Harold got a fright and ran to my rescue. He ran cold water on my hands and attempted to remove the plastic, but I had to stop him as it was very painful. We ran to the house and got a stainless-steel bowl and put cold water in it. I plunged my hands into the bowl and they stayed in there as Harold took me to the hospital.

After administering first aid, the doctor in the Emergency room recommended I see a specialist, saying that I would need skin grafting for the burns. That did not seem like much fun to me, so I did what I do and found a natural alternative. After the initial first aid period, I spoke to my homeopath, Murray from Bio-Ag and he prescribed the homeopathic remedy Cantharis. Ohmer donated a bottle of vitamin E oil to the effort, which I put on the burned areas religiously.

I met with the specialist and was told to return after one month, as it would be healed enough by then for them to do the skin grafting. When I arrived, the doctor looked at my fingers and then called for the nurse to come! He gazed at my hands in awe and exclaimed, "It's a miracle! You are completely healed!" I wish I had a picture of their faces that day; it was priceless!

I always felt like the natural route was the best one. God gave us the tools and it only seems logical to work with nature, instead of against it. This experience helped me gain confidence that I could take my knowledge not only into the pig barn, but also when caring for my sheep. I occasionally needed reminders I suppose – I just wish that they could have been less painful at times!

At the end of January of 1998, my dear, sweet, ten-month-old puppy Chakotay was hit by a car on the road. I ran out to get him with Sue's wooden toboggan dragging behind me. I placed him gently on the sled and wrapped him in a blanket to help ensure he wouldn't fall off. I had to pull him across the snow covered field in order to bring him back to the house so I could take him to the vet.

As I crossed Digger's pasture towing Chakotay behind me, Digger started trying to paw the toboggan I was pulling. Years earlier, when he had lived near Brenda and Shane's place, the folks there had used a toboggan to transport the horse's hay. They had told me that if they left the toboggan unattended, Digger would grab the rope and run away, stealing the bales of hay! They had to run after him on several occasions, to get the hay back before he pulled all the strings off, making himself a huge buffet! Well on this day, it was stressing me out with his memories of hay when I had my beloved injured dog on board!

I managed to get Chakotay loaded into the car. The three kilometers journey to the vet clinic took less than four minutes to drive. After taking a few X-rays, it was determined that indeed, Chakotay had broken his back leg. It was a clear break of his femur bone. Three months and $1000 later, Chakotay's cast came off and he was again fine. Whew!

With Chakotay on the mend, I now had a new issue. In March, my dear sow "PIG" was no longer enjoying her freedom and was uncomfortable with her lameness and other issues. It was a decision that I did not want to make. I had never been in the position to play God for one of my own animals before. I had seen dead animals lots of times. I had taken animals to the butcher and I had even caused death a time or two by accident. I remember driving over my sister Brenda's old rooster with a grain wagon and also pouring a 750 mL bottle of sheep drench down the throat of one of Shane's sheep. It was a medicine that it was supposed to drink, but in error it went straight into her lungs and killed her instantly. It was devastating and sad, but this was different. This was worse, because I saw it coming and had to labour over the decision. Worse, I had to make the call for a beloved friend whose time was up. Thankfully, the vet was a nice woman who was sympathetic to my condition. Digger was standing guard outside, while I was stroking "PIG"'s ear when she took her last breath. She laid in the straw, on her blanket in Digger's house, as the vet helped her pass over to the other side.

It was a huge loss – really huge! It's not like she went around unnoticed - she weighed like 600 pounds! For six months she had hobbled all over the farm, unfenced and unfettered – experiencing the freedom that she deserved. She was going to be missed by all of us.

It was May 11, and I had just finished loading weaner pigs into a trailer to go to one of the other farms and had come downstairs to my office. I was writing in the record book, how many pigs had been taken, when I heard a honk and looked out the window. I saw the truck and trailer blazing down the driveway and my beloved Chakotay, excited by the squealing pigs, running towards the trailer! With the speed of the truck, Chakotay didn't see that the trailer was wider than the truck and I watched as the trailer wheel drove over his head!

Oh dear God! This didn't just happen!? How could this be? I had just spent months nursing Chakotay back to perfect health and he had only been out of his cast for a few weeks!

With my heart in the back of my throat, I ran out to find his lifeless body laying on the gravel driveway. I fell into a heap on the rough ground, buried my face in Chakotay's fur and wept uncontrollably. By this time, the driver had parked the truck in the lane and had come back around to view the damage. He looked down at us and said, "Is it dead?" He confirmed his suspicion by lifting up Chakotay's lips to reveal white gums.

The driver didn't want to get into trouble by Ohmer so he picked Chakotay up, chucked him in the back of the truck and drove away saying he'd "look after it." I never did find out where his final resting place was, probably a manure pile or dumped in the bush. I was extremely traumatized and not enjoying dog ownership very much so far. But I didn't give up on my dream of having a dog... I just wasn't very good at it yet. I'd never been blessed with a dog growing up, so I was learning as I went along. My heart was ripped in two. First "PIG" and now Chakotay. With overwhelming grief, I concentrated on keeping busy with work and trying not to focus on the pain.

HANZ & FRANZ FLY THE COOP

In June, I embarked on an opportunity to bring home something unusual. Actually, it was one of those impulsive auction purchases that leave you shaking your head.

There was a farm equipment auction being held for a retiring farmer, half way between the Hohl Place and the Home Farm; Ohmer had invited me to go with him. He offered to buy me lunch at the food booth, instead of going for dinner at his house. I couldn't turn down a free lunch, nor an opportunity to get "off the farm" for a little while. I had often tagged along with Ohmer to various farm shows and auction sales to see what was on offer. Maybe we actually were looking for something or maybe we were just open to a good deal.

One memorable time, we had gone to an auction house that was located right across the road from my sheep barn, where they had on offer an enormous number of veterinary supplies. Perhaps that was one time I should have bought more than I did! I bought a lot of interesting stainless steel, German made tools like curved scissors and hemostats that I still have today. I also bought a stash of needles and syringes that twenty-five years later I am still dipping into, when needed!

Anyway, I digress, at this neighbour's sale, I thought it was going to just be boring farm equipment and tools, but I was wrong! I walked by a cage with two handsome, one year old Indian Blue Shoulder Peacocks! I pointed them out to Ohmer. He said, "You should buy them." I looked back at the peacocks and thought, I guess I should? Well, whether I should or shouldn't have, either way I did! These two young fellows were sure to add a little colour to my life!

I named the handsome pair, Hanz and Franz. Soon after I brought them home, I felt badly for them. Although their long tails wouldn't grow for another two years, I felt it was mean to keep them in the cage that I had bought with them. Although it had a peaked roof, it was just too short for these tall creatures. If I would have known better, I would have waited at least two weeks for them to get used to me and their new surroundings, but I didn't know I should do that at the time.

Living from my heart, without much more thought about it, I opened the door and stepped way back to give them some room. I watched with delight as they poked their heads out of the little door. One by one, they each jumped onto the ground below.

In the blink of an eye, they were gone. The two of them had simultaneously turned around, ran a few steps, spread their wings and disappeared somewhere in the rafters of the nearby driving shed!

They had up and flown away right before my eyes and I was left standing in front of the cage by the barn, wondering what I had just done. Who even knew they could fly? And how do I catch something large that can fly away, before I even get there!? Some people call Ghostbusters, I call Ohmer.

Once they flew across the road and into the rafters of my neighbour Brian's barn. Ohmer and Brian helped me round them up. Another memorable time, we retrieved them from a back neighbour's sugar shack. This time Sue tagged along with Ohmer and I, in the dark at night and with a ladder. Sue watched as I climbed up into the rafters in the dark. Ohmer would flash a light occasionally so I could see where they were, but not tip them off that I was coming to get them! The light would temporarily blind them and I'd leap forward, without falling to my death, and grab their both feet in one hand and hang on to the ladder with the other!

They were young but they each weighed about twelve pounds and with their wings flapping and carrying on, I was barely able to make my way down to the ground, in order to subdue the birds. Ohmer had a feed bag with a hole cut out of it and would put the bird in the bag, with its head sticking out, but its body safely in the bag for transport. It wasn't perfect, but at least they couldn't get away and could not hurt themselves. Eventually, Ohmer and I made a pen for them in the barn for the winter.

After my purchase, I did some research into Peafowl... its never too late to get educated! I wasn't too surprised to learn that in some countries they are used for both eggs and meat. I was stunned to learn that they can live as long as a donkey, up to fifty years! My boys didn't have their tails yet, but they would grow to be up to five feet wide, helping to make them appear much larger than they actually were. They have ornamental value of course, as they are pretty to look at, but at night when you can't see them, they can certainly be heard! They will shriek quite loudly when danger is present, so they make good additions to the hen house helping to ward off predators. They also protect their territory from many pests by eating ticks, rodents, snakes and amphibians!

They did prove to be very loud creatures and still took every opportunity they got, to fly away. After speaking with the original owner, I found out that the males will always go searching for females, so in order to keep them at home, I was going to have to grow the flock. I added Xena and Gabrielle to the menagerie. They were beautiful in their own right. Sure, they were plain brown and white, but they had some wonderful green colouring on their necks! They took up residence in the old building that Digger had started out in, where I raised my meat birds. When the boys were next let out, these ladies kept a short leash on their men and they never flew away again! The peahens do not lay too many eggs and I never tried to eat one, but they did raise some very nice babies for me! After a few years I did have to find new homes for them, because they were causing grief to the people that looked after the equipment, which was housed underneath where they used to sit and poop, in the rafters of the driving shed!

WYATT, THE COMEDIAN

W ell, they say third times a charm…and so, I embarked on yet another journey to try my hand at having a dog – this time would be different. Although I wouldn't meet him for another five weeks, two days after Chakotay's untimely death, Wyatt was born.

Wyatt was another Registered Border Collie. I had found him through an advertisement in the newspaper. The owner of the female was a dentist and seemed to have done his homework. The parents had been sent away for sheep dog training before being bred, so as to ensure only good working genetics would be passed on, or so this was the hope. These dogs did not live on a farm, but in the city about an hour and a half away.

I was so excited to see the litter of little ones! The mother looked like a real dog of a reasonable size. I had viewed some others where the mothers were scrawny and didn't look like a dog that I would like to have!

A perfectly marked pup ran over to me and immediately started chewing on my pantleg. He had a gorgeous wide white collar of fur, but I barely looked at the pup at my feet. The one that had caught my eye was a little further out. He was calm, the opposite of the little furball aggressively trying to get my attention below. He was slowly making his way over to me when our eyes locked together. I bent down and picked him up and held him gently in my arms; it was love at first sight.

I can hear you saying, "Wait!?"

Yes, I was already in love but, like you were insinuating, the first thing I did was lift up his lips to check his bite. Whew! The top and bottom teeth were in perfect alignment! I could feel this puppy in my soul... I had no doubt that we were to be together.

The first day I met him, he picked me out and I took him home. I named him Wyatt after the character George Strait played in my favourite movie, Pure Country! He was only five weeks old at the time, which was *way* too early to be separated from his family! He hadn't learned enough about being a dog!

Puppies need to stay with their families until eight to ten weeks of age. Socialization is a very important stage of development. They need to learn skills from their mother and siblings as well as be exposed to different situations by the breeder, to help make a well-rounded dog. This step was skipped by the breeder as he said that the younger pup will bond better with the new owner; that might be, but it can also cause issues!

Wyatt's purchase price was more than three times what I had paid for Chakotay. The breeder had spent a *lot* of time with the puppies and apparently, they had been clicker trained from birth. Every time they went to nurse from the mother, the breeder clicked the button.

This method teaches the animal that the exact moment it hears a click, they've done something good and they will be rewarded. The animal learns to do the action to get the reward. For example, in order to teach a dog to sit without the use of a clicker, one might push a dog's butt down and say sit or try other ways to get it to comply. With the clicker training, you would wait around the dog until the moment they were in the exact action of bending to sit down and then you'd click and give a reward. The dog was going to sit because it wanted to – you are rewarding it for doing what it wanted to do. Win-win the dog figures. After a while, with you clicking at the exact moment they are doing the thing that you want them to do, you can add a command – because they are already happy to do it! It makes training easier, because you are very clear at the moment of the click that it is a good thing.

When I took Wyatt home, I continued with the clicker training. By the time he was six weeks old he could come when called, sit, lie down and give me five! Over the next thirteen years, I never did teach him to heel though, no matter how I tried!

I babied my little baby; I never left him alone. How could I?

I still had to go to work in the pig barn, so I bought a baby monitor, in order to be able to keep working. I would put him in his cage when he was sleeping and then go to work. If he woke up, I would come back in and stay with him until he went back to sleep. Because I was always with him, he never had any opportunity to do anything wrong!

When he was six months old, he went in the basement and ripped up a box of Kleenex and made a huge mess. When I walked in and saw white covering the cement floor, I was not impressed, yelled at him and chased him outside. It was my first time getting upset with him and it was his first time reacting to such behaviour. I remember clearly seeing him outside the basement door, his eyes went wild as he looked at me and growled. I had some work to do after that, because occasionally Wyatt would scare me with growling. I eventually taught him to bark and growl on command and then I never asked him to do it! It worked quite well.

Wyatt's most memorable character trait was his ability to lift my spirits and I valued that very much. Wyatt was my comedian, if I got too tense, he would always find a way to make me laugh. I remember one time I was stressed out, driving to my sheep manager job on a farm near Brussels and he stuck his nose into my spit cup for my sunflower seed shells. It stuck on his nose and when I glanced over at him he was just sitting there, next to me, with the cup stuck on his face! I laughed so hard that I had to pull over; it was hilarious.

That year I also tried my hand raising Lincoln sheep. These sheep looked so cool and they came in beautiful colours. Which reminds me of a quick story. In the early years of their marriage, Brenda and Shane had met a government Agent, who was asking them some questions about their sheep. Brenda said they had a certain number of sheep "and a small flock of *coloured* sheep." The Agent thought that was the neatest thing – wow, like pink and green and yellow? Um no, she replied. Just black. Hmm. Not all colours are created equal, I guess. In the case of these Lincolns, they were more interesting than just plain black! They had gorgeous colours in addition to the standard white ones. Beautiful black, various browns and gray with silver being my favourite! Their wool grew incredibly long and amazingly fast, hanging in tight ringlets.

My first Lincoln ram I named "Rasta" as his wool had such beautiful ringlets, resembling the spiritual dreadlocks of the Rastafarian hairstyle. In fact, Lincoln sheep have so much wool that they have to be shorn every eight months to keep them in "good fleece". The wool literally grows an inch per month and is very coarse, the complete opposite of the fine wool of the Corriedale. The Lincoln wool is used in applications like the heels and toes of work socks that need to be much stronger. Rasta sadly bloated on pasture too rich in alfalfa and died suddenly and I needed another ram to get me through breeding season. My friend Bill whom I had bought the Lincolns from, said I could have an older ram that he was going to cull because it had a lump. I named him Clint and after I had used him to breed my ewes, he was immediately sent off to the stockyards. Five months later I had the nicest lambs I'd ever seen. I called Bill and told him of the wonderful offspring saying I wished I had kept him. He said "Well they should have been good, he was past winner at the Royal Winter Fair!" I wish I would have known earlier!

In addition to showing my wool and sheepskins, one year I also showed hay! Ohmer had grown some of the nicest hay that I had ever seen and I had said that he should show it at the Royal Agricultural Winter Fair in Toronto. He responded that it was against his religion to do that. I told him it was too good just to feed to the sheep and asked if he minded if I showed the hay in my name and he agreed.

In November, I entered the hay into the Royal competition. The class was Second Cut or later: at least 30% grass and 30% legume. The hay was judged on several criteria. The overall look of it and the colour was important. A rich deep green colour, with lots of leafy material signifies that it likely has good nutrients, whereas dry brown or thick stems can mean it is older and not as nutritious or delicious. The texture – soft is the nicest, usually means young and tender as opposed to hard and stemmy, which many animals don't prefer. Another thing is the aroma. It should smell sweet and fresh, as opposed to stale or musty. The hay should also be free from dust, as opposed to it making a cloud when handled which could cause respiratory issues for both man and especially women and children! I was delighted when the flake of hay won first prize!!

STRAIT TO TEXAS

It was during March the following year that I made a major, sudden decision to go on a vacation! Now that might not seem like a big deal, but for someone who doesn't even take a day or week-ends off, it *was* a big deal! I told Ohmer that I needed a break; I wrote out about a half an inch thick stack of papers with instructions for someone looking after my pig barn. I didn't have any human to go on vacation with, so Wyatt and I departed on a wonderful adventure on March 26. It was Wyatt, my new pick-up truck and the destination of Texas, USA! My goal was to see Texas and who knew how big it really was! Apparently, it is 1244 km long and 1271 km wide! I wanted to see it all, so I drove from east to west to south and north! There were so many different types of terrain in the second largest state that I would never have guessed.

As for why I chose Texas over any other place? It was surely in my attempt to find George Strait, of course! It seemed like a noble cause to pick up and drive to a very large state and look high and low for him! I brought along his latest album, *Always Never the Same,* just released a couple weeks before, as my soundtrack to our adventures. To this day when I hear those songs, it takes me back to cruising down the highway at 70 miles an hour, taking in the sights with Wyatt by my side. My first thought when I think of Texas is the song *Peace of Mind…*

The chorus sings like I felt at the time:
'I go anywhere that old wind blows

Down a blacktop road anytime
No strings attached, no ties to tie me down.
So why hang around when I can fly?"

Since my mission was to see as much of Texas as possible, but I was too afraid to stop anywhere and leave Wyatt unattended, I ate every meal from drive-thru restaurants. Then one day, I was driving down the highway with a submarine sandwich on my lap. I didn't notice Wyatt pull off the top half of the bun and take it back over to his shotgun seat. There was nothing I could do about it when I glanced over and saw the last bit disappearing from view - into his mouth!

Our travels took us first from Texarkana, that my cow was named after, over to Ozona, southwest down to Mexico, south to Kingsville and the Gulf of Mexico – Mustang Island, north to San Antonio, where I hit an ostrich with my truck on Easter Saturday. I drove west back to Ozona on Easter Sunday and north up through Amarillo. The trip encompassed twelve days, of which I visited only the city of San Antonio, which was the worst part of the trip, and drove the rest of the time – a mere 10,000 km!

For anyone that knows country music, since I was in love with George Strait, my plan was to find him – he lives in Texas don't you know? I drove to the area where he was born, where I thought he lived and to all the places that he sang about in his songs! In the early years I named all of my sheep after words in his songs! I had Amarillo, Adalida, Belle, and so on.

Anyway, I digress. My shearer friend Len had told me of his friends located in Ozona, Texas, so I made sure to visit there. I stayed a day on their huge ranch where they raised, trained and trialed Border Collies. The couple trained their half a dozen Border Collies to herd, using the sheep on the ranch.

They didn't own the ranch but looked after the thousands of acres of sparse land, covered with rocks, live oak, yucca and prickly pear cactus! They had thousands of sheep on the property, but I didn't see any on my visit. The sheep had to cover a lot of ground to find enough to eat, so they moved around a lot. The terrain was nothing like I was used to pasturing animals on – how did they even do it? Somehow, Crockett County, where the ranch was located, is one of the United States leading producers of wool and mohair.

I asked the fellow named Ivan, for his help in getting Wyatt to heel, which had always confounded me. He showed me how to use an evergreen branch to wave in front of Wyatt's face to keep him back and in line. I did try that trick about a hundred times over the next few years, but alas it was not to be! Wyatt refused to heel!

I have pictures of Wyatt at every place we went. Wyatt next to this or that giant statue. At one point, the mayor of a town came out to see my dog perched up on their beloved statue and me trying to take a picture! He was very nice and offered to take a picture of the two of us – so that is the only picture I have of myself from the trip! The best photo though is very picturesque, of Wyatt in Texas at Santa Elena Canyon by the Rio Grande – it's my favourite!

As I mentioned earlier, the whole trip I was only eating fast food while I was craving real food. Imagine my joy at seeing a roadside stand near the Mexican border. We stopped in and I bought a big watermelon. That night we went to a motel and I had the opportunity to sleep in a California King sized bed for the first time! I thought that would be so fun with so much space to spread out! I had my jackknife along, so when I had brought my bags in for the night, I set about hacking apart the giant watermelon for a bedtime snack.

I had the misfortune of letting Wyatt eat his share of the watermelon on the bed; it had seemed like a reasonable thing to do at the time. When I pulled back the covers to climb in for the night,

I saw a three-foot round spot of watermelon juice! I sighed and moved the pillows away and climbed in the giant bed. In order to stay in the dry, I had to sleep across the top of the bed next to the headboard!

As I grabbed all of my belongings from the room the following morning, I was reminded of a job I had one summer when I was seventeen. I had worked at a motel, cleaning rooms. The motel was located eight miles east of where Brenda and Shane lived and I had to ride my bicycle to get there. It was called Wiarton Willie's Motel and on the lawn in a cage there lived the famous albino groundhog that made his appearance every February 2, on Groundhog Day. He was quite the local attraction, but apparently attracted people with a lot of body hair! I only lasted three days as janitorial staff for this establishment, as it was a really disgusting job in my young mind! Pulling the sheets back to find the shape of a hairy man had been the last straw for me and I had quit. Needless to say, I was feeling a little bad for the person that had to clean up the bed from the watermelon juice, but at least it wasn't a three-foot round spot of human hair!

All in all, the trip was an event, but uneventful – except this one time where I made an error in judgement. I wanted to go and take some pictures of the Rio Grande at the Mexican border, but there was no clear shot. It seemed like a good idea at the time to walk unnoticed with Wyatt through the driving lanes at the border and go on the bridge over top of the river. I got some great pictures! As we then tried to walk back through across the now US border – several border agents with guns surrounded us. I was armed only with my camera, no I.D. or anything else to prove who I was! I explained that I had only gone to the bridge to take some pictures and I was parked "over there" as I pointed in the general direction of a nearby parking lot. This was one time that looking very white came in handy – they believed my story about being a Canadian and luckily let us go! My heart was still racing when we made it back to the truck in unscathed.

Wyatt in Santa Elena Canyon

THE ADVENTURES
OF WYATT & HARLEY

I had started out with only a few sheep, but they do seem to multiply! There were so many beautiful female lambs, how could I let them go? Well, truth was, I couldn't and so the flock grew exponentially. Starting with the original five ewes, the flock had quickly grown to thirty-five and now it had grown into a business. Upon my return home from Texas, I thought it was about time for my farming enterprise to have a name. I was selling lamb meat, sheepskins and Muscovy ducks, as by this time I had twelve breeding ducks as well. I aptly named it "Ewe to You."

There had been so many flies in the pig barn and I couldn't stand using fly bait or spraying insecticide, so I chose a natural remedy – Muscovy ducks! For a while I sold the duck eggs as well, since I really liked them, even more than chicken eggs. They are quite thick and rich in nutrients, compared to chicken eggs. After I raised too many ducklings for inside the barn, I used to keep them outside as well. I had one mama duck raise me thirty ducklings in one batch!

I used to let the ducks run around in the farrowing room where the sows were all locked up in the raised farrowing crates with their piglets. I could not let them in with the dry sows as they would have been on the same level and able to go in with the pigs, which would have been extremely dangerous for them! Pigs are omnivores and would have gladly eaten the ducks if given the opportunity!

I remember one time at Brenda and Shane's place, they rented the neighbour's barn to grow their finisher pigs. Their sheep had gotten out of the pasture fence and gone up the barn hill into the second story of the barn. On the floor of the upstairs, overtop of the pigs, there was a large hole where feed and bedding were usually thrown down. Unfortunately a sheep ran up there and fell into the pig pen below, breaking its leg from the fall. They did not find it in time and sadly, the pigs had killed the poor sheep and were already eating it when they showed up!

One day, after I returned from my trip, Ohmer suggested that I get a female for breeding with Wyatt. Hmm. Ohmer often had good ideas, so in May I called up Ivan whom I had visited on the ranch in Ozona, Texas and asked about getting on their list for a female puppy. They had a wonderful female Border Collie named Moy. At the time, she was fourth in standing in North America sheep dog trials. I knew she had recently had a litter and I figured maybe they would be having another litter in a year or so. They said that Moy was older and they might not breed her anymore, but they still had a puppy left from her last litter. I had actually seen two puppies when I was there and even took a picture of them, but hadn't paid too much attention otherwise. The sire of the puppy was Raider, Texas Dog of the Year. She was going to be a good dog. The breeder's daughter lived in Ontario, so in a month or two they would deliver the new puppy.

Finally, in June my five-month-old puppy arrived. I named her Harley Tucker, after Wyatt's girlfriend in Pure Country. Her colouring was black, white and tan. I could not have asked for a better little dog, with excellent working instincts!

Wyatt and Harley always got along, although she was not socialized well with people when she first arrived. Harley had lived in a kennel for the first five months of her life so it took a little bit, but she came around. She was always a serious dog, very intent on keeping her eyes on animals. She had a very strong "eye," meaning always watching the stock with a fixed glare. She could make stock do things, just with her eyes; she was that powerful! Harley was definitely the worker in the family, while Wyatt was the class clown.

July started a disastrous streak for Wyatt. One day he disappeared for almost five hours! I searched all over, phoned Animal Control in three counties, all the vet clinics and was making "MISSING" flyers while talking on the phone to my friend Denise, when I heard the faintest sound of barking! I hung up the phone, dropped the flyers and shot out the door in a flash. As I ran towards the muffled barking, it got a bit louder. I was screaming Wyatt's name as I approached the 75-foot wide, 12-foot deep, liquid manure storage pit.

I climbed up on the cement wall and eerily peered over the five-foot tin fence surrounding the pit. There I saw my beloved Wyatt — well at least the top part of his head! He had managed to find some solids to rest his front feet on — there must have been a pile down below, where the manure exited from the barn into the pit. He was exhausted and was barely able to keep his chin up enough to bark without swallowing manure water. As soon as he saw me, he left his safe haven and started swimming towards me. I took one look at him and went into overdrive. Without thinking about how I'd never been able to do it before, I ripped the eight-foot door off the pit wall and threw it to the ground beside. I ran to the house and called the Home Farm. Esther answered and I asked her to send help. I hung up the phone and grabbed Wyatt's tie-out cable and harness. I ran with such speed that the wind whipped across my face.

First stop was the driveshed. I flew through the door and grabbed a very long, wooden ladder. With the great weight it slowed me down some, but I hauled it across the length of the barn, over to the pit. I managed to get the ladder over the edge and down to the floor below, covered by several feet of liquid pig manure. Luckily it was a heavy enough that it went down without floating.

I secured one end of the cable tie-out and took off my work boots. Without any thought to my safety, I did what any mother would do; I turned around and gingerly placed my sock foot on the second rung and began my descent, into the manure pit to save my baby!

To say that Wyatt was happy to see me was an understatement! He swam over and I managed to get his harness on which was attached to the cable above and helped him on to the ladder. I hugged my completely soaked-in-pig-manure pooch, before we began to climb the ladder. It was harder than I thought. We were resting about halfway up, I had my arms around him on the ladder, supporting him with the front of my body, when the reinforcements reached us. Ohmer's sons arrived, and peered over the edge of the pit down at us. I'm pretty sure one gave me a tongue lashing for not being safe as he hauled Wyatt up – but I wasn't listening. My only thoughts were on getting Wyatt to safety.

As soon as Wyatt had four feet on land, I made my ascent back up the ladder. But lookout! He was concerned that I was in danger and thought he should go back in and now save me! They grabbed the harness and held him tight until I was safely out. I sat on the ground and hugged Wyatt. I think it was several weeks before I got the smell off of my skin – but I didn't care – my baby was safe! But there was still one unanswered question; how did he get into the pit!?

I searched around the entire outside wall and the only possibility that I found was a ten-inch hole at ground level that maybe a pipe had once stuck through. Why he had chosen to take a swim that day and fall about six or eight feet down into the manure below, I'll never know. That trip into the pit was just the first of three things that happened to him in a row.

End of July brought the wedding of my friends I met at Guelph. I was to be a bridesmaid and so for the first time, I had to leave the dogs at home. Whilst I was away, a flash storm passed through.

When I got home at one o'clock in the morning, my truck headlights shone on the place where Wyatt's house used to be. At some point that day, a huge apple tree had fallen on top of Wyatt and his dog house! He was underneath the branches when I ran to rescue him – but again, thankfully he was unscathed. I tried for a couple of days to get someone to help get the tree off his house, but it wasn't a priority to anyone but me. It was funny how quickly it got done after I asked to borrow Ohmer's chainsaw. The same day, the tree got cut up! Funny how no one wanted to set me loose with a chainsaw!

August 14, around 5 PM, my sister Sue and I were chilling on the front porch when we heard several loud bangs, a thud or two and then a rash of whining and yelping. After my fiasco with losing Chakotay, I had gotten an invisible fence for Wyatt and installed it around Digger's lawn. This turned out not to be the best idea because during the next rainy season, Digger's hooves had sunk down and cut up the wires, but that was another story. At this time, Wyatt had been asleep in Digger's house. Digger had turned around to go outside but in so doing, had inadvertently stepped on top of Wyatt's foreleg, but I didn't know this at the time.

Now with this injury, I learned a valuable lesson about trusting myself, and my own judgement. In this case, I did not trust myself, I listened to the words of others, "He'll be fine; you call the vet too much; you spend too much money on your dogs," and so on. So in trying to placate to others, I didn't follow my heart. After all the money I spent on Chakotay, maybe they were right.

I brought Wyatt into my room to sleep that night. He kept me awake with his incessant crying and I got mad at him. I couldn't take it anymore and figured that I needed to sleep! "Shut up already" I thought. I marched downstairs and went outside into the night. I set up a cage on the lawn and then carted him downstairs and outside. As I put him in the cage and shut the door, I told him to

"BE QUIET!! GOODNIGHT!!" And went back to bed, however, only getting a fitful sleep at that point. Was I doing the right thing?

In the morning I got up early to check on him. Wyatt was sitting in the cage holding his paw up to me – clearly saying: "HELP!" How could I have been so heartless? He was my baby! At that moment, I said to myself, "Forget everybody else! I am taking him to the vet!" I called the vet and told them we were on the way.

As it turned out, he had several broken metacarpals – the bones located below his wrist and above his toes. Of four, three were broken and required pins.

I felt terrible. I vowed to myself that I would not make that same mistake again. At least in the end, we got the bones stabilized and he would be okay, but it would require a few months in a cast for sure. At least he would be alright. I didn't balk at the $2000 price tag, I would never give up on him, not ever.

In November, I decided to go on another vacation. Since I worked seven days a week, I figured I had earned the right to ask for a few days off now and then. This time, Len had recommended that I travel south to Louisville, Kentucky for the North American International Livestock Exposition. I was interested in possibly looking for some Corriedale breeding stock for my sheep and went to check out the sheep shows.

My first ram Amos, had been a black Corriedale who I had loved so much. I thought perhaps I could find another one equally as good, and wanted to look stateside. The Corriedale is a breed from New Zealand and was first on the scene around 1882. It was created by breeding the Merino sheep that has very fine, soft wool, with the Lincoln Long-wool with the very strong fibre that I had mentioned before. What a wonderful wool breed to infuse into my flock, or so I thought. However, the sheep at the show did not resemble my Amos.

I was astonished at the sheer size of the sheep there! Over the years they have made show stock very tall so that the handlers do not have to lean over to show them – easier on the back, but what was that? They were not normal farm animals! They were more like ponies! I was not interested in that kind of sheep.

Wyatt and Harley loved to ride in the truck with me. They would sit side by side on the bench seat, looking out the window some of the time. Otherwise they would curl up like cats in a basket, one on each seat – balls of fur. Occasionally, Wyatt would snuggle up with me and put his head on my lap as he slumbered. After the disappointment of the sheep show, I then took Wyatt and Harley to the large herding trial nearby, to watch his grandmother Nan compete.

Nan was great, but I have to say it was not wise to bring two sheep dogs to a sheep dog trial as spectators! They wanted to participate and weren't always silent in the stands! Once again, the trip was fun, but we were happy to go home. I always worried about crossing the border, but on that trip, the border guard waved me straight through without even asking any questions!

In December, I took Wyatt to the vets for his fifth X-ray. He had been out of his splint for a couple of months at this point and they were waiting to take the pins out. Two of the three bones had healed, but one remained broken. They put on a fiberglass cast to stay on for about a month. It had already been four months; we were hoping this would do the trick.

A week later, I went to Kitchener to visit my Mom and Dad and get my snow tires installed on my truck. I stopped at their house to put the dogs in their garage and my mother followed me to the shop. We went shopping at the mall for a while as we were putting in time, until the truck was ready. Just after five o'clock, I suddenly had a feeling of dread come over me and I asked Mom if Dad knew the dogs were in the garage. She assured me that he knew, but I tried to call him at work anyway. He had already left. I wanted to get back there in a hurry and check, but Mom kept reassuring me that he knew.

At six o'clock, Mom and I were driving home from the mall and she suddenly stopped the car and exclaimed, "There's Wyatt!" Actually, it was Harley – but still! She was performing a search pattern zigzagging back and forth down the sidewalk, looking for my scent! I leapt from the car and called her to me. We ran together to Mom and Dad's house around the corner. Wyatt saw me and practically leapt on top of me!

As it turned out, Dad had come home around five o'clock, automatically opened the garage door as he drove around the corner. He backed into the garage and pressed the button to close the door. When he got out of the car, he saw the garbage bin laying on its side and figured that I must have visited earlier in the day. When he stepped inside the house, it was confirmed that I had been there and would be returning, when he noticed the two leashes that had been left on the floor by the door.

He spread out his newspaper on the kitchen table and immersed himself in the daily news. He heard barking a few times and looked out, but there was no sign of my truck. So he went back to reading his newspaper, having no idea that he had let the dogs out of the garage.

My mother opened the garage door as she drove around the corner. We safely put Wyatt and Harley back inside, ensuring the door was closed, before we went in to find my Dad reading a magazine in his chair.

I opened the front door to show Dad that the entire porch and lawn was completely stepped up with dog footprints in the snow! Harley's footprints were even evident on the window sills where she must have been looking at Dad, wondering why he wasn't letting them in! I was just so thankful, that in almost an hour, their first real time in the city, Wyatt never left and Harley was only a few houses away. In the end, the only costly thing was, that I had to get Wyatt's cast redone as he had gotten it wet, being in the snow for so long. All in all – I don't know how, but Wyatt managed to survive 1999!

Nobody's Grandma, Ivy

E arly in 2000, I had worn out my welcome living with Sue and Al at the Hohl Place. I was happy to be able to move into a small apartment that Ohmer had available on one of his other farms. My sheep were now located about halfway between the apartment and the pig barn. I was able to stay there for about six months.

During this time, Wyatt, Harley and I lived in a very small space, without doors between the few rooms. When young Harley came into heat, I was not prepared – but Wyatt was! I needed to know if Harley was pregnant and asked my friend Len who also did ultrasound scanning on sheep, to scan her and see if she was. He found three puppies!

All I was interested in having was a female puppy that looked like Wyatt and Harley. I did all my research and a friend gave me a wooden whelping box. When May 10 arrived, I was as ready as I could be for the coming three puppies. I'd stayed awake all night before with the restless and nesting Harley.

Early in the morning, I thought she had to go pee and took her outside into the darkness. I was keeping a close eye on her, but was veritably unprepared when she squatted to pee and out came a puppy!

I lunged at her and flew through the air like an Olympic diver off a diving board. I landed hands first, by her back end, completely terrifying the young mother! I grabbed the puppy before it hit the ground – but it was still attached to Harley by the umbilical cord!

What a circus it would have seemed to an onlooker – luckily no one could see, because it was dark. I was chasing Harley around the yard, having to stay very close to her, because the puppy was still attached. She was running away because I was strangely chasing her with something! Had I just let her bite off the umbilical cord it would have gone much better, but I didn't want to put the baby on the dirty ground and neither of us would stop running! Eventually, I cornered her on the porch and cut the umbilical cord. I safely got Harley and her new baby back into the house and into the whelping box!

While waiting for the next puppy to arrive, I confirmed the first puppy was male after flipping him over for a quick peek. An hour later, the second male made his appearance. After waiting another two and a half hours, I was getting a little worried about my female puppy's whereabouts, hoping that I wasn't out of luck. Just about then, out popped a slimy green thing. What the heck was that? The puppy and the placenta were green?

When I got the placenta off and toweled her dry, there she was – the perfect puppy. She was perfectly marked and the spitting image of her father. She was instantly named, "IVY" after the wise old Grandma in Pure Country. My next thought was "Great! Now I can get some sleep!" I laid down on the couch and before I was quite asleep, I heard something move about.

I got up to see and there was a fourth puppy, a second female! Wow! I laid down again, but realized that sleep was not to come. Another puppy came instead. And another. And another. Then, when I thought there could not possibly be anymore, I laid down exhausted... but what the heck? Six and a half hours after the first puppy, number eight was born! I promptly named all the puppies in that litter after characters from the movie Pure Country - since the parents had those names already, might as well stick with the theme!

I had Dusty, Lula, Buddy, Earl, Ernest, Tim, JW and of course, Grandma Ivy.

I had been prepared to take care of three puppies and find homes for two, but now there were eight and I had to find homes for seven!

It was a learning curve again for sure! I have to admit that since the litter hadn't been planned – it was planned parents but not planned parenting; I hadn't found homes in advance of breeding. For me, this created a level of panic. Panic is not a good space to be in and I did not make good choices when I found the seven homes. Two of the puppies would eventually need to be rehomed again later. One was returned and one I had to rescue – neither situation was fun.

Puppies open their eyes around ten to fourteen days, but they cannot hear until they are three weeks old. The hearing will continue to develop until five to six weeks of age. Imagine my surprise when the puppies turned three weeks old and Ivy already responded to her name! I was having a particularly stressful day and needed some comfort; there is nothing like puppy love to cure what ails you!

"Ivy?" I said to the group of wiggling puppies nuzzled to their mother's breast. I picked her out of the crowd with my eyes and exclaimed, "I love you!"

Ivy immediately moved away from her mother and siblings towards me. She crawled over to where I was standing by the edge of her pen. I leaned over, picked her up and held her close to my chest. We both sighed. We were together and that is all that mattered; it felt like home.

WHEN THE CLOCK STRUCK MIDNIGHT

While I was living in the apartment, Sue and Al took the opportunity to buy a nice house in New Hamburg. By the beginning of July, I was able to move back home, but this time, I had the whole Hohl house to myself!

With the passing of time, my sheep flock had increased to fifty ewes. I had expanded my business, Ewe To You, to include selling free-range chicken in addition to the lambs, ducks and sheepskins.

It had been a busy year at this point, with the two moves, the litter of puppies in addition to the usual work with the pigs and the sheep. It never had crossed my mind that it would be my last summer with my cat, Midnight. She had been with me for over sixteen years and I couldn't imagine a day without her.

Midnight's little body started to wear out. When I finally had to take her to the vet, she had a raging heart murmur as well as heart and kidney disease. I had to leave her at the vet clinic overnight as they had put her on intravenous fluids, but she began to fill up. Her heart could not pump well enough and this was it. On September 19, one day before my twenty-seventh birthday, I went to the vet clinic to say good-bye to my best friend.

They led me into a room, where I waited while they went to get Middy. They set her on top of a little blanket on the table. The vet gave me a pile of paperwork to read through. I spent the time he was gone, reading all the words on the papers like he suggested. When he came back in the room, he asked if I signed the paper, I said yes. He walked over to Middy, stuck a needle in her and she was gone. He then said, "Now you can spend as much time with her as you want." What?? I had been reading over the paperwork instead of spending time with Middy! I didn't even say good-bye to her? Middy! She was gone! He didn't even say that was what he was doing! I was terribly distraught. I wasn't even holding her or touching her. How could he be so cold?

This was the second time I had to put a friend to sleep. First had been "PIG" and now Middy. This was worse. I had been with "PIG" at the end, the way it should have been with Middy! She'd been with me for so long and had been such a close companion, to have her suddenly gone felt like a knife in the heart.

It took me a long time to get over that loss. At the time, I picked her up and carried her out to my truck and took her home. I made a coffin for her, sized to fit her body, which I had wrapped in a full-size quilt. I realized the error of my ways when I had to dig a hole in clay large enough for this big blanket, inside this giant coffin, but it somehow got done; I never gave up! The next day was my birthday; I planted a tree and a lot of irises to mark her gravesite.

A few days later, Wyatt, Harley, Ivy the chosen one and I, left on an adventure to Grand Rapids, Michigan. I left Harley and Wyatt there for one month to be professionally sheep-dog trained. Harley was absolutely well trained and so amazing when I picked her up, but Wyatt? The trainer said, "Sometimes it skips a generation! Let me show you." Wyatt went on a huge outrun, but just kept on going and didn't go-around the sheep! He never did figure out how to work the sheep properly although he could drive them, sometimes, if he wanted to!

Spiritual Awakening
Notwithstanding Devastation

The year 2001 was a pivotal one. It was time to grow spiritually, whether I was ready or not. I had been hiding out in the pig barn for several years at this point and became inspired to dig a little deeper. At that time, I was a very shy and angry person who was unable to meet anyone's gaze. I was tired of being angry at life, but didn't know that I had a choice. I hadn't realized that I had the option to have different feelings. If anger was the first emotion to pop up – I was stuck with it, or so I thought. This was the year that I would find out that I actually had a choice. Once I could recognize that I was angry, in that moment I had other options. Did I want to continue living in the dark? When given the opportunity, I choose the light.

My dearest sheep and constant companion LG, first born of Georgian, turned fourteen years old in February. By May, I was very dismayed when she started to go downhill. I brought her from the sheep farm to the Hohl place to be close to me and put her in one of the new fenced dog yards. I did what I usually do and called Tanny for help. She was the maker of miracles and that's what I needed.

I had met Tanny a few years earlier, when she was recommended to me after I had gotten hurt on the farm. Although she lived in the city, she created a magical wonderland in her yard. It was always filled with God's creatures, which she helped to take care of in her spare time. Tanny was trained as a registered physiotherapist, but she had put that aside to do her energy work, which included many modalities like Craniosacral therapy. In general, two words to describe her would be "miracle worker" as far as I was concerned. Every time I got injured, she was there to put me back together. Unlike a chiropractor that wants to see you once or twice a week for treatments, Tanny was fine not seeing you ever again! She was so good that she most often fixed the problem in one visit! Occasionally she would be called upon to help in emergencies for animals as well. Sometimes the sheep ended up at her house, like the time we set a sheep's broken leg and put it in a plaster cast. But this time, she was needed to make a house call; LG wasn't going anywhere.

After Tanny arrived, she eased LG's discomfort, but was unable to reverse the hands of time. LG's body was wearing out and she was dying of a natural cause – old age.

Tanny explained to me that LG had been taking care of me for a long time and now it was time for me to take care of myself. What? She was taking care of me? I don't think so! I am the one that fed, watered and bedded her for fourteen years! What did she mean? Tanny said I might not understand now, but one day I would. That day she also explained that animals understand pictures and intent. She said it was a form of communication, but it was not control. I didn't know it at the time, but that one statement would end up changing the way that I viewed the world and my life.

After Tanny went home, I sat in the grass, cradling LG's head in my lap and stroking her head. With a gentle breeze blowing, the warm spring sun beamed down upon us. She took her last breath and I wept profusely.

A few days later, I had to move the finishing pigs around in the barn and I thought about what Tanny had said at LG's deathbed. I would try out what she had attempted to explain to me, that animals can understand pictures and intent. So here I have to admit that I was sort of a short-tempered person back then and occasionally resorted to a standard practice of conventional pig farming. I used an electric livestock prod on the pigs when they wouldn't co-operate and tried my patience.

There was usually one, sometimes two – the last pigs that just didn't want to leave their pen. Pigs are very territorial and you cannot just put a new pig into a pen of pigs that is already established. In order to combine pigs from two or more pens, they must be placed in a new pen, so all are on equal footing. I had to regularly move pigs into bigger or smaller pens, depending on age or size, and so on. On this day, I was moving pigs from the yellow room to the red room.

I put feed in the little pens in the red room where I wanted the pigs to end up. I secured their route from one room to the other and then went back to the yellow room. I stood with the pigs that I intended to move; in my head I saw a picture of the path. I envisioned the pigs running down the alley, out into the hall to the left, then turning left again, running down the alleyway to get to the feed in the pen. I opened the door and the pigs ran out one by one, down the alleyway and around the corner – all but one. Did that ever annoy me!

The last pig was usually always a hassle – fighting for its life to stay *in* the pen. Round and round we go. Here is me, 123 pounds, jumping around with hands through the holes in my sheet of plywood - trying to stop the pig from running back; electric prod hanging from my wrist. The pig, using all four legs under its 180 pounds of bulk, sticking its nose where it doesn't belong, pushing, squealing and making a fuss. For a moment we were at a standstill. Finally, I had it cornered near the door, my plywood up tight against the wall so it couldn't see anywhere to run. We were both out of breath.

Exasperatedly, silently in my head, I said, "All you have to do is go out the open door!" And I swear with no word of a lie, in my head, in English, I heard the pig say, "Okay if you don't shock me!"

I stood there dumbfounded for a moment and then replied, "Okay."

The pig turned and went out the open door, down the hallway and into the pen in the red room. I followed and closed the door behind it. What had just happened?? I think I must be going insane! Perhaps I spend too much time alone!?

It was weeks before I could look an animal in the eye again. I was afraid to know if the other animals had things to say too, so I closed off communication for a while until I could understand better what was going on. I was excited to find out a few weeks later that it was actually a "thing."

In the summer, I remember discovering a really neat alternative store in Waterloo, called the Holly Oak. I went in and noticed a bulletin board just inside the door. I was drawn to a flyer that said "Animal Communication Workshop." There was a line below it that will forever be engrained into my mind – Telepathic Communication with Animals. Huh. I wasn't crazy? It was a "thing"? I wrote down the information and when I got home, I immediately signed up. This was something I needed to know more about!

That summer I also began my studies to become an Acupressure Practitioner. I was beginning to dabble in that which cannot be seen by the naked eye; the world of energy.

Acupressure is using one's fingers instead of needles on the acupuncture points. The energy is run through the practitioner from one hand to the other, each on different points on the subject. The treatment has an effect on both the body and the mind of the individual, dealing with both emotional and physical issues. We were trained to hold the patient's wrists and depending on the pulse felt by our fingers, we would select which "flow" to perform. It was relatively easy to learn, but the hard part was trying to keep my own body's energy separate from the patient and not take on their issues. In my spare time, I practiced Acupressure on people and animals.

By September, I figured it was time for a new species to join the menagerie. I had picked her out earlier in the summer and she was finally old enough to come home. Brenda and Shane had purchased a llama to protect their flock and I thought this sounded like a good idea. I usually followed their lead, like I did with the sheep, chickens and eventually cattle, so this seemed like a natural progression! They introduced me to the breeder where I was fortunate enough to find this special little lady. "Iris" the llama, was four months old by the time she came to live with the sheep. She was the start of a long line of llamas beginning with the letter "I".

Iris was a beautiful dark brown colour, which was accentuated with brilliant white. The front half of her neck was white from her lower lip all the way down to her chest. Her dark face was brightened with a bit of white on her cheeks and white eyebrows! Parts of the back of her ears were white and from the front, her brown ears were highlighted with white around the edges. She was very attractive and she halter trained quite easily.

Over the next few years, some llamas were purchased and some were born on the farm. Baby llamas are called Cria. An interesting fact about llama births is that all crias are born in the day time. Llamas are originally from high mountainous regions where the temperature is very cold at night. They adapted birthing to daytime to ensure the survival of the species! After the cria is born, the mother will hum and gently nuzzle the baby to encourage it to stand up as soon as possible. Any baby laying on the ground is fair game for predators so getting up quickly is always best! In a bizarre quirk of nature, Llamas have an attached tongue, which they can only stick out half an inch! Therefore, the mother is unable to lick off the baby after birth. Newborn crias cannot regulate their own body temperature, especially if they are born wet into a cold or drafty environment. As I found out too many times over the years – if it is too cold, the newborn cria cannot survive.

I could only get males for breeding in the off-season when they weren't in use by the breeder. Add eleven and half months – if you breed in winter, and shockingly you get babies in winter! More than once we had the very tall babies in the house to be warmed up and dried off after birth!

The baby llamas stand about 3.5 feet tall at birth and if you add the ears sometimes 4 feet tall - in line with their mama's shoulder! They were always very curious and amiable when they were in the house. Once they were dried off, warmed up and ready to run around, we would know it was time to quickly get them back to their mama. I knew that I did NOT want to have a bottle baby llama for many reasons and if the mom was going to take it, we needed to get it back out to bond with her as soon as possible.

I didn't have much pasture at the sheep farm, only four acres, but I had so many sheep at this point, that I decided to pasture forty-one of them at another place nearby. It seemed like a good idea at the time, but proved to be one of my worst ever.

One week-end, the owner of the farm was taking care of a Rottweiler-cross dog who was the mother of another Rottweiler-cross that lived on the property. Together they made a mess I shudder to think of to this day.

Saturday, October 13, 2001, I arrived in the morning to check on my girls and my eyes could barely make my brain understand what I was seeing. The bodies of my beloved sheep lay in waste upon the ground.

Finding one dead sheep at any time is bad enough, but when I arrived that fateful day – seven bodies were laid out on the ground. Normally that would have been horrific enough, but they turned out to be the lucky ones. I ran in terror from one body to the next, checking for signs of life, but there was none. Then my gaze turned to the living and my heart sank even further into my stomach. I wanted to vomit, but I had no time. Oh my God! What the hell has happened here?

My hands were shaking so badly I could hardly punch the vet's number into the phone. "Please hurry!" I exclaimed as I begged for them to come quickly. It was only then that I took a moment to take stock of what was in my view.

When the vet arrived, he commented that dogs do so much damage. They pack attack for fun, not for food like a coyote would. This was definitely the work of dogs.

The seven dead ewes were dragged to the middle of the pen, lined up in a row. To me, it looked like a small terrorist attack. It was only one month after 9/11 and as far as my mind was concerned, those were body bags.

The first step was to deal with ewes with the most visible damage. We had no choice but to immediately euthanize poor Wynona. The dogs had literally ripped off her front leg – it was nowhere to be seen. Next to be euthanized was the one of the five ewes that I just bought from my accountant only a short time earlier. Her back leg was broken and she was peeing blood. The remaining thirty-two sheep were each checked over and treated as needed. During the rest of that day, eighteen ewes with multiple wound sites, had to have their necks and legs stitched up. My beloved Milka, died in my arms that evening after succumbing to her many wounds. Of those that lived, four of them did not recover.

I love my sheep and that was the most traumatic day of my life up to that point. If I thought things couldn't get any worse, I just had to wait a day or two.

Two days later, on October 15, one of Ohmer's sons decided that he wanted to take over the pig barn; he just neglected to tell his dad and me. When I went out in the morning to do my chores, I found a pad lock on the door. After five years of exemplary work, my employment as barn manager was halted. Effective immediately – I was unemployed.

Luckily, I was still in Ohmer's good books and my home wasn't hinged on employment in the pig barn. Neither was my rented sheep barn, chicken coop or Digger's house and pasture so at least we could all stay put. My employment in the pig barn had now ended, but only for a time.

Earlier, in July, I had started work on my personal growth and development by completing the Landmark Forum in Toronto. I finished off the year with the Advanced course which helped me realize I have a choice in how I feel. Just because I feel angry first, doesn't mean I have to stay that way. I get to say. I was also able to stop blaming others and take responsibility for how my life goes.

In spring of 2002, I followed up the first two week-end courses with a three-month self-expression and leadership program. I was determined to make something of myself and realized that I could not build relationships with people all alone and locked away on the farm. I was also committed to becoming an Acupressure practitioner, so I finished my third level of Jin Shin.

Sadly, I had to make the decision to sell all of my sows, as I no longer had them in the pig barn. It required a lot more work to keep them on other properties and I wasn't set up very well for it. Dotty was the last to go after her time of living with my sheep and cattle. Another sad time, but it was also a relief, as it had not been working for a while.

From February to April, I worked as manager of a flock of 800 milking ewes. I wasn't actually responsible for milking the ewes, thankfully, but for looking after feeding and caring for the multitude of babies. The lambs were pulled from their mothers after they had their first drink of colostrum and were taken away to live in large groups. They had to drink powdered milk replacer from machines that had many nipples across the bottom of each large box. The machines constantly had mold issues and the babies were frequently ill. I eventually quit working there due to moral and safety issues.

The conditions for the sheep were not ideal, nor for the employee! I tried to get the owners to increase the nutrition on their flock by using products from Bio-Ag, knowing how much they had helped me to turn the pig barn around. When they had put the kelp out free-choice as I suggested, the sheep had gobbled it up like it was candy. The owners quickly concluded that it was too expensive so they quit using it before they could see any benefits. I couldn't stand the way the babies were sick all the time and felt that I didn't want to be a part of any establishment that caused animals to suffer. I tried to help them, but when they wouldn't change their ways, I had to go – I could not support the mistreatment of animals.

I have always enjoyed being with animals, more than I liked being with people. Animals are always present in the moment, which is different than most humans. I most often shied away from groups, believing something was wrong with me, because I felt different when I was with them. By the time I finally found out the reason, I was already an adult. I am an Emotional Empath. Basically, I'm a highly sensitive person, capable of absorbing all of the feelings and emotions in my environment. This means that I often experience another person's emotions as if they were my own. No wonder my feelings often didn't make sense to me when I was growing up! As it turned out, that was not the best attribute to have and especially not knowing about it before training in an energy modality. I knew I was very sensitive to receiving energy treatments from other practitioners, but I hadn't considered that I would also be sensitive to giving them as well.

After finishing the third level of Jin Shin Acupressure in 2002, I attempted to become a qualified practitioner. In order to get my certification, I had to complete a certain number of hours of hands-on treatments with people. In addition to humans, I had learned how to do the acupressure on animals and did that on the side. Although I enjoyed that more, there was no legal certification for animals as it was considered veterinary care and since I wasn't a vet, that wasn't allowed.

Using the Jin Shin Acupressure, I excelled at helping people overcome their sicknesses. At first, it was wonderful to be able to help people – but not for long. The trouble came when I wasn't able to release their energies and was left with their problems!

Jin Shin is an energy treatment. The process is to let the client's energy through the practitioner's body, from one hand on a specific point, to the other hand on another point. The practitioner is supposed to protect themselves from the negative energies; bathing in white light, using Bach Flower Remedies and ensuring the practitioner stayed grounded in their own body were all helpful. I tried all those things, but I am not easily grounded so I was often left with other folk's issues. It was then I realized and learned that my empathic abilities were actually a "thing" too!

Once I remember treating a woman with Multiple Sclerosis. When I left her house, I had a left sided headache. I'd never had a left sided headache in my life and so I knew it couldn't be mine. This was the first time I was clear that something like this can occur. Definitely not mine! Luckily, with that realization, I was able to let it go.

The last Acupressure treatment I ever did was on my mother. She came out to my place for help, because she was sick. I treated her and she got better, but then I was sick for three weeks!! Tanny gave me strict instructions after that - never treat family!! I actually never treated anyone ever again. No person, anyway. It was far too dangerous for me! They say it is better to give than to receive, but in this case, I would still receive an Acupressure treatment when needed, but I had no intention of giving them!

LEARNING TO FLY

In March of 2002, Harley gave birth to her second litter with Wyatt, which included eight more puppies! Two of the puppies were born with their legs all scrunched up! I was told by some people to basically "throw them in the well" because they were deformed. As you might have figured by now, I don't easily give up, so there was no chance of that! I ended up using my new-found skills with the Jin Shin Acupressure to save them!

The non-invasive Acupressure treatment allowed the puppies' bodies to release the blocks they had and come back into balance and alignment with their true selves. After a few treatments, their legs sorted themselves out! They were right as rain and I was very pleased! The one puppy would find a home like the others, but Daisy wouldn't. In this case, Daisy was the darkest puppy in the litter, which suggested that she would be picked last. It went well beyond last; Daisy was simply not destined to find a home at a young age.

I knew the darkest would be last to go, but the right people didn't come. At one point a guy did show up, intent on taking her home. Daisy cowered from him, hid behind me and by the end of his visit she was under the truck and wouldn't come out! Perhaps she was listening to his stories, because soon I wanted to be under the truck with her.

He told me about how his previous dog had been in the back of his brother's truck on the way to get its shots when it had fallen out - breaking most of its bones. The one before that had been run over by a tractor. Before that? Attacked by a bear! No wonder she didn't want to be next in line on the long list of fatalities! I had no intention of sending her with people she didn't want to go with. She definitely would not be going with that guy! It would be five more years before her people finally showed up!

June 8 was a big day for me when I invited the public to join me at the Hohl place! I hosted an Animal Communication Awareness Day as a final project for my self-expression and leadership program. Fifty participants arrived to hear the two animal communicators that drove from Toronto to volunteer their time for the day, one of which was the wonderful Claudia Hehr. The one participant that I will never forget was Brenda. Daisy spent the entire day sitting in Brenda's lap, enjoying the whole experience. Brenda and I became fast friends and remain so to this day.

For the next couple of years, I used to talk to everyone about "my friend Brenda," because I also had a sister named Brenda, it helped stave off confusion. One day, I was visiting Brenda and Shane's farm, I was talking to my sister and said something about "my friend Brenda." She said, "Well of course she is your friend!" I responded, "It's only with you that you know that she isn't you!" That day, I morphed "Friend Brenda" into the name she has lived up to 100% – she will always be my "Frienda"!

The same summer, I also stepped out into the community by running the local sheep 4-H club. I took the children on some interesting excursions and also brought in guest speakers to show the children different aspects of sheep farming, including shearing and showing. The participants either picked lambs from my flock, or already had a lamb of their own. We worked with the lambs all summer, showing them at the fair in the fall. Those were some good times.

I have always enjoyed teaching people how to take care of animals. I especially loved watching the children's confidence develop from the beginning of the program to the end. To conquer their fears, learn new abilities and have fun in the process. Taking home a ribbon at the end of the season – no matter the colour – is a nice memento of their experience.

In September, I created a career for myself and started at Bio-Ag Consultants and Distributors as an Independent Dealer. I helped farmers change from conventional farming to natural farming, selling minerals, supplements, homeopathics, services, and so on. I ended up staying with that great company for thirteen years as our values were in alignment.

When I had first applied to Bio-Ag, they had turned me down. Although I had extensive experience with all kinds of animals, their biggest business was dairy – and that I had little knowledge of, except for milking in Ohmer's barn when his son was on vacation. Due to the fact that I was gaining more confidence in myself through the personal work I had been doing, I asked them to reconsider, and they did.

In an attempt to learn more about dairy farming and also to help keep food on the table, as I was learning the ropes of being a traveling salesperson – I started milking cows. Over the next few years, I milked at many farms, from neighbour Brian's 30-cow tie-stall barn, to much larger dairies, up to 110 cows. Some places milked twice a day and others three times. At one big dairy farm, I remember working late at night for that third milking. Cows produce more if you milk them often, so that extra milking was quite profitable. It was interesting being alone in the big barn late at night, until there were problems. Having to wake up a whole household in order to get help was not that enjoyable.

In 2003, I focused back on my personal growth and development and was ready to spread my wings a little further. I participated in the Landmark Education's Wisdom Course, over five week-ends spread out over several months. The goals were Play, Fun and Ease

– all things I struggled with. Each week we had to meet in groups to complete our homework and take turns organizing social gatherings. For one of our Wisdom parties, I invited a bunch of people to go hang gliding with me near Orangeville. My dream was to fly and this was my opportunity to make that dream come true. Because I brought twenty-two paying customers to the small company, for their gratitude, they allowed me to fly for free. That seemed like a good deal, so I boldly asked, if I were to bring more people, could I fly for free again? Their answer was yes! By the time fall arrived, I'd brought people out nine times and managed to fly for free every time! In the owner's words, at the end of the year, they told me that I "saved their butts!"

Now, I am no daredevil so don't envision me jumping off a cliff with a kite strapped to my back! This hang gliding took place in a field. The glider was attached by a long cable to a winch about 500 feet away. They would start reeling in the winch and the glider would go forward on the wheels. With speed we'd be pulled about 100 feet and then they would release something to change the angle of the wings and up, up, up we'd go!

I was flying tandem, with my instructor Peter, from New Zealand. He had an awesome accent and wasn't hard on the eyes either! There would have been worse people to be strapped in next to, climbing thousands of feet into the air! When we got as high as we could with the winch, it was unhooked and we were free. Sometimes all you could hear was just the sound of the wind, but mostly it was quiet. It was our job to look for and find something that is invisible. To be like a bird and fly on the wind without flapping; then gain altitude with no engine; and find the thermal. Up, up, up we would go when we found it. We would be as high as 2200 feet!

I was so grateful to be able to fly, better yet – for free! I was working my way towards getting my own hang-gliding license.

First hang gliding flight and landing

I managed to rack up ten flights that summer. Now because we were not jumping off cliffs and using a winch to go up instead, that meant that we really couldn't go too far, as we had to be back to land in the same place that we started from. So up as high as we could and then around and down basically is how it went. It didn't matter, I just loved it!

Then one day, Peter invited me to go with the crew on an adventure. We were leaving the safety of the field and winch behind! We were going to be pulled up by a plane!

I drove for an hour or so to the west. It was late in the summer and the corn was tall in the fields. All the people from the hang-gliding school went first. Peter and I were the last to go up and it was getting late in the evening. Even with dusk falling, I was thrilled to get any chance at all.

Up we went into the sky, tethered by a long rope, attached to the small, yellow, propeller plane. When we reached 2000 feet, Peter pointed to the altimeter and unhooked us from our airborne chauffeur. The plane veered off and returned to the landing field. I could feel my heart beating wildly in my chest. We were alone in the sky.

That flight is one of my most memorable moments. We were flying free in the sky when darkness was falling. Gazing down on the earth below, I felt like I was looking at a miniature electric train set from yesteryear. The tiny lights on the little houses twinkled in the night. As we moved lower towards the ground, we could still make out shadows of the unlit fields. The rows and rows of once green cornstalks were now shaded gray with the darkness and the moonlight. How I felt, zooming across the air over the corn that night is something I will never forget. It was the absolute feeling of freedom. I believe that what I felt that night is what a bird feels like when it flies. It is a feeling that I have often longed for since then.

In July of 2003, I sent Daisy away for sheep herding training at Cat Laxton's place near Blythe. The first time was for one week and then again for the entire month of August. When I went to pick her up after the month of training, Cat said, "Make sure she doesn't see you and I will show you what she can do with the sheep." I hid down the driveway behind a tree. Cat went and got Daisy and to my surprise she was actually working the sheep!

I peered around the tree and immediately, up went her nose as she caught a scent on the wind. Cat regained her attention and kept working her. Again, Daisy's nose went up. She stopped, looked in my general direction and ran towards the tree I was hiding behind! She had smelled my scent and the lesson was over! We were happy to be back together, but even though she had the training and ability, Daisy chose never to work with sheep again!

FOR WHOM THE BELLE TOLD

Belle was one of my older sheep, mother of BB and Grandmother to 3Bs. She was a very special girl that had come directly from Brenda and Shane's farm with the originals. Belle was part of the group of sheep involved in the dog attack of 2001, but was miraculously one of the few that remained unhurt or injured, or so I thought! Years later when she was older, she had to go through that which she had hid at the time. If she had shown her damage outwardly, it would have been too much for me to bear! She developed some strange issues that wouldn't resolve. I called Tanny, like I always did, to help me with that odd situation.

Before she arrived, I brought Belle home to the dog pen where wayward animals spent more time than dogs! Tanny explained how a body needs to release trauma, before it can move on and that was what Belle was doing. She was working through her hidden injuries from the incident years earlier! She had brain fluid coming out of her ear, her head was tilted, she'd lost her balance point, she lost her mind and her memory.

I placed a bell on her leather collar. I used to let her out of the pen for exercise and she often went into the corn field. I knew she would always come back, because she was like a boomerang. She was always going in a circle and therefore had to come back. The bell on the collar was my insurance to make sure I could always hear her whereabouts. I spent a lot of time looking after her each day. For a sheep that had always come when called, it was hard to find out that she didn't even seem to recognize me anymore. I had several people tell me that I should just "ship her," but I could not. I remember when I was asked "How can you love such a thing? She doesn't even know you?"

I said, "I just do. My love for her doesn't change just because she can't remember me. I remember enough for both of us!" She was my friend and had done me well over the years, raising lots of lambs and I wasn't about to abandon her in her time of need.

The vet said she had encephalitis – so I did what I knew best and found her the perfect homeopathic remedy! Along with Tanny's treatment, Belle received homeopathic Belladonna for the next several weeks and her recovery was a miracle!

I continued my studies of animal communication that summer, occasionally taking week-end courses with different animal communicators. At my first course we had to work with a partner. The lady showed me a picture of a cat and I was to communicate telepathically with it. I closed my eyes and thought of the cat. The instructions were not to interpret the information, just to relay it. I thought I had failed miserably, when all I had to report to the woman was, that I had seen a bathroom and a roll of toilet paper in a holder on the wall. To my surprise, the woman was very excited by my discovery. Apparently, the cat's favourite toy was an empty toilet paper roll and it could hardly wait for the roll to be done so it could play! That was good for me to have an early win while practicing this new skill. Perhaps I did have a gift and just maybe I could really learn to harness this telepathic communication with animals.

The last Animal Communication course I ever attended was led by a formidable woman named Barbara, in October of 2003. It was a two-day Advanced course and with permission, some of the participants were allowed to bring their pets. Before going home on day one, I approached Barbara with a picture of Belle. I showed it to her and said that Belle had requested to come the following day.

With my Belle

She was sort of gruff with me and said, "It is you that wants her to come, not her." I was still an extremely shy person back then but I quipped back, "Ask her yourself." And so she did…

Belle responded to her telepathically saying, "I would be an asset."

Barbara said back roughly, "What if you drop dead tomorrow?"

Belle said, "It would not matter. I would be an asset."

As it was meant to be, on the second day, I arrived with the Belle of the ball, the star of the show! Harley and Wyatt sat watching from the front seat, while Belle was set up in the bed of the truck with bedding, hay and water.

Everyone gathered around outside as I opened the top door of the cap and Belle stuck her head out.

Barbara addressed the group, "How does the sheep make you feel?"

They all responded with similar words like Joy and Joyful.

Barbara then proceeded to instruct the group:

"Quiet yourself. Be clear for the next few minutes. Have a sense of who you are, encompass that. Look at this big bold sheep, see the beauty, unto Yourself, your life, the world. This is a sheep that has something important to say."

[The following interaction is the actual transcript written down that day by a participant named Lisa. Where you read Lisa, she is talking to Belle. All Belle's answers and communication is noted as Lisa or Barbara sensed it.]

Lisa: Hello, greetings beautiful Belle.

(Belle stops munching)

Belle: I am NOT dying. I am living each and every moment of my incarnation. Dying is like breaking a nail, it will grow back just as beautiful. I AM beautiful. So beautiful as a sheep I am not. I have been a great companion to Beth and others through the ages (decades). I am eternal that goes without saying, but must be shouted high and loud.

[As Beth and Wyatt look out the truck window]

Barbara: Is there anything specific she would like to say, convey?

Belle: Yes always. Beth, pursue your gifts boldly. You are such a good girl. Such a grand soul. Such a searcher. Be who...

Barbara to Beth: Why did you bring her?

Beth: Because she asked!

Barbara to Belle: Is there anything in particular you want?

Barbara to Beth: You have a physical contact with her. Move in with her.

Belle: Oh, tell her the treatment IS working. Trust the process. I will stay as long as I am meant, as I want. I am here. No pain. No real pain.

Barbara: The one thing we can say about Belle is that she is clear!

(Another participant): I asked her to come back. She said she has, "I am my own ancestor" She LOVES being a sheep!

Barbara: The process of melding is a trigger to access more information within ourselves.

Belle: I am grand. Do not have sorrow for me though. Do cry if you need to for other things. You can use me as a trigger to cry, so you may cleanse those pockets of feelings. I am sooooooooooo happy. I have lived soooooooooooo well. It is a good life. I was able to stay a long time this time. I am (sigh) contented. Do not fret, though the love is so what is. Thank you Beth for the love and the care. It is grand to see you love and care for yourself more and more, to be your own project, yay. Ring a ding ring a ding ding. My mind is clear. Royalty? Did you say royalty? Well of course! I have been crowned several times. I loved and love this life. Thank you for being my human.

Barbara: About another sheep who died and did not get found until a few days later.

Belle said: Her work was finished. She left (died) in a way that represented something to you.

Next, Barbara asked Belle about love and about responsibility.

Belle: Oh, responsibility. Well, do not get caught like in the chain link fence about responsibility. It is a glorious role, not a judge, not a rogue, not a prison. Oh rest-ponce-i-bi-li-ti … Yes rest … music, laughter

[*Wyatt looks out the window. So respectful of the process of the focus being on Belle*]

Barbara: With your permission Beth, we'll go around and touch her and thank her.

Lisa to Belle: Dear Belle, bon voyage!

Belle: Always, today and each day, ah what a trip, ah life, ah to be the creation, to be of cre-co-creation, ah celebration ding ding ding ding. Go in Peace Lisa, you can do this, the listener and this life.

You can do this. DO be the Love. Yes trust. Be sheep. It's grand. Be sheep at "times" let it float. Eat grass! Hi hi. Go now, love.

Lisa to Belle: Oh Belle, Grand merci, ma Belle!

Dogs in the truck to Lisa: We are companions, we will support her. We are gentle watchers emanating love and joy for her comfort.

Belle: Wisdom, Respect, Maternal, All encompassing love, power of the group mind, eternal, ageless, Animal as guides, walk with me and we will fly.

Barbara: A wealth of information about living, being present, participating in life. We are all connected. Trust yourself and relax (humour). Trust life, trust yourself. Accept the love around you. Thank you. Listen to the animals.

End of the letter from Lisa from the Barbara Janelle workshop.

That day was the most memorable one for all the people participating in the event. Belle had so much love and information to share with the group. She did not give a prepared speech! Belle communicated something different to everyone. Each person shared their very own connection with her and received what they needed at that time. Several months later I received that long hand-written letter in the mail from Lisa from that course. She exclaimed to me, how her experience with Belle had shifted her life for the better, she was so thankful. When the week-end was over, Barbara thanked me for pushing for Belle to come – she was a hit!

A few weeks later, Belle was back! She knew me again!! She was soon well enough to go back over to the barn and all was well for the rest of her life. She was about thirteen when she passed away. At that point, I somehow knew that there was a lesson for me to learn – and I don't know why I thought this, but it turned out to be true. Perhaps maybe some day my mother might not remember who I am - would that mean that I didn't love her anymore? How could you love someone that doesn't even know who you are? You just do.

A MATCH MADE IN HEAVEN

Six more puppies were blessed to proud parents Wyatt and Harley with their third litter in October of 2003. As was customary, all the Border Collie puppies were picked based on the amount of white in their colouring. The one with the wide white collar, white stripe on the muzzle and white tip of the tail was always first to go and the rest followed from there. George was born in this batch and like his older sister Daisy, was mostly black. He too, did not find a home at the time the other puppies did. I guess his people were not yet ready for a dog! One and a half years later though, I got a call from a friend of Len's, whose nephew was looking for an adult Border Collie. Well, I happened to have one, but said it was not a sure thing – the person would have to pass George's inspection!

Christiaan arrived a few days later and sat down on the couch in the kitchen. George sat beside him. After one and a half hours of visiting, it was bizarre but I felt a change in the energy of the room. Somehow, I had felt that George was no longer mine – he had found his person.

It was seven days before Christiaan was ready to come back and pick him up. During that week, George acted so strangely. He spent most of his time away from the pack and often behind the toilet! He was separating himself from us – cutting the ties with our family so he could more easily move to his next one. When Christiaan came, he opened his truck door and George jumped right in, happy to be moving on to new adventures!

Speaking of adventures – that dog was more well-travelled than most people! His new person used to send me photographs in the mail – back when people still had to have film developed! The pictures were fun shots of George next to this province sign or that one – all the way across Canada! Somehow, I remember that Christiaan ran or biked all across Canada, but I can't remember which it was. All I know for sure is that George got a lot of exercise, was well loved and went everywhere with him.

George supported him from single life through getting married to having children and everything in between! I was very grateful to Christiaan for providing George such a wonderful life for the many years to follow! Christiaan brought George to visit us for the last time when he was sixteen years old. He made it just shy of seventeen years and was still running till the very end. A beautiful love story that was; it always warmed my heart to know they did so well for each other.

With my Border Collies;
(Left to right) Wyatt, Ivy, Daisy, Harley and George (front).

Seeing God

In the summer of 2004, disaster struck my horse Digger for the first and only time of his life. He had been with me already for ten years and never a sick day thus far. Upon rising every morning, first thing I would do is look out the window to check on Digger, mostly to make sure he was still there. His fence consisted of one piece of wire that had never been connected to power. He was so afraid of electric fences, that I could keep him in with a piece of baling twine and often had. This particular morning, my eyes did not quickly see him. Hmm. I put on my shoes and headed out to have a look. Digger was there all right, but not in his pen. He was lying flat on the ground, outside of the fence!

"DIGGER!?!" I yelled his name hoping for a response. As I sprinted across the driveway, I heard faint nickering. Thank God! He was alive!

He laid still, flat on the ground, unable to get up. His legs were wrapped in fence wire, but there had to be something more. Just then, Ohmer's son that had taken over the pig barn drove in. I yelled for him to bring me wire cutters, which he reluctantly did before returning to the barn and tending to his chores. I ran and called the vet. I also called my parents for support, to let them know what was going on.

I cut the wires off Digger's legs, but he still wouldn't get up. Dr. Hordik arrived soon after. He had been on a coffee run nearby, but had doubled back to see Digger first. I had to get some water from the house so while the bucket was filling, I called my parents back to tell them the vet had arrived. This time, Mom answered the phone and said that Dad wasn't home – he'd already left to come and help. I hung up the phone, shocked. I always thought Dad didn't even like animals! I guess it was more that Dad didn't like to *show* that he liked animals. He had grown up on a farm and had not been pleased that two of his daughters had gone down that hard road. No time to think more about that then, I needed to get back out to help the vet.

I had been right. The fencing wire that had been wrapped around his legs was not the issue – he had a bigger one. There was a large cable, a guy wire that ran along the edge of Digger's pen from the ground to the top of the grain elevator leg. We could see his hair on the guy wire that had a hole he must have gotten his leg through. Something must have spooked him and he had jumped over his little fence. Why he jumped out, I'll never know, but what I did find out quickly – we had a problem.

The vet said he has to stand. Come on Digger; time to get up!

With the way he had been laying, the major artery in his leg had been pinched off, but when he stood up – blood flowed like water from a fire hose! The vet yelled for me to hand him the hemostats.

What the heck would he need those for? Thank goodness I knew what they were! I had a pair of my own that I'd bought with that bunch of other medical supplies at the auction with Ohmer years earlier! A hemostat is a clamp-like surgical tool, apparently like forceps for veins and arteries, often used to stop bleeding – especially for surgeries. I actually had no idea it could be used for this purpose! I just thought they were really cool, lockable little clamps that I used for all sorts of things – medical or otherwise. I know I had used them to hold the needle when I used to stitch up baby pigs that had gotten stepped on by their giant mamas! One time I asked Ohmer to hold a little pig in the office, while I sewed up a rupture… to my surprise, he passed out! But here I was now, asked to get the very same tool to be used on my beloved friend. I was very glad that someone qualified was there to use it. I was hoping that *I* wouldn't pass out!

The vet managed to pinch off the artery and he bandaged the hemostats to the leg for the time being. With the blood stopped, he could have a closer look at the injuries that were not visible while Digger was laying down.

Digger had a deep spiral cut, running from the top of his inner thigh, all the way around his leg, down to his pastern – basically from the top to the bottom. The trouble was that it was down to the bone. Dr. Hordyk suggested that I euthanize Digger right then and there, because he may never be able to walk again with such a severe injury. I looked Digger straight in the eye. My best buddy of ten years… we had done everything together! We'd been riding daily for many years and travelled lots of roads side-by-side. He'd never even had a sick day in his entire life!! Why this? Why now? How could I? Could I give up on him without trying?? NO WAY!

I told the vet "I can always *"put him down"* later, but I can't resurrect him!" The vet couldn't help but agree with my logic.

My Dad showed up right about then and was very helpful. It was the most surprising and important moment in my life and relationship with my father. While being the youngest of five children, I had never really bonded with my father and didn't even really know that he loved me. When he came out to help that day, our relationship changed. He held Digger's head and told him that he was loved and assured him that everything would be okay.

The day that Dad came out to help meant so much to me. I actually started calling him Daddy at that time, even though I was grown and had never thought to do that before. It was on that day, I felt in my heart that my Dad truly cared for me. We had never had anything in common. The males in my family always liked to make fun of and pick apart the things that I had a passion for and was inspired by. I was very different than all of them, so at some point I just stopped talking at family gatherings. It was easier to say nothing than to get into a debate about things I didn't want to have to defend. But after that day, when Dad asked at Sunday suppers, "How are things on the ranch?" I knew that he actually did care and it meant the world to me that he asked! We finally had a connection!

Dr. Hordyk worked very hard, stitching up the very long incision made by the guy wire. He had to re-attach the main artery and then close up the leg. We moved Digger into one of the dog pens so that he could stay contained.

While I ate my lunch, I called my Acupressure teacher and asked her to come and work on Digger. Tanny also came when she got my emergency call. She tended to Digger first and then said that she felt the need to work on me! We went in and I laid on my Acupressure table. Tanny explained that I had a "get hurt" energy pattern, stuck in my left ankle from when I was nine years old. I wondered why she hadn't seen it before? She said she had a new technique, that she was always learning and that the body is only ready to release something, when that time comes and not before.

My brother Brian had been fourteen years old when Brenda was teaching him to drive; I was nine and riding in the back of the truck with Bandit. I ensured that Bandit stayed away from the pitch fork as we bounced down the gravel lane, as I had been worried, he would "get hurt."

As my brother was about to park on the lawn my sister said: "Watch out for the rose bush!" and by accident, Brian pushed on the gas instead of the brake. He drove straight into the cement porch of the house. The front end of the orange Ford pickup was pushed in by eighteen inches.

Meanwhile, I was ejected from the centre of the box, into the back window. The left side of my face made an eerie thud as it connected with the glass. My parents rushed from the house upon hearing and feeling the collision. I was standing in the back of the truck, my face, quickly turning gray, was starting to swell up. With all the concern over my face, it wasn't until I tried to walk, that I said my leg hurt. They took off my boot and poured out the blood! The initial thought was that I had hit it on the corner of the tool box. Later, by X-ray, it was determined that I was impaled with the pitchfork through my ankle! I had a hairline fracture and had to stay off it for the whole summer. For years that left ankle bothered me, especially for the action of swimming. Anyway, I must have messed up my energy patterns when, at the time of impact, I had not wanted Bandit to "get hurt" and that is what I got stuck with! My animals had been trying to show me for years, I guess.

When my dog Chakotay got hit on the road, it was the same — left leg. Wyatt's was opposite front, but Tanny said it was the same thing. Even PIG's left hind leg! And now Digger! Somehow Tanny worked her magic and got that subtle energy moving again. I called Murray from Bio-Ag, like I often did in emergencies, who found the appropriate homeopathic and other natural remedies that I could use, in addition to the antibiotics to prevent infection. As you can see, it helps to have friends in many different modalities, to cover all the bases!

To rehabilitate Digger, the total vet bill ended up costing me around $800. This was the same amount I had purchased him for ten years earlier. I was so glad that I used my intuition, stood up for my best friend and did everything I could to save him. I think it was worth the additional investment when you consider that he continued soundly by my side, without incident, for the next seventeen years!

It was winter before I rode Digger again. I remember hearing his loud breath, in and out, as he galloped across the deep snow-covered field. A big smile beamed across my face underneath my scarf. I had not given up on him and I never would.

My parents had instilled in me, the habit of living frugally in order to be able to occasionally have a vacation and travel. After so many summers driving coast to coast, I valued my driving time and enjoyed every minute. But, with so many animals to take care of, taking long driving trips was not very practical. In 2004, I signed up for a Wisdom Vacation Course, where I could do personal growth and development, yet it could be in an enjoyable environment – why not pick my dream destination of Hawaii? That trip had been booked for many months before Digger's accident, so I was still determined to be able to go. Frienda moved in with me, shortly before I had to go away for that week. Digger was doing much better, although still living in the dog pen. There was nothing particular that I needed to do, as he was well on his way to recovery. I chose the course because I would get to be in a safe, although foreign environment.

The most important thing I remember from that trip, was one very difficult exercise that we were asked to do. We were supposed to sit, knee-to-knee with a partner and stare into each other's eyes… for ten minutes straight! Like I said earlier, that was not my strong suit! To just BE *with* someone else like that – didn't matter who they were, a loved one or not. I sat on my chair, struggling not to look away – to cast my eyes down like so many times in my life before. But on this day it was different. I held my ground and met her gaze. After about eight minutes, I got to see what all the fuss was about. I understood what it meant to be human. I have heard it said many times that we are all made in the likeness of God – but on that day, I finally understood what that meant. I could see God through this woman's eyes; I was staring into the face of God and it was beautiful.

Worth the Wait

I don't remember exactly when, but at some point, I started looking after the pigs again when Ohmer's son got tired of the job. My precious sows were no longer in the barn – it was just growers and finishing pigs. Chores didn't take a great deal of time and no longer required much skill, so I just added them to my daily plate. At this point, in addition to the pigs, I was working with Bio-Ag, milking cows, looking after my own sheep and other animals.

If things weren't busy enough, when Iris the llama was safely old enough to breed at three years of age, I started my foray into breeding livestock protection animals. I had always worried about my animals safety, but more so since that horrible dog attack on my sheep. I had been told that two llamas are the maximum that should be kept with one flock. More than that, they likely won't bond with the sheep, preferring to hang out with each other. I didn't listen. I figured, the more the merrier! One day I would discover the error of my ways, but not that day.

Llamas have one of the longest gestation periods of all the domesticated livestock. Pigs are three months, three weeks and three days, sheep are four months, four weeks and four days, cows nine months, horses eleven months and llamas win with eleven and a half to twelve months!

The first baby arrived so long after breeding that I had forgotten Iris might be pregnant! When Isaiah was finally born, I remember seeing him in the barn yard when I first drove in.

What the heck was that? An alien??

My eyes just could not fathom what this tall skinny looking little thing was!

Oh my gosh!? It's a baby llama?

I was as surprised as I was delighted! After he was dried off, he looked almost like a carbon copy of his mother, brown and white.

In addition to breeding llamas, I also had started collecting them! I remember I had wanted a white llama, which is odd because I usually wanted black and red animals, but what I am thinking now is, I want unusual and different species and colours. White sheep are boring, while black sheep are cool. In this case, black llamas were boring, but a white llama would be cool! And so I bought this huge neutered male from the same breeder where I bought Iris. I named him Ishmael.

Covered by a thick coat of bright white wool, Ishmael was huge, weighing over 400 pounds! It was a shame that no one had taught him any manners! He was not halter trained, but I always thought it was never too late for such things. Every time I tried to lead him, he practically pulled my shoulder out of its socket. I was no match for Ishmael.

The following year, one day at chore time, I noticed all the llamas standing in the doorway, looking in the direction of behind the barn. I didn't take the time to go and see what they were looking at. It wasn't until the next day, when I realized that I hadn't seen Ishmael lately and went outside to see where he was. I found him lying on the outside of the fence with his legs caught in the wire. The fence consisted of ten strands of high tensile wire and he must have gotten his legs through it. Somehow, he had thrashed himself through the fence to the other side. It had gone below freezing in the night-time and he must have been in shock, because when I found him that day, he was already gone. I learned another hard lesson; when the animals try to tell me something – I should listen!!

After this terrible tragedy, I always made it a daily priority to make a visual check all around the pens - inside and out. I was reminded of Ishmael every time I looked outside and I would not be so negligent again.

Other than my trip to Hawaii, I'd been working for years without much of a break. In February of 2006, I found a way that I could go to five countries in one trip! I took the opportunity to fly on a plane to Puerto Rico, where I boarded a ship. It was a Caribbean cruise and as per usual, I was by myself. I embarked on an adventure on the high seas - where I learned that the sea life is not for me.

It felt like I was in an apartment building that never stopped moving, day after day. It was a city on the sea, complete with indoor ice-skating rink, movie theatre, rock climbing walls and shopping mall. It was a completely foreign environment and I did not adjust well.

Where were the animals? Where was the plant life? I did enjoy some of the island tours, but mostly it was all an attempt of locals to sell gems and trinkets made in faraway China. I welcomed the change of scenery, but was happy to get home to stable and dry ground.

In the spring, I fell in love with an orphan Muscovy duckling that I named Chinook. He was hatched outside of my house, but his mother abandoned him. I found him huddled cold and alone, next to the old building I used as a crude chicken coop. Why didn't the mother want him? I don't really know. I tried to get her to take him, but all she said was NO! Was it because I was supposed to be his mama? Well, that is precisely what happened.

Chinook was fluffy yellow with black markings. He lived in the house with the dogs and me. When he was little, I had placed a cast iron frying pan on the floor, while organizing the kitchen cabinet. For whatever reason, Chinook jumped in the frying pan. I have the cutest picture of the fluffy yellow duckling, standing in the frying pan! Oh well, I think it is funny anyway!

I used to fill up the bathtub with water, so that he could get some exercise while swimming about. When he got big though, he used to splash around a lot, so I had to keep extra towels close by. Water might flow off a duck's back, but it doesn't off the bathroom floor! Wyatt and Harley always kept a close eye on Chinook while he splash-splashed and enjoyed his bath!

In the end, I had to find him a new home, because he didn't like my new boyfriend! It was another time where I should have listened to the warnings! Chinook would scratch, bite and beat his wings on him. I'm guessing he was jealous? Or perhaps he knew what I would one day find out for myself. I didn't take my own advice. Always listen to the animals!

One day, as I was standing in a field next to Ohmer, my childhood dream was realized. For years he'd been renting this particular farm near my sheep, and I'd been there many times before. Sometimes it was to pick rocks, cultivate or harvest. On this day, we were checking the dryness of the hay to see if it was ready to be baled. I always had one eye on the sky like Shane had taught me long ago, just in case. My many years of persistent observation finally paid off, when high up in the sky, a large black bird caught my attention. I looked up and my mouth dropped open with amazement. I excitedly directed Ohmer's gaze overhead.

He was the first to speak. "Is that a Bald Eagle? I guess they could be around here!"

It was unmistakable and definitely there! This was my first wild Eagle sighting!! I'd viewed Eagles before, but only in a cage at the zoo!

The Eagle was so high up, but I saw it crystal clear. Its dark, seemingly black body and wings were attached to its shock white head and tail. From my perch in the field, for just a moment, I felt like I was flying in the heavens. Since then, an Eagle has always symbolized an upcoming, deeply transformative and unavoidable change in my life.

I started attending a "non-religious" church with Frienda called *The Conscious Living Centre*. They offered guided meditations and treatments, with a very nice group of eclectic people. On the eleventh day of the eleventh month, they offered a movie night and showed a screening of the movie *The Secret*. I didn't know anything about Angel Numbers back then, but it was my first 11 11 moment.

I drank in every word from that movie. Wow! I loved it so much that I went straight home that night and created my very first vision board.

In the top left corner, it had a picture of a brand-new truck with all the specifications that I desired, right down to the vinyl floors. On the top right was a picture from Alaska, with the words Glacier Bay across the bottom. The middle to the right had a picture of a gold ring with small diamonds sunk down in the band. Under that, in the bottom right corner, was a picture of a cowboy, looking down, his face hidden by the brim of his hat, with his horse standing to the side. The cowboy was gazing down at his Border Collies, his strong hands caressing their black and white coats. At the bottom left, was a picture of a red brick farm house, with white lattice, a long driveway and my handwritten words: "100+ acre farm".

This was my vision. Everything I'd ever dreamed of.

MANIFESTING MY VISION

F ast forward six weeks, now it is Christmas Day of 2006. With the plan of the usual order of feeding my sheep before the pigs, I got in my truck and drove down the lane to the main road. I could see something unusual. My heart sank as I turned and drove slowly forward to try and identify it. It was one of my chickens. She had been hit so hard that she was in two separate pieces. To say the least, it wasn't starting out to be the best Christmas.

When I had finished looking after all of the animals, I was still out of sorts and not feeling the best. I lounged around until mid-afternoon and decided I would feel better if I did not miss-out on Christmas dinner with my family. Without concern for fashion and to ensure my comfort, I wore clashing shades of red, elastic waist pants, thick socks, turtleneck and hoodie. I completed the ensemble with a rather large, bulky and warm, green down vest to go over top. I felt very Christmassy and was ready to feast.

My seventeen-year old friend Rachel, was living with me at the time and I was her unofficial guardian. As an independent young lady, ready to go out on her own, it had made sense for her to move in upstairs, since we'd always been good friends and I had lots of room.

She was Ohmer's granddaughter and became one of my family, the same way Ohmer and Esther had accepted me into theirs. She came to all of our family gatherings, as family. On the way to my parent's place, I had stopped in at Ohmer's to pick her up from their

Christmas dinner. She carried some leftover food to give her father, who couldn't make it to the dinner. I had my dogs along in the truck like I always did, so when we arrived, we could obviously not leave the food on the seat with them. We set the box on the hood of the truck and went in the house.

My parents were close friends with a couple that used to come over to their house every year for New Year's Day dinner. My father and the man knew each other since attending the same high school in Manitoba, long ago. On this particular year, for whatever reason, they had come to our family Christmas Dinner. I was in the kitchen, facing away from the door, when I heard the front door answered and someone come in. A man appeared and started speaking with me about the food on top of the truck, wondering if he should carry it in. I turned around and inhaled sharply.

He was the son of the visiting couple and I was surprised to find out that he was apparently joining us for Christmas dinner. Now, I should explain here, that my siblings had all attended a private Mennonite high school in Kitchener, when the family still lived in Scarborough. I only went for Grade 9 though, as I didn't like boarding away from home. My sister Sue had lived with this family during her years in high school. She was one year younger than their son, so they were sort of like brother and sister. My oldest brother Gerry was a little older than their son and all three of them had been at that school together, during the same time period.

I guess this guy was like part of the family? However, I didn't really know him, just *of* him, I guess. My only memory had been from when he was a teenager, about fifteen years old. I remember seeing him once while I stood in the doorway of his house, when I was eight years old. I was along when my parents dropped Sue off at the start of a school year. She lived there for all five years through high school. Now he was suddenly at the door, asking me about Rachel's food.

I somehow managed to say that it was there on purpose and didn't need to be brought in. He had momentarily taken my breath away when he first walked in and I was a bit baffled as to how that had happened!

When it came time for supper, I was the first to sit down and he was the last. He sat in the only empty chair, right next to me. I tried to explain to him that Rachel lived with me. Gee, no I don't mean we live together – I mean she lives in the upstairs of my house. We are not 'together'. Okay that was a rough save... then I was trying to explain to Rachel who this random guy sitting at the table was. We know this fellow because he lived with my sister for five years. Crap. No, I don't mean that he *lived* with my sister! My sister boarded at his parent's home during high school. Okay, not going any better, time to shut up.

Rachel started talking about how she needed to hook up her TV and he responded saying where he could get her a box. After supper, everyone went to the living room to sit down. When I came out of the washroom, there were only two seats left. One I would have had to climb over my nephew, his elaborate toys, move some cushions and it would have been a scene. The other one? The middle seat between my brother Gerry and this guy! So, I marched over there and took a seat. The whole room seemed to fade away. It was just the two of us, talking about this and that. There were actually thirteen other people in the room when I sat down, but it was a surprise to us when someone called to him from the doorway with their coat on, for him to move his car so that they could leave! We were the only two people still in the room! When did that happen? All of a sudden, he was going to leave!? Next thing I know, he told Rachel that he will get her that box for her TV, he just needs my number. He handed me an empty envelope from a card and I wrote down my phone number. And that is how it all began... We started dating and he became my boyfriend. It was the beginning of the best and worst years of my life.

It had been a busy fall and I felt the need for another holiday. Since I rarely ever took a day off and worked seven days a week, another week of vacation was easily granted to me. With Harley pregnant with her last litter, due a couple weeks into January, I took my only chance to get away before the puppies were born. My travel agent told me that Cuba was inexpensive and one of the safer places to go. I took her advice and booked a trip on dry land this time, flying out on New Year's Eve.

I stayed in Cuba for one week. While I was there, I met a Cuban healer named Julio at the resort. Twice on January 6th, both in the morning and in the evening, Julio told me, quite randomly I thought, "You need to have a baby! It's very important!" He went on to explain something about balancing the Yin and Yang energies. "You need to have a baby!" He was very certain. I had just met that guy, seven days before I left for my trip. Perhaps he was the one I was to have this baby with? The only other thing I remember Julio saying to me, was that if someone comes at me with fire, I needed to respond with water. Yin and Yang. I wondered what it all meant.

When I returned home from my trip, it wasn't long and I did get a baby – of sorts! I had decided, since Wyatt hadn't produced the best working offspring, that with Harley's last litter, I would breed her to a champion sheep herding trial dog.

Dirk was born as a singleton. That means he was the only pup born in the litter, so not really a litter! He was the son of Mary Thompson's Hawk, who was very well known with a high ranking at the sheep dog trials.

Harley was a little rough on Dirk, much rougher than she had been when she had a whole litter to look after. I was often interfering when she started throwing him around and such.

Dirk in a lesson with sheep, August 2008

I should have let her do her motherly thing, even if I didn't understand it at the time. Because of my interference and due to having no siblings, he was not well socialized with other dogs. He never really learned how to be a dog. Dirk was a people. He loved people. He loved to work and play. Dirk loved life.

He was also very fast. Even faster than his famous sire was! I remember one day I needed him to bring the sheep in. I sent him on an "out run" by using the term "come by" which means to go clockwise around the sheep, as opposed to "away to me" which is counter-clockwise.

He was running so fast that the sheep did not even see him coming. He was not going wide enough around and collided with an outlying sheep at top speed! Both of them went flying through the air! All concerned were surprised! He was destined to be a long-term, valuable, member of the family.

I had placed a picture of the perfect truck on my vision board. I had directed the salesman at the dealership to order my new truck with all my specifications I had dreamed of, straight from the factory. A week later, I received a call, saying that they were unable to make the exact truck that I ordered. I had wanted to have vinyl floors, not carpet. They said that they had sold out of vinyl floors, so I would have to make a choice. Either get the truck with carpet, or buy a truck that was already made. They had a blue one with vinyl floors if I wanted it? I had ordered Sport Metallic Red. If I was going to pay that much money, I wanted to get the exact one that I ordered!

I told the salesman that I would wait as long as September and if they couldn't make it before moving to the next year models, then I would come up with a new plan. Until then, they were to put forth my precise order.

On the exact day that I had declared I would have my truck by, March 5th, they called to tell me that I would in fact be getting it, as per my exact specifications! On April 13, 2007 I got to pick her up. My GMC Sierra was Sport Metallic Red with an extended cab; the rear doors opened backwards, for ease of letting the dogs in. It had vinyl floors, electric sliding glass rear window, and easy lift tailgate. I topped it off with a beautiful new, matching, high top, truck cap. My unwavering faith had paid off; my dream had come true!

Although my year started pretty well, it went downhill fast. By mid-May, my sweet Ivy, first daughter of Wyatt and Harley had been very ill for over six months. Her troubles had started after I had gotten her spayed, at the same time as Daisy, the previous year. Perhaps it was a complication from the surgery, I think they nicked her kidney, but I'll never know for sure.

One by one, her kidneys deteriorated until there was almost nothing visible on the ultrasounds. I took her to different vets, specialists and natural healers. In my desperation to save her, I tried anything and everything I could. Many times, throughout the spring, I had driven her an hour away to an obscure, natural vet who had an unusual treatment that I had heard Shane talk about in the past. Ivy received, weekly treatments with a Rife Machine, which offers a kind of electric frequency healing - but it was already too late.

Ivy and I only had seven short years together. How was I supposed to make that awful decision to end her time on this earth? She was still high in spirits, but her body was playing its last hand.

As I often did, I requested Tanny's daughter, Jules Hare to help. She had inherited the ability to help people and animals on an subtle energy level. In addition to being a friend, she also became my Craniosacral Therapist. Jules said that Ivy and I were so energetically intertwined, it was like we were one being. No wonder the thought of letting her go felt like cutting off a part of myself. Jules managed to assist us in separating ourselves. Even with her help, May 16th came too fast and it was devastating.

Ivy had been my constant friend, my confidant, my lifeblood. She was that one-in-a-billion kind of kindred spirit. Tanny had explained to me early on, that Ivy was magnetic. People were always attracted to her. We seemed to have been connected not only magnetically, but almost magically! It wasn't until after Ivy got sick, that Tanny had told me Ivy and I had been together before. Apparently, we'd been together for twenty-three lifetimes! Even one time, Ivy had been my steed! It was hard to wrap my head around the idea. It was the first time that I had given any real thought to reincarnation. I knew Ivy had to leave me but deep in my heart I felt that somehow, some way, we would be together again. With all that said, she was the first of two best friends I would lose that year and I thought the hole in my heart was already vast enough.

In June, my boyfriend agreed to go on an Alaskan Cruise with me, so I could fulfill another lifelong dream. Alaska was the destination, but I was not too thrilled with the transportation, after the last ship I had been on. I agreed to the cruise because I was promised it was inland; it would not be rocking on the open sea. It was nice to finally have someone to travel with.

During our trip, my favourite land excursion was to visit an Eagle rescue. We saw many Bald Eagles there and some were wild and free! I was alarmed at the things that people had done to the Eagles that needed to be rescued. I remember taking pictures of one big female and even took a video of her with my new digital camera, that I had purchased before the trip. Someone had shot her – right in the beak! She had such an amazing spirit and to this day, I have never forgotten her. The problem was, that she was stuck there at the rescue, living indoors. She would never be allowed to leave due to her injury. In order to live, she had to give up her freedom. I wondered if she thought it was worth it.

The following month, I was gifted an opportunity to partake in a First Nations Ceremonial Fire-Walk. It was an all-day event, which included building a huge log tower, followed with a lighting ceremony. As the huge stack of wood burned for hours, we chanted to the steady beat of a drum. Finally, by nightfall, the large pile of coals was ready to be spread out into a large circle. The bed of coals spanned about ten feet in diameter. There was more chanting and then it was finally time for the fire walk.

The point of the whole day was to cross the coals with bare feet. They said, if I let the spirit guide me, my feet would not get burned. I was scared as I waited for the *right* time.

At one point I felt something push me towards the fire. Odd as it might seem, it felt like the Great Spirit giving me a nudge. I looked to my left and saw that two ladies were coming in my direction, dancing around the fire. I should have gone when selected, but instead I hesitated, too shy to dash in front of them. As soon as they had passed, with a leap of faith, I lurched myself forward onto the coals. It did come at a cost; the price of not listening to inner guidance.

As I stepped onto the coals with my right foot first, I felt the pain. Even so, I did not give up. I quickly made my way across the hot coals, step after step, to reach the cool grass on the other side. On comparing my feet afterwards, I noticed that only the toes on my right foot had blisters, the rest of my foot and the left one, remained blemish free. I suppose because I sort of listened, I didn't get as burned as I would have, had I not listened at all! From that experience I got that I should not second-guess myself. I am not sure why I didn't take it to heart.

It was shortly afterwards when I found out that Donna, one of my best human friends, had taken a turn for the worse. We had met when I had first started working at Millar Brooke Farm. I clearly remember the day she walked into the laundry room. It was in the grooms' quarters but also attached to the office; I had been sitting on the floor, rolling bandages that I had taken out of the dryer. The bandages were used to keep cotton wraps securely on the horse's legs, after an injury, a workout or for shipping.

Donna seemed strikingly odd, just showing up in my world at that moment, seemingly out of thin air. She had short, yet poofy dark hair, was dressed in a colourful blouse, slacks and had brightly painted fake nails. I was in dirty old clothes, smelling much like something that came out of a horse's back end. For whatever reason, we struck up an unwavering friendship that lasted for fifteen years. Early on in our friendship, she had a cancer diagnosis and had to leave her position as Secretary at Millar Brooke.

Donna went through many years and countless treatments for the rare form of cancer that ailed her liver. We spoke almost daily and I visited her occasionally at her house near Perth, but we saw each other more often when she attended the Cancer Clinic in London, Ontario. That September, Dirk was my traveling companion for the five-hour long journey to visit Donna for one last time. She passed away a few days later and then I had to make the trip once again, this time for her funeral. The hole in my heart was ever widening.

When I was in Grade 9, I attended one year at a private Mennonite school in Kitchener, where I boarded with a family during the week. On the weekends I would ride the coach bus with a few other students from the Toronto area. One of those older students, Ken, contacted me out of the blue in October, almost twenty years later. He and his wife were wanting to move from the city, buy land and start a homestead. They were interested in advice from an experienced farmer, and I was only too happy to oblige.

While we were in the kitchen, chatting about different aspects of farming, there was an important someone trying to get our attention. We were all very surprised when my dear sweet Daisy leapt from the floor to the top of my desk, scattering all of my paperwork!

What in the world? "Get down!!" A few minutes later, a dog that had never been on top of something other than maybe the couch in her whole life, was again standing on top of the desk! It was her attempt to be close to these folks – her people. At that time, Daisy was the only one that knew that fact.

I took the opportunity to ask them if they were looking for a dog. No? Well, this dog was looking for them. They had not been expecting to find a new family member on their visit. They hadn't even known they needed one! They had come to talk about animals and crops, but left with an additional idea planted in their mind instead.

After five years, even though I had always known that it might be a possibility, I wasn't so sure I was ready to send my dog anywhere anyway. I had spent several hundred dollars sheep dog training her, that much again in spaying her. Let's not forget the fact that she was *my* dog!!

That evening, I remember driving in my truck on the way home from feeding the sheep when I received a message. In my mind, I clearly heard Daisy tell me, "These are *my* people".

When I got home, I called them up and suggested that if they were willing to provide her with a loving home, they could pay somewhere between zero to $300 for her. After careful consideration they told me they would pay $300.

A week or two later, Daisy was getting restless, wondering when they would be coming back for her. To help her out with her query, I put a backpack on Daisy's back and took a picture of her sitting by the end of the driveway. I sent them the picture, with the caption, "She's packed and ready to go!" They got the message! When the time was right, they came back to get her and took her home.

On that day, it was hard to let her go, but Daisy was very sure of herself. She jumped right in the back seat of their station wagon, sat in the middle seat, and stared straight ahead. She would not look at me. She was being very clear that she would not be swayed from this choice she had made. By not giving up on Daisy when she was young, I allowed the time she needed for her people to come. It turned out to be the best decision for all involved. The ten years that followed were the best of Daisy's life! Sometimes, it is worth the wait!

WELCOME, PRECIOUS CHILD

It was a stormy winter day at the end of December, when I married the man that I had met at my parents' house one year earlier. At that time, my personal family had consisted of five Border Collies, Digger, my fifty sheep, llamas, cattle, chickens, ducks and likely others I am forgetting to mention. I guess I had figured maybe it was time to settle down and take the plunge.

Since I had very little interest parading around in a spectacle in front of a large group of people, we opted for a small wedding. To avoid a crowd, we had a total of twenty-three people from our immediate families only, including my friend Rachel.

In addition to my fear of the spotlight in general, there was no way that I would be caught dead in front of any amount of people, wearing a frilly, bright white dress. The way I figured it, farmers and white were like oil and water. I have never understood why animal handlers are expected to wear white shirts and sometimes even white pants in the show ring when parading livestock around during a competition. I certainly wasn't going to wear all white at any time, no matter what wedding traditions say!

I purchased a full-length, crimson red wedding dress instead! I also had no intention of freezing on my special day, so I wore thick winter socks in my brand-new cowboy boots. With staying away from traditions, I also did not walk down the aisle, so we got married in a circle of our family.

In September of 2008, we planned an adventure, aligned with the successful intention of conceiving our child at Tuweep, in the Grand Canyon. A special child deserves a special entrance!

It was during my pregnancy that I finally gave up my work in the pig barn. Not only was there a danger of me getting hurt, but my biggest issue was the smell! My pregnant body could no longer take the distinctive odor, day in and day out. I was several months along when I stopped working full time with the pigs.

When I was seven months pregnant, Rachel and I drove Dirk to Sheep Dog training Camp in Michigan. When we returned to pick him up a month later, it became apparent that the person had gone on vacation for a week, and only trained him for three instead of the four weeks as promised.

The trainer released all the dogs from the pens she had in a shack. Dirk was running around outside in the pack, sniffing around and whatnot. He had a wild look in his eyes, unseeing – which changed the moment he saw it was us. We were all so happy! Dirk was always a hard worker, but still I wished he would have had the full four weeks of training. It would have made a big difference in the fine-tuning of his skills! After we returned home, I continued to work on the farm and do all of my chores, right up until our child was born.

On the first day of June 2009, I woke up in the morning and thought I felt a "little something." It was a curious sensation, so I put my feet in my Birkenstocks and stood up. No sooner had I reached a standing position, my water broke, filling my favourite shoes and the floor. With the breaking of water, I called my midwife and let her know.

Nothing happened for much of the rest of the day and my midwife instructed me to take several homeopathic remedies in succession, every fifteen minutes. I did so and laid down for a nap. No sooner had I laid down, my contractions started. They were already five minutes apart. I called the midwife again. I was home alone, hoping my child wouldn't arrive before the midwife did!

Very early in the morning, in the living room of the Hohl Place, I gave birth to my son, Clayton. He weighed in at 8 pounds, 7 ounces and was so very long, at 23 inches!

For about the first few days of his life, I was almost afraid of my own child! I hadn't really been around children much and was worried that I would break him! It didn't help that I was really sore and could hardly get out of bed.

I had looked after many newborns in my life, but none as important as this one. I struggled a fair bit at the beginning, but after I found a book at the library on Attachment Parenting, things got easier. I'd found a way to raise our son that really resonated with me, which included carrying him everywhere. He would be attached to me in some way, on a carrier on my front, or a backpack on my back. He was always with me, day and night.

I did all of my farm work while carrying Clayton. We installed a car seat in the tractor and he accompanied me to work. The trouble was that he slept most of the time while we were in the tractor. This meant that he was awake all the rest of the time, but that was okay; I was just glad that we were together.

I had heard people warn us about having a child sleep in the parent's bed, because then they don't learn to sleep on their own. That wasn't what attachment parenting taught though. It was more about children that didn't have their needs met when very young, that then needed more comfort when older. This is how the ten-year-old ends up not being able to sleep alone in their room, since they didn't get what they needed when they were a baby. The attachment theory was that the child, around the age of twenty-four months, would want to have their own independence and their own room – thus getting out of our bedroom. And so it was, when Clayton turned two, he got his own bed in his own room. He hardly ever came in to our room after that. That was cool. I was glad that I had gone against the grain and used my own intuition on that one.

It was on Clayton's first birthday when we moved to our very own, 100 acre farm property near Flesherton. It was the exact replica of the one pictured on my vision board.

How could this be? All my dreams from my whole life had come true! Amazing! Or so I thought.

In order to set off on our own, I had to leave the comfort of my home at the Hohl Place. I'd spent the previous fourteen years there, most of my adult life and then moved far away from my family and friends. I was home alone each day with no help, while caring for our young child. Our property was next to a busy highway, where lots of strangers happened to stop by for various reasons. We were far away from neighbours and it was tough to make new friends. We stockpiled the farm right away with many different species, in addition to the animals we brought from Wellesley. It should have been happy times, but I was overwhelmed, with little support. There was so much work to be done and most of it, on my own. I felt isolated and all alone.

Have you ever had the experience of having all your dreams come true? Everything you ever dreamed of in your whole life since childhood, suddenly right there before you?

I had such an experience; I was living my dream. Because I'd had the same dreams for my entire life, when I finally achieved – all of them at once – what then? I had the experience of feeling flatlined.

This is it? This is life? This is all there is? Forever more?

It wasn't all that it cracked up to be. Fulfilling my life long dreams had not brought the lasting happiness like I had anticipated. I had no new dreams to inspire me – I had nothing to look forward to. With no outside help or emotional support, things started to go downhill.

OREOS WITH BUTTER?

I had to take care of and manage our herd of rare breed Galloway beef cattle, a couple of milk cows, several pigs, chickens, turkeys, ducks, laying hens, a flock of 100 sheep, some horses, in addition to having a large garden to grow most of our vegetables. I had a young child – no babysitter or help for the farm and all of the household responsibilities.

But at least my wonderful dog Dirk was happy!

He had much more work to do after we moved to that farm, on Clayton's birthday, June 2, 2010. Dirk was so skilled and smart, that if there were multiple species in a field, such as horses, sheep, cattle, llamas, ducks, and so on, he could bring in just the ones I asked for! "Bring the sheep, Dirk!" If it was time to do the milking and the cow was way out in the field... "Go get Butter!" If the sheep were in, but not the protection animals, I'd tell him to "Bring the llamas Dirk!" He was brilliant.

Speaking of llamas... in all my twenty-some years of having them, I only got spit on twice and kicked one time. Ida, an all-black llama that was born back in Wellesley, was the only llama to ever kick me. It was purely in self-defense when I had her cornered and came up straight behind her. At least it was winter and I was wearing my insulated overalls at the time, so I was well padded on my legs! I didn't really blame her - I probably had it coming! As far as the spitting goes, the only one to spit was Iris. The first time was when my friend Len – the sheepshearer, was scanning her for pregnancy. He was reaching around with his instrument in places she didn't think was appropriate. I was holding onto her halter when she turned her head and spit in my ear! The only other time was when I was hand feeding her whole corn. Ishmael had come up alongside her, looking to share the treat! She meant to spit at him, but I was right there and got caught in the cross-fire!! FYI - Projectile dry corn hurts!!

Llamas can be dangerous creatures, but mostly they are curious. They are very capable guards, but their biggest asset is their height and their curiosity. Since llamas stand at the height of a person, they can see a long distance. If they see something lurking around, their curious nature has them run over to see what it is! Predators are not used to being run at by large beasts, so often that is enough to scare them away. If the predator is determined on a meal, count on a llama having a whole bag of tricks to use on the hungry attacker.

In addition to spitting a warning, llamas can bite, kick, smash into, roll on top of and scream like a human! I have heard stories of them screaming so loud, they woke up a family to save them from a fire. I have heard of llamas rounding up their sheep and putting them in the barn. They then lay in front of the door to make sure no animal gets in or out! They are truly remarkable!

Not long after we moved to our very own farm, we bought a purebred, three-year-old Guernsey cow to whom we gave the apt name, Butter. She was a medium sized cow that had a beautiful fawn coat with large white spots. We were excited that she would give us rich yellow milk, higher in protein and butterfat than what is produced by the common, commercial Holsteins found in modern dairies.

Guernseys and other old-style cattle also come equipped with the sought after A2/A2 milk gene. The milk produced from A2 cows is highly digestible and more like goat milk in that regard. At the same time, we also bought a young, bred, Milking Shorthorn heifer that we named Cheddar. She sported a dark red colour with the characteristic white forehead of dairy cattle.

Butter – the Guernsey, standing in the strawberry patch

The Milking Shorthorn cattle are good milkers in addition to producing meatier offspring than many dairy cattle are capable of. Their milk is good for cheesemaking as they have a higher protein to fat ratio compared to other breeds. The Milking Shorthorn also does very well on pasture, so it was a good addition to our 100 acres of hay/grass.

My sister Brenda had suggested that I hand milk the cow, if I was milking just one. She explained that lugging around the milker and cleaning it, takes a lot of time. So I tried that. Butter had never been hand-milked and she did not prefer it! She would kick away my hand once, then twice, then a thousand times. This was not working!! I had to have a machine! Butter gave a lot of milk, so we decided to get a little Jersey calf to suckle her. Jerseys are known to be good nurse mothers and I just figured that a Guernsey would be the same! Not so! Remember how Butter kicked me when I tried to milk her by hand? That is how she felt when the strange calf tried to suckle her. She kicked him away repeatedly and it wasn't long before she had stepped upon his head!! I had to remove the poor thing, before he would be killed by his evil stepmother!!

We were not very original with the name we called the calf at first. We didn't want to get attached to it so called it CALF. Then as you know, people add an "ie" or a "y" to names and we started to call him Calfy which soon turned into "Cathy." Cathy the calf for a male? Yes, well, so be it.

Cathy was with us for one year when he came to an untimely death. I was putting hay in with the loader tractor and dropped a 500-pound bale in the cattle feeder. It was a good system in that I didn't have to drive in the pen with the cattle, but not a good system in that I couldn't see where the bale landed. After putting the tractor in the shed, I had to go and look after Clayton. Driving the loader tractor was the one job where he couldn't come along. I guess Cathy must have been hungry and put his head in the feeder, before I put the bale in. It was later in the day when I walked through the cattle pen and popped my head outside to make sure everyone was okay, but they weren't. Cathy was standing at the feeder, but his head was under the bale and he was already gone. A year's worth of beef wasted and a life snuffed out too soon; it wasn't a good day.

As for the milk cow, Butter, I didn't like her too much at the beginning. That soon changed and she became my favourite one! It turned out that she also loved me as well – even too much sometimes! Butter was a wonderful cow who always came when I called. She did make things a little awkward though, when she came into heat and would come when I didn't call. She would always be looking for me. She would stand at the gate and moo for me. If I went in the pen, I'd better be running because she would be chasing me! Why? Because when cows are in heat, they mount each other. If there are no other cows, sometimes they choose other species. One time I remember riding my beloved horse Digger in a field with my cows, when a Jersey cow almost knocked me from my perch! She randomly ran up behind us and jumped on Digger's rump! Hey watch it!! No room for both of us! So, let me just say that I wasn't too keen on having 1200 pounds of Butter jumping on my back! I made sure to run away - really fast!

In addition to Butter and Cheddar, we ended up buying quite a number of rare purebred Galloway Cattle, both belted and solid. These cows were not fun in temperament, but were amusing to look at! The black belted ones looked like Oreo cookies! They had pitch-black hair with a distinctive, wide, white belt all the way around their middle section! I also had some extra-cool, Dun coloured cows with the white belt. The belties ended up being a little nutso-in-the-head and were terrifying to me. The solids seemed to be a little more "solid" minded with a more even temper. In solid colours we had black, dun and even a red one for a time. All of the cattle, whether solid or belted, had thick wavy hair with an undercoat like a beaver. It helped protect them from the elements.

Those Galloway Cattle were purchased from a farm that had no barns. These were pure range cattle and knew how to fend for themselves. Poor Dirk could not herd them. If I needed the cattle, I would send Dirk out after them and soon *they* would be chasing *him*!! I would call Dirk to come in the direction I needed the cattle. Although more dangerous than herding, it worked every time!

We inherited three gray, standard-sized donkeys with that farm. We should've guessed the reason they let us have them for so cheap, was because they were impossible to work with! The two females, known as jennies, were three years old. They had been born on the property and no one had ever taken the time to handle them. Donkeys especially, need to be handled at a young age, as they are very capable of biting, striking with their front legs or kicking with their hind legs. If they don't learn any better, they can be quite a handful.

They could barely be haltered. I had a farrier come to trim their hooves and they kicked him; he promptly said not to call him in future. They were not tame or friendly. The third was a male, that they had recently bought for breeding. A male donkey is called a Jack. He lived up to his name and was a real live jackass! And man were they loud! Their braying could be heard three kilometers away! What were we going to do with this bunch?

It was after dealing with these "untouchables," that I decided I would rather have a nice brown donkey. Wouldn't that be much better than these plain Jane gray ones? I'd actually never thought of having donkeys prior to inheriting these ones, but I was certain brown would be way better. I always liked black sheep instead of the usual white, so why would I settle for a gray donkey, when there was a brown one to be had?

We sold the gray ones. Or did we? The selling was the easy part, but we still had to get them off the property, somehow! The buyers brought an enclosed car trailer which I didn't think was the best way to transport livestock, but I really wanted them to go away. Although I did voice my objection, I didn't stop the transaction. I was actually on my way out the door to buy my beautiful brown donkey Celeste, so there was no time to waste. But, they would NOT go on the trailer.

We had halters on the donkeys and they tied a rope through a pully inside the trailer. I am certain that they were the most stubborn animals ever born. One inch at a time. The rope with a bungee cord attached, kept tension on them, as the donkeys would pull back as hard as they could. The bungee cord would help bring them in. As soon as a donkey moved its head forward even a fraction of an inch, the rope was again pulled tight. In the end, I left my husband to deal with it. I had to go and buy sweet Celeste - the good one! One inch at a time and they eventually got the donkeys in and away! Good luck was wished to all involved!

THE DEATH OF COMEDY

By 2011, we bought three Berkshire crossed with Tamworth pigs to fatten up with the extra skim milk that we had leftover from Butter's incredibly creamy milk! My sister Brenda had been raising Berkshire pigs for many years. They are black with white on their muzzle, feet and tip of their tails! The Berkshire meat is known for being uniquely marbled. I personally have always liked the Tamworth pigs – because they are red! The Tamworth breed is known for being the "bacon" pig. I believe it is because you can get the most bacon out of them of all the breeds! I love bacon! They have fine-grained lean meat and can be used as a grazing pig. Together I thought that crossbreed would be the perfect combination of fat and lean! It also made for beautiful red pigs with black spots. In later years I stuck with pure Tamworth, since I had found a breeder that I knew and trusted.

Butter gave about six gallons of milk per day and as the year progressed, it would get more and more cream until fall, when it was conceivably half and half! I would often get a headache if I drank it straight, because I wasn't getting enough liquid in my diet. Milk is my beverage of choice, but in the fall, it seemed like it was only cream! I remember walking by the pig pen one day after I had put the pig chop in the long, metal trough. There was my toddler Clayton, sandwiched in between the pigs! With his butt sticking up and his head down in the trough, he was having a snack *with* the pigs!! After that, whenever I turned my back on Clayton in the barn, he was always eating the animal's feed!

As a family, we had been occasionally watching the *Little House on the Prairie* Series. With knowledge I gleaned from one episode, I managed to stop his behaviour, permanently, with one sentence. In the next show, rats had contaminated Walnut Grove's grain supply and residents started to get sick and die. The next time I saw Clayton eating the chicken feed, I told him he was going to catch "The Plague." He never ate the feed again!

In 2011, at the age of thirteen my beloved Border Collie Wyatt passed away. The vet had recommended that I give him Tramadol for pain and I had followed the directions. Within an hour and a half, I found him lying dead under my desk in the dog room. I believe he suffered a heart attack, as a reaction to the medication. Finding him dead so suddenly, was beyond shocking and my heart immediately broke in two; the comedy he brought into my life was gone.

It wasn't long after Wyatt had passed on, that he wanted to show me he was still around. It happened as an extremely strange occurrence, when Wyatt's spirit took over Harley's body from time to time! First, she would be howling or barking the exact same way, that he did. She would do things comedically, that were totally uncharacteristic of her, but exactly the way Wyatt used to do it! Although I loved the thought of Wyatt still being with me, he started putting Harley in harms way. I had to ask Jules for help in communicating with my spirit animal!

Once, Wyatt brought Harley out into the field in front of the haybine mower, which I was using to trim the tops of the grass in the pasture. A large reel pushed the grass towards the fast-moving knives that cut it, putting Harley in grave danger. Another time, Wyatt took her across the highway in front of a transport truck when I was cutting the hay across the road. I had to ask Wyatt to leave and not to inhabit Harley's body anymore.

Clayton & Freckles with my truck in behind

I loved him but he needed to go – his time had passed. I missed him terribly but luckily, I still had Harley and Dirk!

In July, we had gotten an old pony for Clayton to ride, named Freckles. The poor old guy must have been fed on sand or something, because his teeth were all worn down to nothing. Nonetheless, he was a wonderful old soul. One day, my three-year-old Clayton was leading Freckles around on the back lawn. Freckles really wasn't interested in walking. Instead, he wanted to eat, so he held his head down, munching on the grass. When Clayton started to get frustrated, because Freckles wouldn't walk forward, I said, "It's okay, just give him a little *tug*." He dropped the lead rope, marched up to Freckles and put his arms up around his chest. I asked Clayton what he was doing. He said, "You told me to give him a little *HUG!*" I have the cutest picture of him hugging Freckles that day. Hugging *is* way better than tugging any time!

I was out in the barn one morning and found a cold lamb laying in the pen. There was a mom who already had two new born babies and she didn't have any interest in that extra one. I scooped up the little lamb and ran with her to the house. I hollered in to my husband and Clayton that a little lamb needed their help! I handed her to Clayton and said that he must get her warmed up. Could he do that? He thought he could. They got a hot water bottle, put it in a box with some towels next to the fireplace and placed the lamb inside.

Clayton stayed with the lamb, playing quietly next to the box. When she finally roused a couple hours later, the first face that Lambie saw was Clayton's. "Mama?"

When I came in from chores, I put my finger in Lambie's mouth to make sure it was no longer cold, before she was fed. Clayton had managed to bring her back from hypothermia and her mouth was now warm! I heated up some colostrum that I had milked out of the mother for Lambie to drink. I handed the bottle to Clayton and he gave her the life-giving liquid.

From that day on, the bond between Clayton and Lambie was strong. Clayton had a little lamb; her fleece was white as snow. Everywhere that Clayton went the lamb was sure to go!

And let's not forget old Harley, she did her job too – following the lamb! Clayton, Lambie, Harley…they were inseparable!

When Lambie grew up, she still didn't know she was a sheep. She was more like a dog. She would jump in the Jeep with the dogs and go out to the back of the farm, to help with fencing or whatever we happened to be doing. She simply had to be with Clayton, so she might as well go along for the ride! Lambie only lived for a short four years and sadly died of tetanus in 2016.

I say four short years for Lambie, because Georgian's daughter "Q" lived for over nineteen years! Lots of sheep farmers think ewes are old and cull them after the age of five! A sheep at the age of ten is ancient in most flocks.

Clayton & Lambie, March 2012

I didn't even start keeping records on Q until she was six years old, after I had moved out on my own and brought my originals from Brenda and Shane's farm. *After* the age of six, she produced *twenty-six more* lambs for me! I retired her at the age of sixteen and much to my surprise, she still managed to have babies twice more, at age seventeen and eighteen!

As I previously mentioned, back in 2001, there had been that dog attack on the sheep I had been pasturing at a different place. So many of my sheep had been hurt or killed and it had been very traumatic for me. I already had a couple llamas at the farm where I usually kept my sheep, but hadn't taken any along to that pasture. After that fateful day, I started collecting livestock protection animals, figuring the more, the safer. It was a grand notion, but in practice, it doesn't really work. Having one or two llamas that bond to the sheep is much preferable; more just bond to each other. This was the first farm where we suffered actual losses from coyotes. At first, we didn't even notice that coyotes were taking our sheep, because they would eat the entire carcass and leave no trace.

One day I walked into the barn and there were only a few lambs in the one pen that went out to pasture. I wondered where my pen full of 80-pound lambs had gotten to!? I ran to look and they were just gone – none to be seen anywhere.

I called the county inspector and we went out looking for evidence to piece together what had happened. In the field next to the barn, we found one lamb skin and when we picked it up, there was part of a bone beneath it. They paid me for that one. We walked through that field and to the one behind and eventually found a depression in the grass with a few tufts of wool. They paid me for that. The coyotes had eaten every scrap. I was missing eight lambs, but they paid me for two, because that was all I could prove.

Later that same year, I noticed quite a few turkey vultures out in the field, lined up on a fence. Other than thinking it was neat, I didn't really pay much attention, until the sheep didn't want to go out to the pasture. They were fighting against going – but again, I didn't pay much attention.

The following day, nine baby lambs went missing from the field, without a trace. The county said if I could find a leg or an ear or any part, they could pay me, but just knowing that they were gone, was not good enough for them.

At that time, I had seven llamas and two donkeys out protecting them!! I remember driving around in our farm Jeep, looking for my special lamb. I yelled her name "Lucky!" in desperation, hoping that she would come. As it turned out, Lucky wasn't really lucky.

Another time, the coyotes somehow got into the barnyard during the night, even though the walls were ten feet tall. They killed one ewe and ran off with another baby lamb. That was it. I had too many llamas and donkeys and not enough protection. It was then that I started my search for the perfect dog breed.

Clayton & Cria, March 2012

IN SEARCH OF PROTECTION

It was time for a new dog breed. Not just any breed would do – it had to fit all my specifications. Ideally, I wanted a herding breed that could guard, but soon realized that dogs have specific purposes for a reason, so that they can be the best at what they do. I had always wanted a big dog – but it needed to be compatible with livestock and have a low prey drive.

We had people coming and going, buying eggs and meat as well as a little homeschool group and therefore needed a breed that would not bite someone, just because they showed up. We needed a tough, yet smart, friendly and loving dog.

I looked at breed after breed – all sizes, shapes and colours. Big dogs seemed to have short life spans and health challenges. There had to be something out there for us. I completed all the online "help you pick your perfect breed" questionnaires that I could find from dog food and other pet companies.

Late one night, I found yet another online questionnaire. I learned that most don't ask appropriate questions, such as; if you have livestock and things of similar nature. This one seemed to ask at least relatively intelligent questions and it suggested twenty-six breeds for me to choose from. There was one breed that I had never heard of, that caught my attention.

The breed was giant-sized, a very rare livestock protection dog from Spain. My eyes just about popped out of my head when I saw the pictures. I had to know more, so I read everything I could find, which wasn't too much. I knew in my heart without a doubt that I had found the perfect breed – The Pyrenean Mastiff. Now all I had to do was find one!

There was only one breeder in North America at the time; *De La Tierra Alta Kennels* in California, owned by Karin Graefe. As is often the case when I set my mind to something, I wanted a puppy… instantly!

I was placed on Karin's waiting list hoping to get a puppy from the November 2011 litter, and was so disappointed when I didn't get one. I had to wait until the April 2012 litter. Some things are worth the wait and this definitely was.

On April 18, four puppies were born; one of them would be ours. I looked at the pictures and saw three nicely marked puppies and one darker one. I said to myself pointing to the dark one, "Any pup but that one." Every week, new, individual photos were posted of the puppies. Clayton was almost four years old at the time and looked at the pictures each week as well. His response was the same, week after week. I would say, "Which one would you like?" He would point saying, "The cute one." And my response to that would be, "Any puppy but that one." We were talking about the same pup.

Finally, the puppies were seven weeks old and the determinations of which were to be pet-quality and which were to be breed-quality were complete. Karin sent us an email with pictures of the puppies from which we were to choose from.

There was only one picture, since there was only one available puppy. She was, as Clayton referred to her, "The cute one."

I had gotten the one that I have given my attention to - whether I had wanted her or not. "Any pup but that one…"

From our choice of one, we made our pick. It was the best decision that we ever made. I picked the breed; Clayton picked the puppy and my husband picked the name. She was named after the warrior woman from *Lord of the Rings* – Éowyn. Her full name would be Éowyn de la Tierra Alta, and she was perfect.

My husband was often gone for his job and Clayton and I were mostly left alone on the farm, day and sometimes also at night. One day, a couple stopped by wanting to look at the lambs that we had pasturing on the front lawn. The Border Collies were behind the fence, but the lambs were in front of it. Clayton and I went into the front yard to speak with the couple.

My son was always an extremely charismatic little fellow and made friends easily. The man started playing with Clayton, swinging him around, giving him airplane rides. He was acting about like an uncle would be with a nephew, except I didn't know these people at all. Their car was parked at the end of the driveway, on the side of the road. There was a moment that the man said to Clayton, "I'm taking you with me in my car" and with Clayton laughing, picked him up and started running for his car!

I was astonished! I ran after them and the man stopped and said he was just joking. Had they have stuffed Clayton in their car and driven away, I wouldn't have even known what kind of car it was and I could not see the license plate with the way it was parked.

Clayton was only three years old and it terrified me, because if that same person were to come back again – Clayton would see him as a friend, someone we knew. I tried to convince Clayton that he should never go in anyone's car without Mommy or Daddy. He thought why not? He liked riding in the car! I knew I needed help. I needed a backup. I needed someone to watch Clayton when I couldn't. It was impossible to be with him every minute and still do everything I needed to do, while my husband was away! Luckily, it wouldn't be long before Éowyn would arrive to become Clayton's guardian.

TAILS OF FANCY

Digger was always fine as an "only horse." At times he had not gotten along with others, but had done fine on the lawn at the Hohl Place for many years. We had each other. When I got married that bond stayed strong, but my husband also wanted a horse of his own. First, we bought him young Sammy. He was a large, beautiful black, untrained Thoroughbred crossed with Percheron, with a gorgeous silver mane and tail. A Thoroughbred is "hot blooded" like the ones you see on the race track, while the Percheron is "cold blooded," a draft horse. It could have been a great combination, if we had wanted to do a sport of some kind with him. Not having any knowledge of horses, my husband let this big lug learn a few bad habits. I was pregnant at the time and was unwilling to risk stepping-in to help. Sammy's feet were as big as dinner plates and he would choose to lean his giant body onto whomever decided to pick up one of his feet. In the end, he was just going to be too much horse for us. We found him a wonderful home.

Next, we bought a quarter horse foal we named Rocky. He was a sad little thing we fell in love with at an auction sale. We bought George, when Rocky was still quite young. He was an Oldenburg gelding that used to be an "A" circuit jumper. The owner was retiring him and wanted a good home for him. I used to look after Lonesome Dove for Ian Millar and this was only the second Oldenburg I'd ever seen, so I thought it was a sign. George was so big, almost eighteen hands high! If you are not familiar with measuring the height of a horse, one hand equals four inches. They are measured from the ground to the top of their withers, which is located just below where the mane and the back meet. Therefore, to ride George, the rider was perched, six feet in the air! He was a sport horse that was extremely well trained, but was lost without a job, and was shoved into retirement on a sheep farm. He could easily jump over the fences so it was hard to keep him in sometimes. A new disease was developed in the newborn lambs. I wrote it in the record book under Reason For Death, "Equinitis." Yes, I made up that word. I didn't know what else to say, when it was a horse that had stomped the baby lamb to death.

I took both horses, Rocky and George and placed them into a separate paddock. One day when I drove in, I saw giant George biting little Rocky in the back! CHOMP! What was going on with him? I asked my friend Jules for help. What was wrong with this big guy?

George was a sensitive character and he didn't understand why there were a lot of animal spirits hanging around. Some animals that had passed over the years, still lingered around. He felt like he was taken away from the jumping he loved and put in to a graveyard. He was extremely unhappy, which in turn, made *us* also extremely unhappy. When the farrier came to trim the horses' hooves, she said that her little sister was looking for a new horse. I said that we had signed a paper saying that we were not supposed to jump George, but that he was so unhappy for not having a job. He and this little thirteen-year-old girl ended up being the perfect team. He only had to jump fences that were eighteen inches high so it was easy for him. By allowing George to still have a job, to jump, to do what he loved – they both flourished.

When Rocky grew up, we had him trained properly at great expense. He was a gorgeous horse – red, chestnut hair, white blaze and four white socks. My original beloved horse Digger and Rocky got along pretty well. One day my husband saddled up Rocky before I had Digger ready, so he went on ahead for a ride. Once they got to the field, Digger, still by the house, let out a loud whinny for his buddy. Upon hearing his elder's call, Rocky started bucking and my husband flew off, bruising several ribs. After that, he didn't want to ride Rocky anymore and we had to find *him* a new home! I rode Rocky only one time and it was like riding a rocking chair; so smooth compared to Digger's incessantly choppy gaits. I still loved Digger to bits and no matter what he did, we would never be separated until God made that decision and took him away from me, ten years later.

In the summer we purchased two off track Thoroughbreds, Jockey Club-registered horses that were previously racing and had been retired. They had issues and were sort of being rescued for a cheap price, I guess. They were supposed to be our riding horses but "what were we thinking?" We never did get to ride them and they became just more mouths to feed.

After that it was Jack, another quarter horse, so quiet and perfect but we didn't notice the bone chip in his knee and didn't get him examined by a veterinarian before purchase, because he was coming from a breeder. We thought if we paid the big bucks from a reputable breeder for a horse this time, we would be okay - but we weren't. That was incredibly disappointing, because Jack was a very special three-year-old, who now could not be the riding horse we had envisioned. We tried to get the breeder to take him back, but they would not.

That long list of horses, would not be complete without the one that was in the middle, following Rocky. While we waited for our Pyrenean Mastiff puppy Éowyn, we purchased another horse for my husband – his name was Fancy. He was small in stature, but had a big personality. Fancy was a Spotted Saddle Horse, which meant that he was also a "gaited" horse.

When "gaiting," a horse moves each foot independently, leaving one foot on the ground at all times. A gaited horse can walk normally, some can trot and canter like any other horse, but they also have this special gear – almost like overdrive. It's a running walk that helps the horse to conserve energy, while giving them greater endurance and stamina. Due to the smoother, easier motion, it is easier on the rider's body by not having to bounce along at a trot.

Fancy had been kept for most of his life all alone in the previous owner's garage, while his only friends were human. Little Clayton could lead this horse around with just a handful of his mane – no halter required. Fancy would hold his head low and walk alongside him. He was the perfect horse around people and was wonderful to ride, but he was not socialized one bit with other animals.

I will always remember the first day we brought him home. We had a two-year-old bull named Brent that I think could sense, that Fancy was not a normal farm animal. We let Fancy out in the pasture with the cattle. Clayton was just a little fellow and we were standing in the middle of the field, when Brent saw Fancy. This bull whom we had had since he was seven months old was now grown up and big. In all the time we'd had him, he'd never moved faster than a lumbering pace. He was in the far corner of the field and in a blink of an eye, he was across the length of the field and halted to a stop right next to Fancy. Lucky for Fancy, that Brent had stopped first, before smashing his head into Fancy's side. Therefore, it was just the head action and not the full weight of Brent, giving Fancy a warning. I had no idea that a bull could run that fast!

Never again did I go into the cattle pen with Clayton and it wasn't very long before we sold the bull. The cattle were soon to follow, because we had a severe drought that year and there was not enough feed for all the cattle and horses, besides, we had no bull to re-breed the cows.

Fancy

Fancy ended up being a short-lived member of our family. Not that his life was cut short, but his time at our place was short. We had to keep him in a pen separate from the cattle and other horses, because he chased and picked on them. But even in his separate pen, if a small animal was unfortunate enough to get near his grasp – they were in for it. Once I saw him grab a cat by the tail and swing it into the air! Another time I saw him grab a red hen. He got a mouth full of feathers and shook her!! He had to go. I found him a more suitable home.

There had been so many horses at this point that we had bought and sold. It seemed like we failed. In another way, it was good because they always found better homes than the places we had bought them from. In the end, I figured my job was being the intermediary.

ÉOWYN, THE SHIELDMAIDEN

In June of 2012, at thirteen years old, my sweet Harley was feeling her age, I inadvertently gave her two cups of straight chicken fat that I had skimmed off some stock. She had a sudden attack of pancreatitis and didn't really recover. The vet wanted her to have Tramadol, but I didn't want to give it to her. I was certain that drug had killed Wyatt, but I didn't listen to myself and again followed the instructions.

Harley was soon paralyzed and after a few days I had to make that uncomfortable decision to euthanize her. I was again, heartbroken.

I already had Éowyn on order and she was coming, but with feeling the loss of Harley's untimely death, I was no longer excited about our new puppy's arrival. I hadn't planned for Éowyn to be a replacement for Harley, for she couldn't be. I didn't feel ready to have another dog at this point in my grief. I was so sad, missing my sweet Harley. It was only for a couple months, but Dirk had quickly become an only dog. I swore that I would never get so many dogs again, it was too heartbreaking, especially to lose them so close together.

Éowyn would have been old enough to fly at the end of June, but it was incredibly hot and there was a ban on flying dogs. Week after week, we waited, hoping for something to change, but it was a very hot summer and we were getting antsy. She was getting bigger every day! We ended up having her ground shipped by van, which took six days for her to come all the way across the country. She got to ride most of the way with her brother who was going to Wisconsin, then the rest of the way to Detroit by herself.

Clayton and I crossed the US border and got a hotel in Detroit, awaiting her middle of the night arrival on August first. The next morning, after not getting much sleep, with precious cargo on board, we travelled back to Canada. On the way home, we decided to break up the long drive with a quick stop in Kitchener, to visit my parents. Clayton got to spend some time with his grandparents and it was a nice pit stop for the puppy and me.

When we arrived, my father, whom I'd always thought of as not generally fond of my dogs, was sitting in a lawn chair in the garage. I asked Dad if he could hold on to the leash and watch Éowyn for a few minutes, while I went inside to use the bathroom and get Clayton set up for a snack. He agreed.

I came back about five minutes later and they were gone! I went running out the cul-de-sac to the street, looked left and could see no one. I looked to the right and was relieved to see my Dad! He was down the street, getting his mail from the community mailbox, with Éowyn in tow!

I love the picture of my father that I took right then – it's my favourite. It was just him and Éowyn walking back from getting the mail! I believe he bonded with her that fateful morning. Previously, my father never had much interest in my Border Collies or any dog that I had ever seen. After that day, whenever we talked, Dad always asked how she was. Éowyn had even won over my father!! The breed was a winner and this particular girl was a miracle worker.

Only twenty-five days later, Éowyn was entered into her first dog show. It was actually my first time as well, so you can imagine my excitement when this new rare breed of mine, managed to win Best Puppy in Show! I guarantee it was nothing that I did to help with it!

Years earlier, when I'd left the pig barn for the last time, I had taken a piece of plastic chain, as a memento of my years there.

Éowyn's first day – with my Dad, August 2012

I'd eventually gotten the smell out and it had become a plaything for Clayton. The night before the show, I stepped on that piece of plastic chain that he had left laid out in the living room. I slid uncontrollably across the floor and in so doing, had mildly sprained both ankles. So, it was at my first show, that I limped horribly around the ring, with an untrained puppy. Éowyn alone with her charm won the day!

It was the first time a Pyrenean Mastiff had been shown in Canada, but I was fortunate to have a judge from the US that had seen the breed before and knew what it was supposed to look like! I went to one or two more shows that year, but the last one in October was where I got my first education on showing dogs.

I was sitting with a woman I'd just met and we were watching the other dogs, awaiting our turn in the ring. I commented to the woman, "Look at how those other dogs stand so beautifully! Wow! They must come by that naturally in some breeds!" She had been munching on potato chips, but stopped in mid chew, swallowed, looked at me and began speaking words I could hardly believe. "They are trained to do that!! It's called *stacking*!"

That was a thing? The book I had bought on showing never even mentioned that I had to train my dog! Well, you learn something new every day - I was at my third show before I even knew what I was supposed to do! But it didn't stop me from showing. I would be better prepared the next year. I'd do better with the next one, or so I thought.

We had brought Éowyn into our family with a specific purpose. She was to be Clayton's protector and took her job very seriously. We had to spend a week-end in a booth for my Bio-Ag business, during the fall fair in mid-September.

Having a puppy and a four-year-old along, helped to keep things interesting! People were astonished that a little boy could walk such a large dog, in, around and through the crowds. She never pulled or pushed him anywhere. While I was in the booth, Clayton would sometimes ride his rolling horse around the arena, with Éowyn watching very closely. If he were to go out of sight, even for a moment, she would pull me in his direction. Although barely five months old, she knew her job and did it well.

Éowyn grew at an alarming rate. She surpassed Dirk's full-grown size very quickly and soon dwarfed him. She liked to pretend that Dirk was a coyote and practice her craft on him. Dirk would run away at his very fast top speed; his little legs going so rapidly they could hardly be seen. Éowyn would take off after him with one giant stride after the next and slowly overtake him. While running, she would open her big mouth and place it over the back of Dirk's neck, as if she was going to kill him. When they would return, he would be soaked with slobber and look like a drowned rat, but he was never harmed in any way!

We loved Éowyn so much that we decided perhaps we could breed these rare dogs. We thought about using artificial insemination, but that would be very expensive, so we opted to get a male instead. It was the year following the drought, we'd sold the cattle so it was time to find another enterprise.

I looked all over the world for a male. I searched high and low, but in the end, settled comfortably back with Karin. We trusted her and she had unrelated stock available in an upcoming litter. Gandalf was born December 12, 2012.

GANDALF, THE WIZARD

When sweet little Gandalf arrived from California in February of 2013, he was only ten weeks old. Being as he was my second Pyrenean Mastiff, I thought I would be more prepared, but that was not the case. From the first moment I set him down in the dog room, he immediately started to hump the other, older dogs. Humping is a sign of dominance that I hadn't expected from this young newcomer. I thought, "Uh oh." What have I gotten myself into?

The original plan for Gandalf was, that he was to live in the barn and protect the livestock. The timing of his arrival was such, that we were deep in the winter of Canada and we did not have an insulated barn. The puppy was worth more than all of our livestock put together, so we opted to keep him in the house. Even with sleeping in the house, as he grew, he instinctively knew that the livestock were his and took his job very seriously.

That spring, I started Gandalf's show training. I'd gotten a new book that was much more explicit and explained in detail how to show and stack. Now I knew what to do, but *he* wouldn't do it. He would NOT stand still… for anything. In my determination to get it right this time, I hired Nicole, a young lady from the dogs shows, to come and help me.

After arriving at the farm, the first thing she did was attach the leash to Gandalf's collar. He was already wearing the standard show, snake choke chain. Immediately, he started flopping around on the ground, pulling on the leash and squealing in terror!

I exclaimed, "Stop! You're hurting him!"

She said, "He'll stop when he's ready to. I'm not pulling on the leash; I'm just standing here."

I watched and listened in horror as my beautiful puppy acted like he was being tortured or killed. It felt like forever, but it probably wasn't quite that long, before he eventually gave up and became reasonable to work with. Wow, just like that. Not saying that it was the end of his issues, but I didn't have any more trouble walking him on the leash after that!

My hope was that he would be Gandalf the Gray, but ended up being Gandalf the beige. A bit disappointing as I had really wanted a gray one and had so far ended up with mostly black and now beige. What I have learned from animals over the years is that they often live up to their name. When you say the animal's name, you form a picture with intent in your mind and *that* is projected to them. If you call your dog "Killer" for example, it is more likely that it will be aggressive than if you call it "Daisy." I remember hearing about a horse that had been named "Sly". She used to open the stall doors and escape regularly! When they changed her name to "Lisa," she no longer did that!

Gandalf was a wizard. He lived up to his name in being able to get from place to place unnoticed. He could find a way through any fence or open any door. This would eventually become an insurmountable problem.

During the previous August, Summer Rain, one of our off-track racehorses, had gone on a month-long vacation to visit a beautiful, black and white, Spotted Saddle Horse stallion. Other than Digger, she had been the first horse I had purchased with myself in mind. Since she was unrideable, I was hoping to create a gaited horse of my own.

Gandalf, the wizard

I went out one morning to find a tall, white and brown spotted filly, standing brightly in the field next to her dark liver chestnut mother. I named her Summer Breeze. We called her Breezy for short. That is what was felt when she would zip by… I'd feel the breeze! She was energetic, high-spirited and certainly not gaited! Again, not the best backyard horse, but it had been worth a try. Our vet Angela purchased her from us and began Breezy's training.

The next dinner party we had; Angela came over sporting not one but *two* black eyes! We were almost afraid to ask why! In the end, she did admit that Breezy had knocked her out! Oops! At least Angela still continued to work with her and thankfully, didn't give up!

Also in 2013, my sweet Butter gave birth to a beautiful brindle heifer calf, sired by a Jersey bull through artificial insemination. I was so happy to have a female calf this time and named her Clare –

shortened from Clarified Butter. We'd had trouble getting Butter pregnant in the past and the last calf that had been born was male. We had tried eight Artificial Insemination services and hadn't gotten a pregnancy. First, we tried Guernsey. After giving up that dream, I had changed to Jersey semen, hoping for some hybrid vigor. We thought we'd finally gotten the job done when she didn't return to heat a ninth time.

To my surprise, when the calf was born, I could clearly tell that it was neither Guernsey nor Jersey! He looked like a carbon copy of our bull Brent! Both were black with a white stripe down their middles! I could have saved a lot of time and money and just had Brent do the job in the first place! At least my plan had worked this time; I was going to keep Clare as another milk cow. As she grew, her markings became even more striking! The white with the brown patches had the marvelous black stripes through it. She was a beauty!

Meanwhile, in addition to the fun on the farm, I continued to keep myself busy with the monthly dog shows, on various week-ends from May to October. I loved getting out and educating the spectators and the judges on my rare breed! I was very happy when Gandalf won Best Jr. Puppy in Show that August!

In October, Éowyn became the first ever Pyrenean Mastiff to get a title and was the first to be a Champion in Canada! I was so proud of her!

Although I had distant plans for Éowyn and Gandalf to become parents, I guess I hadn't made the "off in the future" part known to them. I had made a signature on the bottom of my emails, that said something about being a breeder of Pyrenean Mastiff puppies. My plan was to wait until Éowyn was two years old, to ensure all of the health tests would be completed before breeding. We could do preliminary hip X-rays on Gandalf when he was eighteen months of age, at the same time.

One morning, early in November of 2013, I needed to walk out into the field to get Butter for milking. Éowyn, who was eighteen months old, was in heat so I locked Gandalf, who was ten months old, in the front field. There were five acres to run around in, surrounded by six-foot-tall elk fencing. I was only going to be gone for a few minutes, but the cow was a little further afield than I originally anticipated, so it took a bit longer than I'd expected. As soon as I had locked Butter in the milking stall, I went out to check on Gandalf. Apparently, I was away too long, because Éowyn and Gandalf were tied together on the lawn!

What? OH NO! How could this have happened? I didn't even think that Gandalf was old enough to get the job done! His sire Quark had been three years old before he was able to do that! Oh crap. I didn't know what to do. I did the only thing I could do; I called my breeder Karin and admitted that I had messed up. What do I do now?

At that time, I did not know of any person in the whole world, other than Karin, that had Pyrenean Mastiffs. Except for my own two, I'd never seen another Pyrenean Mastiff in real life; barely even in pictures, to be honest! I didn't have a website. I didn't even have Facebook. I was totally unprepared!

With only two months to get things in order, I had my work cut out for me. Against my better judgement, I joined the world of social media and got a Facebook account. Whoa! The whole world opened up! Who knew that there were so many Pyrenean Mastiff owners out there!

I found hope creeping in with the worldwide support for my first litter! Although I had raised several litters of Border Collies previously, I was completely unprepared for the endeavor into the world of the giant breed, Pyrenean Mastiffs.

ARAGLAS, MY CHAMPION

The year of 2014 started with the birth of my first litter of Pyrenean Mastiffs. On January 2, over the course of fourteen hours, Éowyn gave birth to thirteen puppies, each with beautiful markings. All of them were white, with a dark mask and ears, with irregularly shaped patches all over. Of the thirteen, sadly two were stillborn. In subsequent litters, I would find out that seemingly dead doesn't necessarily mean irreversibly dead – but in this case they were, because I didn't know life might have been an option.

When Éowyn got pregnant, my vet had told me to ensure that I didn't give her anything raw. I tried my best to comply and fed her the best kibble I could buy. After the puppies were born, she struggled to feed them. They chewed up her teats and she lost a lot of her hair. We had to wean the puppies early, so that Éowyn could have a break.

The puppies were not a picture of health either. They had worms, constant ear infections and diarrhea. I treated each condition conventionally with the drugs prescribed. If I did everything right, according to accepted ordinary methods, then why did I have such a mess? If I only knew then what I learned before I had another litter, it would have been much better. But one only knows what they know, and can only do the best that they can, with what they know at the time.

I had been overjoyed with the birth of the puppies, more so than even I was expecting to be. I had felt graced with the return of my beloved Ivy! She was marked so neatly with a keyhole shaped patch on the back of her head. She definitely held the key to my heart! I was so happy to have us reunited again – it had been too long in my opinion. I am sad to say, that my joy was short-lived.

When the puppies were seven days old, I asked Clayton to hold them up, one at a time, so I could take individual pictures of each one, for the website. I went around the corner to the computer, barely ten feet away from the whelping box. Uploading pictures to the website took a long time with my rural internet connection. I'd only ever put one picture of each puppy on there; the rest were posted on Facebook because that was super quick and easy.

It took a whole hour to post those few pictures. I then went back around the corner to count the puppies like I always did. One was missing. The pig rails around the edge of this newly constructed whelping box, were made of solid two-by-fours. We hadn't known that if they were solid, it could cause a problem; there was nowhere for the puppies to escape if they were underneath it.

In that short hour, with no sound made, Éowyn had laid down on my favourite little girl, my Ivy reincarnate!! Her body had been safely under the two-by-four, but her head and upper body had been sticking out. She had been smothered. Without a sound, I didn't know there was a problem. I was right there! I could have done something!!

I couldn't believe it. I'd waited so long for her and she was already gone after only seven days. From that day forward, in this and subsequent litters, I never again left the puppies alone. I stayed with them day and night until they were well over three weeks of age.

I remember the first time I left them; it was to attend church. I cried the whole time we were gone. It affected me deeply that I had not only lost some puppies during birth, but then this beautiful vibrant life force, snuffed out so quickly when I wasn't watching.

The pig rails were remodeled before the next litter. I would not make that same mistake again.

My first litter of Pyrenean Mastiffs were the first to be born in Ontario. There were only three other puppies ever born in Canada before, one in Quebec and two in Alberta. My puppies were as rare as they were wonderful! We even had the county newspaper write an article about the miraculous birth!!

With the article coming out in the newspaper, I learned a few things about "free advertising." Finding lifelong homes through people buying on impulse was harder than it would have seemed. After seeing the article, each of two local families purchased a puppy. About a year later, both puppies needed to be rehomed. One was returned to me as per contract and I found him another home. The second one was rehomed, without my knowledge, in violation of the contract. It was several years before I was contacted by the second owner, and it was news to me! Thankfully they were doing right by him and it was surely a better home than the first.

My first litter wasn't well planned and history had repeated itself with the Pyrenean Mastiffs as had happened with the Border Collies. Both times, two puppies had to take a detour to get where they were going. Maybe it wasn't the wrong place, maybe they were just temporary steps that were needed to get to where they were supposed to be. The universe works in many strange ways that we do not always understand.

After losing my little girl, to distract myself, I picked a rebound puppy. Not only is it not a good idea in general, it really didn't make much sense that I picked a male! If I was going to keep a puppy, I should've kept a girl for breeding. Trouble was, I didn't much like the other two girls. One was on the small side and not show quality. The other was scary smart, too much like her sire. I couldn't have two Gandalfs - one was more than enough most days!

I named the puppy Sunshine, because he made my world brighter. As it turned out, he had some pink on his lips, which is a disqualifying fault for showing. I still wanted to keep him though; I didn't want to let him go!

It was the strangest thing, but Sunshine did not want to be kept! He attacked Gandalf and once he even bit Clayton! There was no way that I could keep him afterwards, it was three strikes against my pick. I found a great home for him when placing the other puppies. I made sure that they knew of the way that he had acted with my son. They said they were not usually around children and they were okay with it. Checking in with them years later, they said he was perfectly even-tempered and never once had any kind of outburst. He just wasn't the right dog for us and he wanted to be clear that he had other plans!

One day, a client of our vet friend Angela, came to see the puppies with the intention of taking home the best show quality male that I had. Their heart was set on Araglas and they had come, cash in hand, to get him. Araglas took one look at the lady and went around the corner, laying down out of sight.

I wasn't expecting that reaction – what then? I certainly would never make a puppy go with someone they didn't want to. I didn't have to do anything. The show quality female puppy was all over this woman. There was no way that she could leave without her! Araglas was to find his forever home with us.

He was perfect in every way, the epitome of the breed standard. I called him my sticky dog because he followed me everywhere. He was my protector. As a puppy, he walked so closely behind me that he would be stepping on my heels! If I stopped suddenly, he would bump into the back of my leg.

My favorite picture of Clayton and Araglas

Since I had been taking Gandalf and Éowyn to the shows for almost two years at this point – about once a month for half a year of good weather – the judges were becoming more familiar with the breed and its standard.

In May, at his first outing, first time ever off the farm, Araglas went to three shows in one day. He did everything I asked of him even though he'd had virtually no training in advance. He made me proud with winning all three – Best Puppy in Show titles! He started out a true champion and never let me down.

I was also very proud of Gandalf when he won Reserve Best in Show and became a Canadian Champion! Now he was the second Pyrenean Mastiff in Canada to become a Champion. When we got home, I had to laugh at Gandalf. He immediately ran to find his best friend, the brindle heifer Clare! I felt like he was just bursting to give her the good news, how he did good for once!! She had grown up so beautiful with her striped coat, seeing them so happy together was a joy.

Right from birth, Araglas stood out from the other puppies. Part of the breed standard is to have "bright white, snow white" colouring and Araglas had the brightest whitest coat wherever the mottled black patches were not. He was in all ways, a perfect Pyrenean Mastiff. They are often considered the quietest of the livestock guardian breeds. They often do not bark unless there is something important to say. They have a "deep dark bark, from deep inside their chest." I had actually been quite worried when he was young that perhaps he wasn't as perfect as I thought, with being silent and all. Araglas was seven months of age before he uttered a sound! I guess he figured his parents had things under control and he didn't have anything pressing to say! After he started barking, he didn't go all crazy – he only barked when it was important and I have to admit, if Araglas barked, I listened!

On my birthday in September, I took this beautiful boy of mine to the show. Sometimes, I was nervous about showing and felt that Paul, whom I'd met at the shows, could do it better than me. Paul was a nice young man who was a seasoned showman. He always dressed in formal business attire and looked sharp. Some women at the shows wore fancy clothes and dresses, sporting pumps on their feet, which I thought was insane! You wouldn't ever catch me running around on rough grass covered ground in uncomfortable shoes! At some shows clothes are important, but these shows were more laid back and you could still win, even while wearing jeans and running shoes, thankfully. Paul looked very professional when showing and was often hired to show dogs for other people. I wanted to win and didn't have the confidence that I needed, so I occasionally traded him a bag of Bio-Ag dog food for his effort. He didn't have to get Araglas ready or train him – he was already there. He just needed to run him around in the ring and show him.

On this day, I think maybe I had a sore knee – real or perceived, I don't remember. I asked Paul to show Araglas for me. My eight-month-old puppy, one of the rarest breeds at the show, did me proud! I stood at the ringside bawling my eyes out when the judge handed Paul the BEST IN SHOW ribbon for Araglas!! Oh my goodness!? Best in Show! Over all the other breeds, my baby, my first born, my perfect puppy – BEST IN SHOW!! As I walked by the President of the show, I heard her say how he was much better than either of his parents – what an excellent job of breeding I'd done! I could not have been happier.

I didn't even get Araglas to too many shows that year and he still managed to make it to the Top Ten dog of the year list!! Coming in at Number Ten, but it was still an honour!

THE ART OF LETTING GO

My father passed away suddenly, at the end of April in 2014. Being far away from family, it had been hard to grieve alone, especially when I was always so busy. That summer, my husband was between jobs and became distant, first emotionally, then physically! Although he found employment in October, it was several hours away and he moved in with his parents during the week, leaving us alone once again. I longed to go back to Wellesley, although it didn't seem like we ever could or would.

The farm really carried us that year, but I had to work extra hard. Eventually, we had to put it up for sale and look for a new one in the area where he had found employment. The new farm I really, really wanted was much cheaper, had a wonderful home, but did not have the best outbuildings. My husband thought we should move to the farm that we finally ended up buying, but I did not. It did not feel right to me at all. I cried every day, because I didn't want to move there; but to no avail.

We had to make some hard choices and let some of our animals go before the move. Angela helped us find good homes for our three, unrideable horses Summer, Thunder and Jack. It was sad to see them go, but I was glad that they were going to good homes. It was the next decision that was much harder.

On December 16, I had to let my beloved Butter go, although it broke my heart. I loved that cow so much, but we could not risk taking her to our new farm. She had been struggling with a severe case of highly contagious staph. aureus Mastitis, which I could not get a handle on. I had done everything I could for her, but when we were moving to a clean farm, I had to make the hard decision. Yes, she was my friend, but contaminating our new farm, possibly putting Clare and other future cows at risk, would not be a wise choice.

The day the truck came to take her to the stockyards was one that came too fast. I knew with my head it was the right decision, but my heart did not feel so sure. Had I really done absolutely every possible thing for her? It was very distressing to put her on that trailer for one last time. The worst part for me was that she loaded beautifully, without issue, just jumped right in the trailer. I almost wanted it to be a struggle so that I would be glad to have her gone, but that was not the case. My sweet Butter, who was only seven years old, was going away and would not be coming back. As the trailer pulled away, I laid down in a heap on the barn floor and wept.

Thinking back to that day still brings a tear to my eye, but I know it was the right choice. Some folks will say that I shouldn't get so attached to the animals. Other folks will say that it is cruel to send your friend to the stockyards. Sometimes we just have to let go of what others think and do what is best for ourselves, and our animals. We are always doing the best we can with what we have at the time — but it doesn't always end up feeling warm and fuzzy.

In the case of keeping a cow that is not productive, let's consider that a cow eats approximately 18 tonnes of feed per year. Therefore, it would not seem too practical to keep a cow that is not producing. Maybe you keep one as a pet, then what about the next one? Then you'd need 36 tonnes of feed for your two unproductive pets? It can't work, unless you are blessed with unlimited space, time and money.

It was sort of the same scenario that I had once in the past with my sheep, when I used to name every one of my black sheep and sometimes the white ones. I always kept the named ones — forever. It wasn't too long before I had fifty ewes that were all related to my first sheep. All had mothers and sisters that I loved and I didn't want to part with any of them! Finally, one day I realized that I had nine sheep that weren't pulling their weight, not producing well like the others. They were all related to the second Corriedale ram I had purchased, after Amos. His daughters were basically duds. Culling was very difficult, but necessary. Afterwards, instead of just blaming a poor choice of ram, I blamed myself for being too attached and stopped naming sheep.

Interestingly enough, by removing what I found the most fun about farming, there became a point where I stopped liking sheep! They just became a mass of wool with legs; a chore; bodies that needed to be taken care of.

I like knowing the individual animals by name, by character, by who their mother is or was. It didn't have to be every one, but I had to find a happy medium. Now I am back to naming sheep, because I like to be personable with them and it brings me joy. I don't recommend naming animals soon destined to be meat, though. I do have a new policy of naming all the meat lambs the same name, like Steve for example. I can then talk to them or about them, able to give them love and so on, but I don't get attached to "Steve" in particular. To me, it's all about giving the animal the best life that I can, while they are entrusted into my care. If they one day end up in a box destined for the freezer, so be it. They were happy and well cared for while they were with me, and that is the best that I can do.

No Rain in Spain, Only Snow

When we first moved to Caledonia, we locked all the dogs in the barn to keep them safely out of the way, when the big water truck arrived for the first delivery. After I had opened the gate, letting the truck through, I closed it again. The truck drove up to the house and parked, just as Gandalf got the barn door open and all of the dogs suddenly burst out.

The dogs ran over and thoroughly checked out the truck as well as the driver. When they were satisfied that all was well, each one disappeared from my view around the side of the house. I was standing on the porch in my slippers, watching the driver as he started to take out the large hoses. Clayton was watching the events unfold from where he stood, several feet behind the driver. I watched as the large hose suddenly went in Clayton's direction! It was just registering in my brain that I should react, when out of nowhere Éowyn flew in and put herself between the big pipe and Clayton. She didn't knock Clayton over, she didn't bite the pipe or the driver, she just stayed between to make sure that he was noticed and not harmed. As I said before, she took her job very seriously.

One time, all the dogs were in the barn repeatedly barking at something and wouldn't let up. That was unusual, so I went out to investigate. When I entered the barn, I saw it was a raccoon. I told them to stop barking and eventually they did. I was trying to get them to back away from it, since the raccoon was not acting right. Gandalf laid down on the cement floor in front of the raccoon. The crazy raccoon must have been sick as it went and climbed right on top of Gandalf!! The Pyrenean Mastiff in general won't attack unless there is a threat, so he just let this wild animal walk on top of him! It was a sight to behold. I quickly got Gandalf and the other dogs out of the barn and called my neighbour to help "dispatch" the poor sick creature.

Araglas had seventeen ear infections in a row upon moving to this new, southern property. He seemed suddenly allergic to all kinds of foods and environmental stimuli. I ended up taking him to a natural type vet and she suggested a raw diet. I remember being flabbergasted at the thought! Raw? That wasn't safe! How could that be healthy? My vets had always said that a diet of kibble was balanced and good nutrition! I'd given my dogs really good kibble too! Hmmm. It was suggested that I read a book by Dr. Ian Billinghurst, Give Your Dog A Bone. It was a real eye opener and I highly recommend it to anyone considering feeding a raw diet to your dog. I started with feeding raw slowly by transitioning them to raw at one feeding and kibble at the other.

It was soon after this, that I found out from my sister Sue, that she had used a natural treatment to eliminate her own lifetime of suffering from allergy problems. It was called Nambudripad's Allergy Elimination Techniques, but most commonly referred to as NAET. I was able to locate a natural vet in Pennsylvania that could treat Araglas from a distance. I made an appointment with Dr. Deva Khalsa and she was able to help him eliminate his multitude of new found allergies.

I had been searching for a mate for Araglas, for over a year. I had been waiting on a couple litters from my vet friend Ixaka in Spain. Finally, a litter had been born and I was in line, second pick, for a show quality female puppy. There were three females born in the litter. Sadly, one female was squished early and one had an overbite, so not breed quality. That only left one suitable female in the litter and I had second pick behind the breeder himself. Ixaka hadn't been sure if he was keeping the puppy and was very slow on making up his mind.

I loved this beautiful gray girl! I thought for sure that she would be mine with a name like Georgia! I heard from several people about a big Pyrenean Mastiff show, held yearly in Spain in March. I so wanted to go there! I had never seen another Pyrenean Mastiff before, only my own that I imported and the puppies that had been created by them. I would love to meet Pyrenean Mastiffs, talk to other breeders, ask them about how they feed their dogs, watch the show, see Spain and meet the folks that I had spoken with online! Wow – that would be so awesome... so I planned an impromptu trip to Spain! We decided to leave in two weeks for a five-day trip!

I contacted Ixaka and told him that we were coming to see Georgia. He needed to decide if he was going to keep her, or if we were going to be picking her up! Luckily, my new neighbour John and another neighbour Blain, agreed to do the chores at the farm, so we were able to go. Clayton was happy going to my sister Sue's for a week, because he was getting to visit daycare for the first time, which sounded much more fun to him than driving around!

We booked our tickets, got updated passports and each bought a new camera for the trip. I left Dirk at home, with the door ajar, so he could go in and out himself. Gandalf, Éowyn and Araglas were taken to a kennel. It was my first time leaving them in such a place. By the time we flew out, we already knew that Georgia was not going to be coming home with us, but I was still thrilled to be able to go!

How exciting! My first time going overseas! The forecasted weather in Madrid was 22°Celsius each day! Hey, we don't even need to bring coats! We packed up a few clothes and headed off to the airport.

After a long flight, late in the afternoon we arrived to the perfect temperatures of Madrid, where we spent the night. The following day we had a long trek north, to get to the small town in the mountains, where the show was being held. We stopped at a castle that was supposed to have been the original template for the Disney Castle. After leaving there and a bit of sight-seeing, we headed towards the place where we were scheduled to arrive for the Welcome supper.

I was so excited that we would be with the other breeders and see real live Pyrenean Mastiffs! It seemed like a long way to follow the highway around to the west, so we thought a more direct, scenic route was in order – straight north and then across. The main highway would have been fine, but I wanted to see what the real Spanish countryside looked like, off the main track.

At this point I am reminded of Carrie Underwood's song Jesus Take the Wheel, that says "It was still getting colder when we made it to the shoulder and the car came to a stop." We drove as far north as we could, and then all we had to do was go west a way and we should be there. But the road did not look like a very well-travelled route. It was not as big as I would have expected. We clambered on, as I didn't want to be late for dinner, since we had come a long way to be there. But as we progressed, my mind could not understand why there was snow? What happened to 22° Celsius?

It was already dark when we came around a corner and bumped into a rockslide across our lane! Yikes! We made it around and back to our side, just as an old tractor came around the next corner! Whew! That had been too close. We drove more carefully moving forward.

Finally, we made it to the little town where we were supposed to be hours earlier. We pulled over after locating a parking spot. Deep breath... I was so glad to be there! I glanced around at my surroundings and saw a couple people walking a few dogs down a dimly lit street nearby. As my eyes adjusted to the scene, I burst into tears. They were Pyrenean Mastiffs!

My husband was concerned because he couldn't reach the AirBnB we'd booked for the night, so we had to go there, before going to the dinner event. It turned out to be a hair-raising experience and we decided not to make the return trip in the dark. I was extremely disappointed.

The next morning, we drove out of the little town and back to the main road. We stopped and stared in awe at the scene. The road we had driven on the night before was right next to a huge cliff and we were very high in the mountains! It was stunning to see the sights in the daylight. Apparently, we'd been lucky to have made it alive the night before, as there were no guardrails anywhere along the winding path and we had encountered random farm animals on the road; from donkeys to cows and even pigs!

We found the show the next day and I was able to meet a few of the breeders. I was so excited to be able to see over eighty Pyrenean Mastiffs of all shapes and sizes! I was surprised at what some folks were considering show quality, but I drank it all in just the same. I was in awe.

I was also freezing cold. We were in the mountains and although the show was held under cover, it was basically open to the air. I had only a light jacket and no sweater. If I would have been at home in the same temperature, I would have at least had insulated overalls on and a parka! One lady lent me her thin scarf, which was a bit helpful, but I was still cold.

After the show, we went to the awards ceremony where I was able to talk to a few more of the breeders and ask them my questions about feeding, although there was a huge language barrier in some cases. Luckily there were a few English speakers to help translate and we did learn some interesting information.

The breeder that won overall at the show that year, was one of the only two breeders that were choosing to feed raw; I was sold!

After we got back home, I confidently switched the dogs over to an all-raw diet.

After the dinner, we had one more trek up the mountainside to our Airbnb. In the morning we headed north and drove through some beautiful countryside. I felt like we had stepped back in time. The clothing on the men we saw seemed like something one would see in a movie of days gone by. We passed men in old fashioned hip waders, carrying fishing poles made out of sticks with string hanging from them. We passed by a family butchering a large sow, that they'd tied down on a large platform near the road. The men were wearing fedoras with feathers in their caps!

Before we got back on the main roads, we still had deep snow to contend with in places. We drove up and around the north shore before heading east. We stuck to the main thoroughfares after that, as we had a lot of ground to cover. We needed to be in Zaragoza by the next day to meet Georgia, before heading back to Madrid for our flight.

When we arrived in Zaragoza, we met Ixaka at a rural gas station located randomly in the middle of the countryside. We followed him out to his country place where he kept his dogs. He is a vet and lives in an apartment in town, but travels the 30 km each way to visit and care for his dogs daily. The dogs had free range of the basement of the house and a fenced compound outside with ten-foot-tall iron gates surrounding it.

It was mostly concrete, but there were some grassy areas and several almond trees completing the lawn. I had been picking Ixaka's brain for a long time about wanting to find a new herding breed. I had only ever had Border Collies and I believed the breed was being ruined in North America. I was interested in the herding breeds of Spain. At the time he had a rescue dog there – a Basque Shepherd. A beautiful dog really, but it had issues so it wasn't a great specimen for temperament.

Ixaka was a big proponent of the Basque Shepherd, because that is what he had grown up with in the Basque Country. I enjoyed meeting his Pyrenean Mastiffs, especially Georgia. It was heart-breaking to leave her there, but there was nothing more to be done. We took a quick trip to meet another breeder and then we had to get back to Madrid, for a few short hours of sleep before our flight home. In total, we drove 1850 km in the few days that we were there. I sat in the passenger seat and took pictures of the Spanish countryside. Since the majority of our travels were on the main roadways, most of my pictures are of the wide variety and often very funny road signs. Except for the show and the visit with Ixaka, my trip pictures were basically all of signs!

Upon returning home I was very distraught to find out that Éowyn was sick and even worse, she just started her heat cycle. It was figured that she had contracted a Urinary Tract Infection from sitting on dirty concrete in the kennel. The vet said that it could be problematic to breed her this time, if that wasn't properly cleared up. We opted to treat it and hoped for a good outcome. When we had the vet's okay, we brought Gandalf over to "visit" with Éowyn. That did not seem to be enough... maybe it was stage fright?

He could not seem to get the job done, even though it had appeared so easy for him when he was much younger and wasn't supposed to! At one point I locked him in a barn stall for safe-keeping, so he could rest and be apart from Éowyn. Now to explain, this stall had been built originally for Clydesdale horses, so it was solid planks five-feet up, with wrought iron bars about four-inches apart, to the ceiling above that. No way he is getting out of there – or so I thought!

I came back later and he was not in the stall. I found a tuft of white hair clinging to one of the iron bars. In one corner, there had been a small horse feeder attached at the top of the wooden planks;

the iron bars in that particular spot had been previously bent slightly to one side. Gandalf, who was probably 140 pounds at the time, climbed up and fit through a six-inch gap! Later on, I locked Éowyn in a different barn stall, with a wooden handle that pushed a long rod in to lock it tightly. I then closed the barn up tight. Outside, there was a six-foot-tall fence surrounding the outdoor dog paddock, and Gandalf was supposed to be on the OUTSIDE of that fence. When I thought both dogs were securely locked apart, I left them. I returned a short time later to a big surprise! Gandalf had jumped over the six-foot fence, opened the barn door, opened the stall door and let Éowyn into the hall. He had bred her and they were tied together!! *That* is persistence! The funny thing was, he couldn't seem to do it if she had been standing right in front of him. He seemed to have to overcome some big obstacle in order to be able to perform! Any which way, he got the job done!

SEEING DOUBLE

I had a friend, whom I had met by driving in his farm lane thirteen years earlier, while I had been cold-calling for Bio-Ag. His was one of the last places I ever door-knocked and I was blessed at that time to meet him, a friendly sheep farmer. I had been maid of honour at his wedding and now he was going through a divorce, a move, dating new people, and so on. I had supported him on the phone for over ten-hours a week during the previous months! I had needed an outside connection to the world and I got that through supporting him; we both talked while we worked! It was seemingly fine until I got laryngitis and lost my voice for 23 days, leaving no one I could to talk to!

I remember sitting on the stool, milking my cow, contemplating my existence. I texted and told him where I was at. We'd been texting instead of calling after I lost my voice. Who would even care if I was gone? The new farm was not what I had expected and it was so much work. My marriage was crashing. I was giving everything I could to others and my well was long since dry. Perhaps it was time to pull the plug and call it a day on this life.

I remember very clearly, the moment I thought about someone telling my mother that I had committed suicide and, that same someone telling my son. I made a decision in that moment that I would choose life. I was not going to give up; I would never give up.

I made an appointment with Jules, my Craniosacral Therapist and told her where I was at. She helped me work through some stuff, energetically. When I finally got my voice back and wanted to talk with my friend on the phone, he said he'd rather just text. I needed to talk after being silent so long. It was so odd after thirteen years, but I never did speak to him again. I guess when I chose to live, one chapter of my life ended, but not my life.

One night I did chores very late and my heifer, Clare – Butter's daughter, didn't come over to get her grain. I didn't think much of it because it was late and I thought if she doesn't see me, who am I to cause myself more work? I had made it very complicated to feed her in another barn, because I was trying to train her to the new milking stall, as she was due on May 12. The next morning, I went out and saw that Clare was in labour. There was a small red sack hanging out behind her! That was great except as the day wore on, no baby was coming and I was home alone with Clayton. Just after noon, we saw a white water sack break, but still no action. The trouble was; I couldn't call anyone for help, I still had no voice!

I was hoping that my neighbour John would be home to come and help me. We had walked over to John and Lois's place, but they hadn't been home for lunch. He would know better if we needed to intervene or wait. I had reached into Clare and found some big feet and a nose, but I could not budge the calf! At around 4:30 pm we saw John's truck pull into his driveway and I had Clayton go in and call him. Thankfully he came straight over! We managed to get Clare into the other barn to the milk stall, but it wasn't easy. He tied her up and went to work getting that calf out!

Keep in mind at this point in the story, that Clare wasn't due for three weeks! It was no wonder I wasn't prepared! I had been hoping for a heifer calf as we had bred Clare back to a Guernsey. Clare was the only heifer that Butter ever had, so we thought we were due! I was certain I was getting a heifer!

John reached his arm inside of Clare and ensured that he had two front legs and a nose in the right position. He left the cow standing, whereas with the sheep I was used to laying them down. Good luck forcing something that weighs 1000 pounds to lay down without a fight! John tied a rope to the calf's front feet and used all of his weight to hang on to the legs in his attempt to pull it out. With much effort, the calf finally broke free and landed on the floor in a heap. I cringed. John jumped up from his place on the floor next to the calf and lifted it high by its back legs. That was something I'd done with smaller animals like lambs and puppies, to get their airways clean and get them breathing – but I'd never seen it done with such a large animal! The calf still didn't breathe, but John didn't give up! He went above and beyond the call of duty when he gave the calf mouth-to-mouth resuscitation!! When he had tried every thing he could think of, he admitted defeat. He lifted up the calf's leg to check out the sex. It was a heifer, now dead. We put Clare in a horse box stall and when John left, I gave her some hay and water. I went to the house and cried.

I was so sad and disappointed! I was inside the house doing dishes when my husband came home from work. I asked him if he could please remove the body, as I didn't want to deal with it anymore! He came back a few minutes later and said the calf is up and looks fine to him.

What? How cruel of a joke is this? Of course, she is dead! She looks fine?? I thought what does he know! I put on my boots, went out to the barn and looked into the stall.

Clare was licking her new baby calf! What the...?

I stumbled over to the milk stall, because I could not believe my eyes. There laid the calf, just as we had left it. I ran back to the stall. What the...? There was an identical live heifer calf in with Clare!! Because it is an unusual occurrence, in my grief I hadn't even considered the possibility, then it suddenly dawned on me ...

TWINS!! I named my living miracle "Leche," which means milk in Spanish!

The birth of an animal can be a joyous wonder or a great stress, depending upon the situation. When everything goes well, often it is because the parents had the right nutrition at the times when it was needed. Troubles can occur when certain nutrients are missing, or there is too much or not enough feed. Occasionally a mishap happens, a baby gets misaligned or is too big, or what have you and it's possible to have a difficult birth. If you have more than one animal experiencing a difficult birth, you'd better check your feed ration, test your feeds or give your head a shake. If you overfeed early in pregnancy, the babies will grow too big and then they just can't get out! Sometimes it's specific nutrients that could cause problems, including the ability to become pregnant. Occasionally as in the case of Clare, there is a multiple birth and one offspring comes out and one remains in, but no one guesses that there was still a baby left inside. If the baby dies inside, the mom can go septic and without medical intervention, she will also die. It's most important to pay attention, before, during and after birth.

ÉOWYN'S DYSTOCIA

It was the end of May when my new friend Christine, who had ordered a puppy from my next litter, had offered to come and help at whelping time. I would otherwise have been home alone with Clayton who was almost six years old at the time, so I gladly accepted. Éowyn started being restless and nesting Wednesday night, so Christine came over on Thursday. We were up all night, expecting the birthing to begin, but it didn't. Éowyn did not want to stay in the whelping box to have the babies. I couldn't figure out what was wrong. Finally on Friday morning, Christine who was exhausted after being up all night, decided to go to town and get some coffee; I don't drink coffee and never have. I stayed with Éowyn of course, but she did not want to remain indoors. She wanted to get out of the house and so I figured, that I would take her for a walk and maybe get things moving.

Éowyn went directly out to the barn and into a stall that had straw on the floor as bedding. I thought she was just going to pee, but she had other ideas! Puppy number one was born right there in the barn at 10:40 AM! I did manage to catch it before it hit the ground and she chewed the umbilical cord off right away.

I rushed Éowyn back to the house and made her get in the whelping box with her baby! When Christine returned from town, she was delighted that the birthing had begun. I didn't realize until later, that it was actually probably Christine that was the problem! Éowyn did not want to have her babies with a stranger in the house. I think she had only met Christine once before. From then on, the labour was slow going. It would be exactly three hours before puppy number two made an appearance. It was about an hour between each for the next ones. Boy oh boy, I mean boy after boy! Where were the girls? I found out about twenty minutes later with the birth of puppy number five, girl number one. This perfectly marked, sweet thing would become my Brandybuck and she arrived around 3:30 in the afternoon! The puppies did not come any faster after that. It was more than an hour before the next boy and then three hours before the next! All seven puppies were alive and well at 8 PM.

It was Friday night, and since things were still progressing so slowly, I asked the neighbours John and Lois for some oxytocin. Sadly, theirs was old and expired. I had never used the product before, so I didn't feel comfortable trying it. I knew there were more puppies and they had to come out, but weren't.

It was twelve hours past the first pup when I managed to pull out a stillborn male puppy. I was trying to help Éowyn when she needed it, but at some point, my hand became numb and I was struggling myself. When I had rolled up my sleeve to reach in and feel if there was a puppy needing help, Christine noticed a thick red line on my arm. It started at my shoulder and was moving down my arm. Apparently, a little infected hangnail had somehow turned into blood poisoning, but I didn't know that at the time! I didn't really know what it meant to have a red line on one's arm, but I sure knew I didn't have time to worry about it; I had to get these puppies out!

By midnight, I made arrangements to drive Éowyn to an emergency clinic about a half an hour away, expecting that they would want to do a C-section, since she had been in labour so long. On the way there, at 12:15 AM on Saturday morning, I heard Éowyn making slurping noises in the back seat! I pulled over and retrieved the puppy, but it was a small female and she was stillborn. I hurriedly made my way to the vet clinic.

The people at the clinic were very unkind and treated me like I was putting them out by being there. They did blood work and took an X-ray. They said that there were four more unborn puppies still inside. They did not want to do a C-section and instead gave Éowyn a shot of oxytocin. I asked if I should wait there and they said no, that I could drive the half an hour home, as it didn't work that quickly. It was not long after pulling out onto the street when I heard Éowyn giving birth in the back seat again! It was just before 2 AM so there were no cars around and I just stopped the truck right there on the four-lane-road and jumped out!

I opened the back door and grabbed the puppy. It was also stillborn. With my heart racing, I got back in the truck and kept going, albeit a little faster.

I was about five minutes from home, when I heard birth happening once more! There was not much shoulder to the road, so I got over as much as I could and jumped out. The rear door of my truck opened backwards, so I had to open the front and back doors at the same time. I was so happy to see that she was alive! I unceremoniously snatched the 20.8-ounce, slimy, black little body and slipped her inside of my sweatshirt to keep her warm, while I drove home. I had just barely gotten my door closed when a pickup truck came around the corner and barreled past, over the line, only inches from my mirror. Had he have come just a few seconds earlier, I would have been killed! Somebody was watching out for me!

First thing Saturday morning, when the local clinic opened, I was on the phone with them requesting an appointment. I waited in a room for over an hour while they were waiting to get the vet records from the emergency clinic, when a vet finally came and looked at Éowyn. He didn't seem too impressed nor worried. I told him about the long labour, the trip to the emergency clinic, the X-ray results, about the oxytocin and how there were still at least two puppies still in there. I said that I thought she needed a C-section and he said, "She probably ate the puppies when you weren't looking."

Pardon?

I suggested he should take another X-ray?

He said, "Here are five doses of the strongest oxytocin... Go home and give her one every hour or two, if the puppies still don't come out, come back on Monday."

Pardon?

I took the five doses home and diligently gave it to her as directed. A few hours after starting the Oxytocin, puppy number twelve was stillborn. I spread out the last doses completing around 7 PM. Still, one puppy was unaccounted for.

I was quite upset at this point and had called my sister Brenda to talk it out. In passing, I happened to mention the red line on my arm and my hand being sore. About two hours later, my sister Sue knocked on the door. That seemed random, because she lived an hour and a half away!

"What are you doing here?" I wondered. She said that Brenda had called her and said that she needed to come and take me to the hospital.

"No way! I am not leaving Éowyn!" I proclaimed!

Eventually, with much persuasion, I accepted Christine's offer to watch Clayton, the puppies and Éowyn, while I took a little trip to the hospital with Sue. We restlessly waited there long into the night. Eventually I was given some medication and sent home, but not before I got a text from my vet friend Angela, whom I had updated on Éowyn's situation. Angela said for me to take her to Graham Animal Hospital, that they would help. I turned to Sue and asked if she would please drive us there. She looked at her watch - it was one o'clock on Sunday morning. I had been awake since Wednesday morning at that point and I would not have been able to make the trip alone. Christine offered to stay with Clayton, so Sue and I picked up the puppies and Éowyn and drove to Graham Animal Hospital. We would meet the vet there at 4 o'clock in the morning.

When we arrived, that vet was none too excited to see me either. She said that the C-section should have been performed on Friday already, not at 4 AM on Sunday. I told her of my attempts to get her help and of the other clinics I had been to. She took another X-ray and one puppy could be seen, in the wrong direction and as far up inside as was possible. Sue was tired after the 100 km drive, so she went to sleep on the hard-wooden bench in the waiting area. The vet later commented they had never seen someone sleep there before!

I sat on the floor of the surgery room while they opened up my girl. The vet said that the puppy was breech and had crawled all the way to the wrong end and died. It was already decaying and she figured that Éowyn might have been dead by Monday, had I taken that second vet's advice. I was grateful to Sue and Chris for getting us the help we needed.

Sadly, soon after getting home, puppy number one, who had only weighed one pound at birth, started losing weight instead of gaining. We lost him on Clayton's birthday, June 2.

BRANDY WAVES

In June, I purchased two books by Rhonda Byrne, *The Power* and *The Magic*. I had been down too low in recent months and figured it was time to get back to some positive thinking.

A few weeks later, with the puppies safely looked after, I took Araglas, who was eighteen months old at the time, to another show. All the way there, I only thought good thoughts. They were the most positive thoughts I have ever had. I didn't allow anything negative in. I knew in my heart and my soul that Araglas would win Best in Show. I saw it in my mind. I lived it. I breathed it. I was excited for it…

It was a cooler day, which was good because Araglas did not like the heat of the summer shows. He missed his fan on the porch and usually just did his best to avoid heat stroke. But today was different, it was even raining. Now I have to admit, that some of the competition did not look very good – wet. Fancy dogs with their poofy hair just do not do well with water falling from the sky on them in the ring. My most memorable dog that day was the usually beautiful Afghan Hound with its flowing hair; dump a bucket of water on that dog and it is a different story! That poor dog looked like a drowned rat, so it didn't offer a lot of competition to Araglas!

Araglas, on the other hand, on a cool wet day, was in fine form. His hair stayed its beautiful snow-white self and he looked gorgeous. I couldn't help but smile all day. I was uncharacteristically grinning from ear to ear when the judge pointed to us, declaring Araglas Best in Show!! I KNEW IT!! I was ecstatic! So happy that my boy had grown up and done it again!

In August, I entered Araglas in the Working Dog Specialty. This was always the largest show and so many breeds and champions came back for this special class. Araglas was his usual shining star self and I was so proud of him! The show included fifteen top quality working dogs, twelve of which were already at least Champion status. In order to progress past Champion, a dog must win over fifteen other champions in order to get to the next level, which is Master Champion. That day, they handed the ribbons out, starting with fourth place. Then third followed quickly by second. Always look at the judge, don't let your attention waiver, even if you think you have lost – you just never know. The judge briefly glanced over the lineup and then looked me straight in the eye and pointed at us. WE WON!! We won first place in the esteemed Working Dog Specialty!! Since Araglas had already won over a few champions, adding the eleven champions he just beat – he was also declared Master Champion!! The first and only Pyrenean Mastiff to ever become Master Champion in Canada! My heart was full!

Our house was quite small and the whelping box was not. Located in a central point, it took up the entire dining area. Basically, in order to get to anywhere in the house, a person had to walk past the whelping box. I began to notice that one puppy was acting differently than the others; the puppy was *waving* at me! Every time I glanced in, this beautiful, show quality female, named Brandybuck would wave her paw at me; every time. Then after a while, while waving, she started blowing me kisses! She would stick her tongue out and lick the air and wave at me! I took the hint and got the message. Brandy was a keeper!

My vet friend Angela, came quite a distance to this new property to do the puppy vet checks at my request.

Brandy at one day old

As she was examining each puppy, she asked questions like, "Didn't they get diarrhea? Are you sure that you should be feeding them raw food? I don't think it is safe. Didn't you deworm them?"

When she had checked each puppy over and looked in the last puppy's ears, she exclaimed in surprise, "Clean as a whip! Every one of them!" I knew in my heart that feeding raw was the best choice I could have made. I had clinical evidence, the difference from one litter to the next was marked, like night and day. We were on to something.

In October of 2015, Brandy was at her second show week-end. At the first one in September, she had managed a Group first, with her first time off the farm. This particular day, it was only the second chance she'd had at showing, but because it was the last show for the year, it was her last chance showing as a puppy. Baby puppies were 3-6 months of age whereas Jr. Puppies were 6-12 months. This was a particularly cold and rainy day. Normally, I'd prefer better weather for an outdoor show but if I'd learned anything, it was that my dogs performed well in adverse conditions, whereas some other pampered dogs did not.

I will always remember the Judge's reaction to Brandy when she was giving her reasons after the show. I had taken Brandy around the ring with the others at a trot, like we were supposed to. The cold rain had started to come down heavily and Brandy had sped up. She started to do this beautiful, but not breed characteristically extended flying trot. She had the most graceful and large flowing foot action that I have only ever seen in top quality show horses. We did our thing in the ring and then the competitors huddled together with our puppies under the little canopy tent, where the judge was standing to give the results.

The judge was beside herself, almost speechless yet trying to grasp for words to describe what she had just witnessed. She was using her hands and arms as descriptors. She gracefully extended her arms one at a time trying to mimic what she had seen Brandy doing. She finally exclaimed that she had never seen such a beautifully moving puppy! She caught herself and said that the other puppies were also beautiful, but this one… and she kept moving her arms in front of herself in disbelief!

Brandy is a beauty and I was very upset that the photographer refused to get her expensive camera wet, so that I could have a picture memento of our special day! Best Puppy in Show and New Puppy Champion… I was very proud!

By the following spring at the first show of the year, Brandy only had one chance to show as a Jr. puppy, before she would be considered an adult at one year of age. As it turned out, Brandy was not a fan of showing. She didn't mind the running bit, but she had no use for the standing still bit! Somehow, she still managed to get Best Jr. Puppy in Show and I was extremely proud of her!

Late in the year of 2015, a good friend of mine died and we had to drive six hours round trip to go to her funeral. We left the dogs on duty, free to roam throughout the fifteen acres of fenced property, as usual. When we came back at night, the dogs lined up across the gate, but several eyes were missing! When we parked up by the driveway, we found a note on the car that said, "We have your dogs in our shed."

What??

Apparently, Gandalf who could go over or under any fence and open any door, had done just that and had gone walkabout – this time taking Éowyn with him for the adventure! I was not impressed when I went to get them six km away, but I was sure grateful to have them back safe and sound! Around the same time, Gandalf started fighting with his son Araglas on a regular basis. I had the misfortune of getting between them one night in the dark. I tried to stop them, but somehow my hand ended up between them full of large holes and pouring blood like a bad B movie! It really hurt, and I should have just wrapped it up and stayed home, but instead I drove myself to the hospital. As soon as they found out it was a dog bite, then it became a rabies issue. I told them it was Gandalf, but didn't have a clue which teeth were the cause of my distress. By law, Gandalf was to be quarantined for ten days.

Since Gandalf could legally only be near me and no one else, I tied a twenty-foot lunge line around my waist and to his collar, while I did my chores out in the barn. It was fine until Araglas showed up. He loved to be with me and usually followed me around like a shadow, so he was upset because now Gandalf was following me around and they started to fight. I was panicked, because I was attached to one of the fighting dogs and I couldn't get away. I was so upset afterwards that I realized I couldn't do it anymore. I was so afraid of them fighting and Gandalf kept getting out and causing trouble in the neighbourhood, I realized I had to make a choice. It was him or me, and it couldn't be me, so it had to be him.

Gandalf was to have a new chapter in his life, he'd go from being a livestock protection dog to being a pet dog in the city, but he adjusted well. We would be able to breed him one more time with Éowyn, so all was not lost.

THE TROUBLE WITH GOATS

In searching for happiness through exterior circumstances, I decided that the sheep must be the problem. I'd had them too long; they were not interesting to me anymore. Goats were something I had never ever wanted before in my life, but I thought that perhaps they were the magic solution to farming bliss. When I was growing up, Shane had always said that goats and sheep do not mix, but perhaps he was mistaken? In November of 2015, I bought a few unregistered pregnant Boer goats, to see what the craze was all about. I loved those goats! They were so personable and the babies were so cute!

The Boer goats are raised for meat production, being hardier and more adaptive than some of the other breeds. From the top of the neck down, each goat had a shock white body with long ears, that droop down beside their reddish-brown head. Two horns stuck out the back of their head, with a slight curve down. I did not realize it at first, but later found out that the goats I bought carried diseases — some of which were contagious to sheep!

Three days after I bought my first goat in November, I photographed my first Bald Eagle. It was flying over the Grand River near our farm. It had been many years since I had seen that first Eagle with Ohmer in Wellesley. Apart from the ones in Alaska, this was only the second one I had ever seen in the wild. I didn't think much more of it at the time, not realizing the significance the Eagle would have, later on in my life.

Early in 2016, I added quite a few, very expensive Boer show goats to the menagerie, several for $1200 each! One of note was a $1500 triplet buck, named Trivago du Biquet.

He was still quite young, but had started growing a nice set of horns. They were thick at the base and stayed close to his head, hugging around the ears. Just past his ears, the horn spiraled straight out, making him several inches wider on each side, than the rest of his body.

He had a wonderful temperament and was very people-oriented, growing up pampered and well-fed in a show barn. I still remember the day that Clayton and I were out in the pasture field with my camera, taking pictures like I sometimes did while checking on the animals. The goats were always way more people oriented and were looking for treats and petting, while the sheep generally ignored us or ran away. I pointed the new buck Trivago out to Clayton as he was making a bee-line towards us. Normally rams and bucks can be dangerous and he knew that from the past. In this case, I wasn't worried but Clayton, then seven years old, took off at a run before I could say another word. Trivago thought, "Hey!? Wait up!" and went after him. Clayton was booking it across the nine-acre pasture, Trivago hot on his heels. I did what any good mother would do and turned on the video camera…

Clayton was running full speed while screaming "MOOOOOOOOOM!" over and over. If there had been an exciting sound track playing in the background, I think I would have peed my pants from laughing so hard. When Clayton got to the end of the pasture, the four-foot page wire fence did not slow him down. He scaled it with ease and flew over to the other side, still screaming to me for help! When I stopped laughing and composed myself, I made my way over to where the two were watching each other through the wire fence. Clayton was *not* impressed.

Trivago smiling

I explained that Trivago had been raised in a fancy show barn where he had been mollycoddled. Trivago thought that he was a people; he was running *with* Clayton, not *after* him! Clayton soon did realize though, that Trivago was a big teddy bear and although he needed to be respected, was not to be feared.

After getting the Boer herd together, we decided to have all one-size of animal – just sheep and goats. I sold the last of the cows, which included my beloved Clare. My husband and Clare did not see eye to eye. He was happy to see her go, but I was not. In addition to her unmatched beauty, she provided us with the most delicious milk of any cow we'd ever known. She had been the best of her two breeds, Jersey & Guernsey. I was sad to see her go but in order to get milk, I purchased eight, show Nubian goats instead. They supposedly had the best tasting milk and highest cream content.

Nubian goats have long pendulous ears, round roman nose, tall legs and are elegant in appearance. They can be black, brown, white or any combination. They really were beautiful to look at, but these crazy goats drove me to distraction. They were not regular farm animals; they were show goats. I guess you could call them goat royalty. They thought they were princesses and should be treated as such. They had absolutely no ability to fend for themselves in anyway and expected us to wait on them, hand and hoof. They didn't want to be left alone and followed us everywhere. They did not want to graze in a field... no way! They had no intentions of lowering themselves to such hard labour! They wouldn't stay in the field, but would find a way out or cry very loudly at the gate! They became extremely annoying very quickly.

They needed me and paid attention to my whereabouts. Goats are extremely needy; Sheep are much more independent! Where sheep will nicely subsist on pasture, goats start with your trees as high as they can reach! It wouldn't be long and they'd be back in the barn yelling, because they'd destroyed all the branches they could eat and now what else was there that I could offer them? Fifteen acres of pasture? There was no need for it. These goats would not be caught dead out there in the sun, or the rain.... Way out in the field?? No thanks... Maa...

I've had sheep forever and there was a hole in the barnyard area where the dogs could go from the front field and house area into the barn and pasture area. The sheep never bothered with the hole — not once. A sheep would not venture off by itself, because that would be a death sentence. Sheep feel safety in numbers. Three or more is preferable for them. A goat on the other hand? When *wouldn't* it venture off by itself or with others? So, that meant I had to close off the hole that the Livestock Protection Dogs (LGDs) needed to protect the stock, and those Nubians needed to be protected! The Boers on the other hand would just as soon kill a dog as look at it – and with their big horns it was quite dangerous for the dogs to be enclosed with them anyway.

It wasn't just the constant personal attention they were after; their nutrient needs were higher than other animals – especially in the area of copper. They needed to have copper boluses shoved down their throats on a regular basis, just to keep them thrifty and alive. A plastic balling gun was the tool of choice for inserting the bolus into the back of the goat's mouth. It was basically a long plastic stick that the large capsule was placed on one end and gently inserted past the point of no return. By ejecting the capsule so far back, the goat couldn't help but swallow it! Copper is so extremely important to a goat, as it is needed for proper organ function and bone growth. A copper deficiency in a goat can be a death sentence. They can be overtaken by parasites, may develop bowed legs, swayback or spinal injuries, their offspring may be compromised, they develop poor haircoat, and so on. Proper amounts of copper provide vitality, health and productivity. This is not so with sheep, although a sheep does need a little bit of copper, it is a fatal if they get too much of it.

Then, it was the constant foot care. Goats' hooves grow so incredibly quickly. I guess it would be great if they lived in the mountains or on rough ground, they would file them down on the rocks. This is not so with domestic stock. If a sheep requires yearly foot trimming, you twist the sheep's face around to its shoulder and lift up the haunches, so it falls on its bottom. Then with a heave-ho you set them up on their behind, resting their back between your knees. With the legs protruding in the air, you can trim the feet. Done. Once a year. Goats? Not so.

Having the experience with sheep, it was quite memorable the first time we attempted to trim a goat's feet and tried the old heave-ho method.   The goat and its legs moved so fast that one could hardly follow what happened in a fraction of a second! My husband was going to hold the goat, while I trimmed the feet.   In that one quick moment in time, my husband was on the ground and the goat was on top of him!! It didn't exactly go as planned!

I then called a goat breeder friend for some advice about trimming their feet. Apparently, you trim them like you do a horse, with the goat standing. So that is what I did, but boy is that ever hard on the back. And the other issue was that they didn't need yearly but *monthly* foot trimming!   I had thirty-one goats, so I basically had to do one goat a day just to keep up with it. It was not fun and I didn't enjoy it. I loved goats yet also hated them.

With the Boers I had bought more and more of them and kept the daughters as well. There were lots of health issues and I had to give them extra copper, because of the high sulphur content in the water.

The fresh Nubian goat milk, once cooled, tasted similar to cow milk. Palatability became a problem if it wasn't cooled quickly or was left out for any length of time. The milk, if uncovered would absorb everything from the air. In addition, it could only be stirred a bit, not shaken, otherwise it tasted like an old goat's foot.

Clayton was used to leaving his milk cup on the table for hours after a meal and then putting it back in the fridge for later use. With cow's milk, that works out just fine. Do that one time with goat milk and soon an aversion to milk develops! Clayton stopped drinking milk!

Now what do I do?

These Nubian show goats did not have very much milk either, especially not compared to a cow, but not even compared to a goat. I milked the goats by hand each day and my child wouldn't drink the milk? And my beloved cow is sold to another home!? I had so loved the goats - at first.

Both breeds of the goats had various degrees of sickness and health. It took quite some time before I got everyone in tip-top shape. In the end, the Nubians were the ones that threw me over the edge. I have never met more time-consuming animals, ever. I managed to survive only two months with the Nubians. My days of goat ownership were numbered. I lasted precisely eleven months with the goats and then I sold all thirty-one of them in one week. They were all in good health by then and people were impressed with my top-quality herd. I had nursed the sick to health - I had made it through the hurdles, or so I thought.

Little did I realize at the time, that having the goats would eventually cause the demise of my sheep flock, as Shane had forewarned me, when I was a child. After the goats had all left, my sheep started to have their babies. The stress of birth caused many of them to turn yellow, bleed out and die. I called the vet in when the second one died. She said, "It's copper toxicity."

The copper that goats need in great quantities in order to survive, had built up in the sheep's bodies. At times of stress, it overloads their system and they die horribly. One by one, my sheep were passing away. I was left with a large quantity of newborn babies to take care of! If the ewes didn't die after birthing, they died at weaning or when changing pens, shearing, and so on. Any stressful event became a problem.

I purchased a homeopathic copper remedy and tried to treat the survivors, but soon found that it didn't work. I consulted with the natural vet from Bio-Ag and realized that they needed a different homeopathic copper. I put the new remedy in their water bowl over the next few weeks and managed to save the rest. After the goats were long gone, I had lost 70% of my sheep. Having goats was a long hard lesson to learn.

After all that effort, I still did not have any milk. I needed to find another cow and was wishing that I hadn't sold Clare. With the goats gone, I did the flip-flop of species; we flipped back into cattle after flopping with the goats. I went to a ranch near Peterborough and the farmer let me walk around in the fields to see which ones I liked. I didn't like too many, but picked a couple of quiet, Charolais cross cattle. They were the only ones that weren't afraid of me walking through their field! I had wanted red cattle, because red is my favourite colour, but these cows were big and white. Well, one was white and one a golden cream colour. Charolais cattle happen to be one of the largest breeds, mainly raised for meat but historically used as draught animals. They were both characteristic of the breed, and had very broad bodies with heavily muscled loins and haunches. In addition to the two Charolais, I also purchased three Jersey cows.

In the summer, we had another misfortune to deal with. Clayton's beloved sheep Lambie had contracted tetanus. We tried desperately to save her with homeopathic remedies, but it was not to be. Lambie lay stiff legged in the barn and succumbed to the disease after a short battle. Clayton was distraught losing such a good friend. I had no good explanation of his question, "Why Lambie?" She was only four years old! I thought Clayton would want to keep the collar and bell she wore, but he was terrified of it. We hung it in the closet and he'd freak out if I brought it out. When he was older, he later explained to me that he was afraid that the disease would get him too! Poor guy.

We lost a couple sheep and lambs to tetanus at that property in the first year we arrived. Tetanus is a disease caused by an organism commonly found in soil. It was years later when I found out, that it is much more prevalent on farms where horses have been kept. The previous owner raised Clydesdale horses, so I figure that's where it came from. Tetanus can infect sheep through wounds that might be caused by shearing, docking tails or castration. Lambie may have been the last one to succumb to this disease, but she was not the least. She was definitely missed the most!

That was also the same summer that I bought a British Suffolk ram from a supposedly high health herd. British Suffolks are a stocky, terminal meat breed, meaning; that they are often used on other more maternal breeds to make meaty, hybrid offspring. They have white wool on their bodies and black legs. Their heads are also black and their long ears stick straight out the sides of their head. I don't usually like to bring in stock from other farms, but it is necessary in order to get new bloodlines. I misread the cues from this farmer.

The fella was concerned that I would be driving to his place after going to the stockyards in Waterloo. There were deep puddles in the parking area that was driven through by so many vehicles, from different farms dropping their animals off at the yards. When I arrived at the farm, he wouldn't let me see his stock. I should have seen this as a red flag, but I was buying the story about the high health status and not wanting any diseases to get in his barn. The ram in question was located in a trailer in the driveway. The ram was of good bloodlines and looked reasonable from the outside, so I paid the man and took him home.

I should have quarantined him, but I skipped that step because he came from such a high health herd. I would never have even considered buying him if I thought he might need quarantining! I turned him directly out with my sheep and goats.

He ended up fighting with my buck Trivago and I was concerned that he would hurt him. Trivago was young and very expensive and not the toughest of animals, as bucks go.

By fall, this new ram developed a lump on the side of his face. When I saw it, I exclaimed "Oh no! It isn't – is it??"

It was. Caseous Lymphadenitis or commonly referred to as CL, is a chronically infectious disease of sheep and goats, that is caused by the bacterium Corynebacterium Pseudotuberculosis. It is a very contagious disease to both animals and humans when the abscess breaks open. A very high death and cull rate can occur from this disease. I was very upset and I called the fella that sold me this ram and found out why he didn't let me in his barn!! He said that it wasn't his fault, and blamed a shearer, who supposedly brought the disease to his flock through dirty shearing equipment and as a result his flock was terribly infected!

In addition to some diseases, shearing equipment may carry ecoparasites such as keds or lice as well, so it is expected that shearers will clean their equipment between flocks.

The man said that he didn't know the ram was infected prior to selling him to me, but it was hard to know for sure. All I did know for sure was that I had to get rid of that ram as soon as possible, but it was not before his abscess ruptured. Every goat that got the disease was separated, and their abscesses drained and flushed. They remained separate until they were healed. The damage was done. As sheep got the disease, they were sent immediately to the stockyards before any more abscesses could break open. Later on when I finally sold the goats, I made sure that potential buyers knew which goats had been infected and were healed from it. Other less expensive goats were sent on their way to the stockyards. The rest of the sheep seemed to be immune to the disease and never got it, thank God.

In November of 2016, I bought a beautiful Appaloosa mare whom I named Happy. Happy the Appy. I had gone to the place to purchase a gorgeous looking chestnut gelding but, he was not for me – she was. Happy seemed quite large compared to my compact friend, Digger. She was 15 hands and two inches tall and was a colour I had never seen before. She had a progressive silvering effect called Appaloosa Varnish. The majority of her coat was a light pink in colour, but her legs, part of her face and neck, forearms, knees, hips and stifle, were all shaded in with red. It was like the artist had made brush strokes with the darker colour on the light. She was striking to look at.

After our experience with Jack, I wanted to pay the $300 to the vet to ensure that the horse was in good shape. My husband thought that it was too expensive and suggested I just take a trainer along to make sure she is good for riding. I should have listened to my head on that one but didn't. I bought her with my heart and loved her all the same.

About the first week in I was lunging her around in a circle. I managed to let her get too close to the fence and she smashed her shoulder directly into a cedar fence post! I had no idea that she couldn't see well! The vet informed me that she apparently had moon blindness. Dang it! Now the vet also didn't know if she was lame because of the post or was already lame and perhaps drugged or something. Damn. Why didn't we ever learn that $300 preventative is cheaper than the $1700 blind horse that then had a $300 vet bill? She had been a way more comfortable ride than Digger, but as it turned out, I never rode her again.

Moon Blindness, also known as Equine Recurrent Uveitis, can be quite painful. There is no way to know what caused her eye damage, as it could have been from any number of things. A virus, bacteria, pollen, vitamin deficiency, fungus, autoimmune deficiency, physical injury or tooth abscess are just a few possibilities. It is important to note though that Appaloosas are more prone to moon blindness than other breeds. I wish I could have known in advance or at least have known a way to help her.

THORIN EMBRACES HIS NEW IDENTITY

We had attempted to breed Éowyn with Gandalf in the fall, but taking her to visit him in the city hadn't worked out that well. We were given one more chance in the winter and Gandalf came out to the farm for a few days instead. On February 20th, Gandalf had possibly bred Éowyn naturally, but I hadn't seen it so I didn't know for sure. I really had to be sure, so I took Gandalf and Éowyn up to Graham Animal Hospital to see Dr. Rasa. She accomplished a "side-by-side" which means the sperm was collected from the male and then deposited, fresh, directly into the female. I had my fingers and toes crossed!

For years I had been searching for a mate for Araglas and after his younger sister Brandy had been born, I had also searched for a mate for her. I had been in line for a puppy seven different times, from seven different litters in three different countries; still I couldn't find one for either of them and Brandy was already of breeding age.

Ixaka, my vet friend in Spain, sent me a *for sale* post from a woman in the Czech Republic. She was selling a three-year-old male, with A/A hips, that had Ixaka's Pyrenean Mastiff breeding lines in him. I jumped at the chance! I had to hire an interpreter since the lady in the Czech Republic was very upset about having to re-home her dog, due to her own health challenges, and we could not seem to communicate through Google translate. They called the dog Nessi and a few other variations of his registered name. He had to be vaccinated for rabies before travelling, so we had to wait a full month for him to be able to come. He was so large that there were no commercial crates big enough to fit him! We had to pay the travel company to construct a custom one for him.

I hired the animal communicator, Claudia Hehr, to contact this new dog and explain to him what was going on. He was going to have to leave his family which included a young boy, travel across the world, to come and live with us. We let him know that the arrangements had already been made for him to come and that we would be changing his name. He wondered what his new name would be. We told him, "Thorin".

I had Claudia let him know on the day of transport that this was the big day. He was loaded up and transported to Germany and then overseas. It took him two days to get to Toronto. On March 27, Clayton and I drove to the airport to pick him up. He had been taken to a cargo bay so we had to wait a long time; finally we were able to retrieve him.

We took him out of the giant crate and the workers loaded it into the back of the truck for us. He could hardly stand up after laying down for so long. We walked him all over outside, to let him pee and stretch his legs. When it came time to go home, I opened the door of the truck and instructed Nessi to get in. He would not.

I had Clayton open the opposite door so he could see his way through, but still, he would not get in. I had Clayton pull and me push, but he would not go in. I tried using every variation of his name that I had ever seen written but still, he would not go in.

We were attempting to get this 180-pound male dog that we have never met, onto the floor of the back seat of the truck with Clayton who was at this time seven years old! What other option did I have? I was more than an hour away from home, stuck outside this warehouse with a child and dog that outweighed me by 55 pounds that refused to get in… What was I to do!?

Well, when all else failed, I reasoned with him! I explained the situation and told him what needed to happen and why. He stood there looking at me with a blank expression. Then I tried begging.

I pleaded, *"Thorin, please!"*

I will never forget the look in his eye when he realized he was finally home. After his long journey and all the different people along the way, I had used the name that we had told him about and then he knew it was us!

He immediately tried very hard to get in the truck; it was a big struggle for him. In addition to his huge bulk, I think his hips were out of place due to laying on one side for so long. Clayton, Thorin and I were much relieved to have him on board and heading for home.

I hadn't given enough thought to his living arrangements once arriving though. I already had a male, Araglas, similar in age and size. I had heard that if they met elsewhere and then came back home together, it would be easier for territorial issues. I had believed in my heart that Araglas would be alright with the new arrival, as he was extremely even tempered. I had not even considered that it would be *Thorin* who would not be okay with another male. Araglas wouldn't start a fight, I knew that, but he wasn't about to be picked on either. Thorin pushed his buttons at every turn. If I tried to ward off a situation and get Araglas quickly into the house, Thorin would bite him in the butt when he turned his back to comply. I was quick to find out that I hadn't created a fun situation.

When Thorin had first arrived, he was about twenty-five pounds overweight and his hair had been all tattered and matted together like felt made out of wool. We had tried to get him groomed at the local pet shop, but their facilities could not handle such a large dog, considering that the pet needed to be lifted into the wash-tub. No one was lifting this 180-pound guy off the ground! We ended up hiring a mobile grooming truck to come to the farm and help us with Thorin. What happened next was almost like something you'd see in a cartoon. Take the dog, throw him in the washing machine and out pops a fluffy pup! The two groomers worked for several hours, washing and brushing the giant dog... the camper was rocking back and forth like it was in a wash cycle! They came out with a garbage bag filled with wet fur and a beautiful boy with flowing hair, looking like he just stepped out of the salon! Of course he didn't stay that way, but at least long enough for me to take a few pictures! After the initial cleaning, it was much easier to wash and groom him for the show season.

He was not used to eating raw and really wasn't into it for a while, so he did drop some weight right out of the gate. By the time September rolled around, Thorin had lost about forty pounds and was moving around the show ring very easily while attracting attention from the judges. He was crowned new Canadian Champion, to go along with his previous Czech Jr. Championship title.

Thorin's first day coming with us on a walk in the field, was the same day that our big old Jersey cow, Bossy, gave birth to a new calf on the pasture. While Thorin was running about in the field, Clayton and I went over to look at the baby calf.

Bossy began posturing, with her head held down. I realize now, she was just being protective. I asked Clayton to find me a stick and he came back with a useless dead branch. I wanted to check out Bossy's udder, because it was huge and distended. I instructed Clayton to go stand far away, which he did. Next, I went around behind Bossy to look at her udder, when all of a sudden she disappeared. I was left standing there looking at the little calf. Where did she go?

Bossy had made a beeline for Clayton! I guess he was bopping around in the field, doing what youngsters do and she had taken offense to it in some way. I ran after Bossy, but she got to Clayton before I did. She had him down on the ground, was stepping on him and smashing him with her head!

What do I do? I didn't have a proper stick, only a branch! What if she turned on me next? I didn't think past that and began to scream at her and hit her with the branch. Eventually she relented and I told Clayton to run and run he did. He ran very fast to the edge of the field and fell up against a tree. I chased Bossy so that she went back to her calf and I ran like crazy to see if Clayton was okay. He had peed himself, which I would have too, if I'd had an angry 1000-pound cow pummeling *me* into the ground! I asked him if he could walk and thankfully he could, so we went out of the pasture field as fast as we were able to.

When we got back to the house, I checked him over and discovered that he was a very lucky boy. He had been stepped on, foot prints on both of his upper legs. It was so close, if she had stepped on his reproductive or any other organs, he could have been in real trouble – thankfully he just had a few scrapes and bruises.

The next week, Bossy and her calf were on a truck heading out to pastures elsewhere. I could no longer trust her and although I realized afterwards that Bossy had shown us all the signs that we should stay away, I hadn't been qualified to read them. For some reason, after that, Clayton no longer liked cattle – actually, he became terrified of them. Our beef cows were Charolais cross, which made them very large. They were not tame and when startled they would run – thus making them a little more dangerous. I had always been cautious of large animals, knowing what they are capable of. Now I needed to re-think what I was doing with these cattle.

At one point, we had the vet visiting us for pregnancy checking. She was standing in the chute behind our biggest cow, Emma. The vet was shoving her arm, covered by a long plastic glove, up into the rectum of the cow when my husband asked, "Don't you ever get kicked?" No sooner had the words come out of his mouth and she was starting to say, "Not ..." Emma lifted her foot up and swiftly retracted it. Her right foot sprang out with such power that the vet – when the collision of the foot hit her knee – flew up into the air, back about six-feet and landed on the ground in a heap. From her position on her backside on the ground, after a moment she said, "Not usually!" Luckily nothing was broken and she was able to hobble back over and finish the examinations. After that, we always put a pipe or two-by-four, behind the back legs of the cows, when they were in the chute. That was much smarter.

SAVING MY SHIELDMAIDEN

É owyn was restless. It was Thursday, April 20, and I knew it would soon be time to welcome the new puppies from Litter C! I stayed with her continuously throughout the day and night. The first puppy didn't arrive until late the following afternoon. He was the biggest puppy we've ever had, but he was green! Green placenta usually means the nutrients are being cut off so I was quite worried, since this was only the first puppy! This time, I was going to drive up to Graham Animal Hospital, but I had been awake for two days already. I called GAH and there was a new vet on call, so I decided to try a different, local emergency clinic.

While Éowyn tried in vain to deliver the next puppy onto the concrete floor of the waiting area of the Emergency Vet Clinic, I cradled the first-born puppy for one and a half hours. The vet finally took an X-ray and found five more puppies. Unlike the last litter, this vet wanted to start with a Cesarian, although she did admit that she had never previously performed surgery on a dog this size. I should have thanked her and driven on to GAH. I could have made it there in the time I had wasted in the waiting room! I was then worried about waiting another one and a half hours to drive to GAH before getting the puppies out, so I agreed with the vet, but obviously wasn't thinking straight. It was a decision I will regret for the rest of my life.

Since it was the middle of the night, I was allowed in the room, taking pictures to show Clayton for educational purposes. The vet anesthetized Éowyn and placed her on her back, with her legs spread-eagle and strapped down. The vet made a large, deep incision in her abdomen. Imagine everyone's surprise when Éowyn suddenly woke up! There was my beautiful girl, flopping around with her belly wide open, terrified and in pain! I almost dropped the camera as I watched in horror! The vet and tech were apparently also in shock, running around like chickens without heads. I was going to be sick and had to leave the room. They eventually got things under control and induced Éowyn back to sleep. I could hardly believe what had just happened.

It wasn't long before the vet came and requested my help. I stood by as she pulled out the first puppy and handed it to me, still and lifeless. With increasing sadness, I rubbed it with a towel before handing the dead puppy to the technician. We repeated the process for all five puppies. All five, dead! How could this be? I felt a rock in the pit of my stomach.

As I handed over the fifth puppy, something caught my attention behind the technician. I noticed a little face wearing an oxygen mask, peeking out from under a moving towel! The tech handed me a different puppy back again and gave me instructions on what to do! What? They were alive!

I exclaimed, "But they were all dead?!"

She said, "Never give up on a puppy! Not for at least twenty minutes!"

Oh, my goodness! How many precious puppies could I have saved from the first two litters had I known that dead doesn't necessarily mean dead!?

A few hours later, the six puppies, Éowyn and I went home. That tip and saving those puppies were the only good things to come out of that night, I would soon find out.

On Monday, April 24, first thing in the morning, I called my large animal vet that had a small animal clinic. Éowyn had not been eating well and had vomited on Sunday around noon. I called back several times throughout the day to speak with the vet about the Cesarean and subsequent troubles. She did not get back to me until the evening. She then chastised me for not making an appointment and bringing Éowyn in, although throughout the day, it was not even once suggested by her staff that I do so.

I noticed that Éowyn's belly seemed larger than it should be and she started to be less than careful with her babies. At one point, they were all in one pile and she went over and laid right down on the lot! I dove on the situation and saved all but one from harm. The firstborn I had to pull hard to get out. I was reaching over the side of the whelping box and pulled him instead of lifting Éowyn up; so he was damaged internally. This happened just before the vet called. It was then past the time of regular business hours – so now both of them would have to go back to the Emergency clinic *again*!

When we first arrived at the clinic, the sweet little puppy started to bleed out of his nose. As I held him with love next to my heart, he passed away a short time later. What was I even doing back at this vet's office??

The vet took an X-ray of Éowyn's enlarged belly. Either the uterus or the bladder was the size of a watermelon and she didn't know which. She instructed me to take her to OVC – Ontario Veterinary College in Guelph. It was just past midnight Tuesday morning, when I drove the hour in the rain and parked near the door. Since they didn't know if it was a bladder or uterus issue, when Éowyn squatted on the grass to pee - without thinking - I shoved my hand underneath her to check the stream. Nothing.

I went inside and gave the information to a vet student. I told them she couldn't pee. They took her to another room, leaving me behind. Later they said she peed three times in the room! What? She would never pee indoors or barely even away from home. When we went to a show, she would most often wait until we got back!

After waiting for hours, completely alone, a vet came and told me they had to wait for the Reproductive team to make the diagnosis in the morning. He said it could cost $3500 and I had to pay half down; it was 3:30 in the morning. When I got home an hour later it was time to feed the puppies, so there was no time to rest.

The experts at OVC determined Éowyn had metritis and they would likely need to remove the infected uterus. They bumped her surgery to another day and although I researched about taking her someplace else, I left her in their supposedly expert care.

Éowyn's surgery was booked for the morning of April 26, but again postponed to afternoon. When the surgeon finally called, she explained that the uterus seemed in good condition, so they cut it out and sent it away for testing!

What??

After removing the healthy uterus, they were surprised to see the biggest bladder they had ever seen in their lives! Since she was open anyway, they checked out the bladder and it seemed to be okay, albeit watermelon sized!

Why had they spayed my extremely rare breed show dog on her way to becoming Master Champion? Oh, they thought it was a crossbred Pyrenees x Mastiff.

I was very upset that they cut her open for the second time in four days and removed a perfectly healthy organ – when by inserting an eight dollar catheter they could have quickly surmised that it was her bladder, not a uterine issue! I had even told them that when I arrived! OVC is a teaching hospital so Éowyn was cut open from chest to vulva and now sported staples the entire length of her belly. Her showing days were over and the kicker was that they still didn't have a clue to the problem - she still couldn't pee!

After the surgery, they finally put a catheter in. They wanted to keep it in there for a couple days, as there was blood in the urine.

Later in the day they said she was out of ICU, so I tore down the road to see her.

I was able to be with her for over an hour before visiting hours were done. She staged a jail-break and we snuck out a back door to the great outdoors! I thought she had to go pee, but she was looking for the truck! They eventually found us, laying in the grass outside under a maple tree. I had to pet her with both hands, because one wasn't enough! It was wonderful; we were together. The warm breeze was blowing through our hair.

The next day, OVC called and said she was blasting through the doors that morning. Although they had not solved the problem, the consensus was that perhaps she would do better at home, because she would not pee for them. I had explained that at a show, she would hold it all day, until she came back home. I so desperately wanted her back home though.

Éowyn did come home, but was still unable to pee. Why had she been cracked in half for nothing? Thousands of dollars wasted for the removal of a healthy organ? My husband sewed her a halter top to cover her sutures, so she didn't have to wear a cone. Due to the multiple medications Éowyn now had to endure, she was unable to nurse her puppies, but the halter top enabled her to have monitored visits.

The halter top also applied pressure, so that after about twenty-four hours she started to leak urine. OVC still did not have the urine cultures so it made no sense to take her back in. My team of alternative therapy practitioners went to work in hopes of getting her back on track.

With time passing, on May 4, I took Éowyn to the local vet clinic for an ultrasound. With much difficulty, they placed a catheter in for a few days. Éowyn wasn't to be left unattended, lest she pull the catheter out. We didn't have any help, just Clayton and I to look after everything. Some of the puppies had been struggling, but we managed to pull them through.

Éowyn had been peeing pink, filling diapers every three to four hours, while the catheter was in for the three days. The following day, she tried to pee about twenty-five times and not even a drop came out! I was distressed that after two weeks she was no further ahead, but I was not going to give up.

I drove the 200 km, three-hour round trip to take Éowyn to GAH, where I knew I should have gone in the first place. They were shocked at the length of incision and the pile of staples that lined her belly. Bloodwork was done and the urine cultured again; I had no idea that this was just the beginning.

On May 10, I requested the help of Dr. Deva Khalsa, my natural vet in the US. She made several recommendations including homeopathic remedies. I was very thankful that my Dr. Rasa at GAH was willing to let me combine both philosophies together. The mutual diagnosis was that during the Cesarian, while flopping around, she must have pinched her bladder nerve – it was all they could think of.

The next day, I went back to GAH. She was still not peeing, not even a drop. I was already so exhausted, that when they gave me the results of the cultured urine, I couldn't even comprehend them. There were seventeen antibiotics listed and all but one had an "R" beside them – which meant there was only one that could be used, the rest were resistant. I immediately forwarded the results to Dr. Khalsa and within five minutes she was on the phone with me. The only antibiotic to which this particular bacterium was susceptible was rarely used, because it was a carcinogen. She said we have to get the urine pH level down to five in order for the drug to work, or it would be the end of this story.

Dr. Rasa wanted to keep Éowyn overnight for intravenous fluids, but they did not have overnight staff. I suggested I could give her subcutaneous fluids at home as I'd done that years earlier for my Border Collie, Ivy. Éowyn was also started on the awful antibiotic. I was prepared to let her go if there was no hope to save her, but there still was. I was not going to give up on her, but I would follow her lead on what she wanted to do. The next day, I took her to Dr. Jodi, a chiropractor I found that treated dogs, to see about freeing up the damaged nerves.

It was already May 18, almost a whole month since the fiasco had begun. After a few more trips to GAH, Éowyn was sore in the back end; something wasn't right. She no longer wanted to go out to pee, only wanted to sit or lay down. The catheter had been in for a week and wasn't meant to be indwelling. I increased her subcutaneous fluids to two liters per day and she started to protest having the countless needles in her back.

I was giving her pills around the clock. The total was forty-four a day in addition to probiotics, silver, and homeopathics. I commissioned the animal communicator, Claudia Hehr, to communicate telepathically with Éowyn, because I really thought we were nearing the end. Éowyn told her that she wanted to live and I recommitted to never give up on her.

I had called one of the owners of the Emergency clinic where Éowyn had first been harmed, asking for some compensation after explaining the spinal as well as nerve damage and the events that had transpired. His response was baffling. He said, "That happens a lot when I do knee surgeries." I continued saying that Éowyn and I were traumatized that night, he said, "You were probably more traumatized than she was!" Really? All that just made me mad and increased my desire to help Éowyn. None of this was her fault.

On May 19, I got up at 6 AM and drove to GAH. They pulled the catheter and placed Éowyn on intravenous fluids for twelve hours, delivering four Litres. I was camped out with a sleeping bag right next to her the whole time. While I was at the clinic, a friend Linda, who I'd met at the dog shows, started a GoFundMe to help with expenses. It was very thoughtful of her and much appreciated. That night I had the first six whole hours of real sleep since before the puppies were born! The puppies were starting to eat and drink from a dish, so that freed up a little time from bottling them.

In the little bit of time that I actually spent with the puppies, I of course had a favourite. She had a fancy name, ColourFast Celandine but my husband used to call her Spot. I sometimes wondered if Éowyn would even live through it all. I wanted to keep Spotty for sure if her mom passed away, but I didn't want her mom to *have to* pass away to keep her either. I talked to my husband and he said a puppy couldn't just wave at me like Brandy did. It would have to do something more. He said it would have to *double wave*... at him!

I remember sitting in the whelping box late one night after feeding the puppies. Spotty was three weeks old at the time. I held her close to me and I whispered in her ear. "I love you but I can't change his mind... It's all up to you!" And I left it in her court.

The very next morning, I was standing next to the whelping box while my husband was having a coffee and looking down at the puppies. I saw it with my own eyes... Spotty left her siblings and went over to the edge of the whelping box, so that she was in front of him. As he looked down at her she put her little paws up on the pig rail and steadied herself to sit upright. She pulled her paws from the rail and waved at him! First the little right foot and then followed by the little left foot. I could hardly believe my eyes!

I pointed and exclaimed, "You saw that!! You saw that didn't you?"

"Saw what? He questioned meekly. He saw it. Spotter my daughter was mine!!

Spotty at eight weeks & Clayton at eight years of age

A three-week-old puppy had gone away from the others, marched over and double waved at him! It was specifically what he had asked for. Who could argue with that?

A week later, I remember it well as "The day Éowyn wagged her tail!" She did start peeing after receiving the four litres of fluids – but now she had another bacterial infection! On a good note, where it had said "R" resistant to 16/17, now it said "S" for susceptible – to all but one antibiotic, which was the nasty one she'd just come off. I gave her daily fluids for another week, until she plainly asked for no more needles. I continued her chiropractic and other treatments in between trips to GAH for the next few weeks.

It occurred like all of a sudden, that the puppies were leaving! I had barely spent any time with them and hardly had any pictures of them! The puppies going to Michigan, US and Quebec were picked up and the other two flew together, but to different homes in Saskatchewan. Spotter my daughter was to stay with me.

On June 28, more than two months after the ordeal began, I cried with joy when I saw Éowyn rolling around on the grass with her older daughter Brandy! Her crazy pacing gait was all but gone and I even saw her trot when she went walking with the others to the fifteen-acre pasture field. I was grateful for the miracle; I never gave up!

THE MIRACLE SIXTEEN

In early September, my vet friend Ixaka, in Spain, sent me a picture of his first litter of Basque Shepherd puppies! We had been planning to purchase a pup from Ixaka, but I'd had let him know during the summer that I had to cancel, because of all the expenses that I'd occurred with Éowyn. He was so impressed by the lengths I went to save and take care of Éowyn throughout her ordeal, that he generously offered me a female Basque Shepherd, as a gift. I would have to wait ten weeks until she could come home; I had a bit of time, or so I thought.

On the second week-end in September, I took Thorin to a dog show, where he earned his title of Canadian Champion! When we got home, he managed to breed Brandy too! That was two ties, one each day. Gandalf and Éowyn had only ever had one breeding and had produced thirteen puppies twice and six puppies the last time with the side-by-side. After living through the fiasco of Litter C, this time, my extreme commitment and intention was for 100% turn-out for both the mother and the pups.

During one of my consultations for Éowyn with Dr. Khalsa, she had mentioned about some homeopathic remedies that should be given during pregnancy; also ones that should be given during labour. I was going to set the record straight and was going to do it right this time. After the C-section with Éowyn where I thought all her puppies were dead and then watched them be resurrected, I'd promised myself that I would make an extra effort to keep everyone alive and healthy. I researched and asked questions of experts and compiled a list of the tips and tricks of the trade, on ways to keep the babies alive. Little did I know at the time, that I would need to use so many of them!

Before the litter was born, one of the couples on our waiting list came to visit the parents, Brandy and Thorin. I mentioned that I was looking for a new living arrangement for Thorin, because he didn't get a long with Araglas. He needed to still live close by for when we needed him for breeding, but he would be better off with his own family and get all the attention he deserved. They decided that in addition to a puppy, they also would like to add Thorin to their family. He went to live about half an hour away.

After the goats, I had gotten a few beef cattle. Although they were sort of calm for beef cattle, they were big and scary. I had ended up purchasing four young jersey cows at one point, to go with the three Jerseys I already had. I was going to make my own beef breed, one that was smaller, quieter, with lots of milk. After Clayton had been attacked by the rogue Jersey cow Bossy, I had been on the hunt for the perfect breed. I researched all kinds of cattle, all sizes, shapes and purposes. We love our raw milk, so ideally I wanted to have cows that could produce milk in addition to making good quality meat. I especially needed a breed of cows that was inherently calm. We already had rare breed dogs, so I thought that perhaps it would be sensible to follow up with a rare breed of cattle.

After much research, I found the perfect breed; Red Polls — they had it all! They were considered the BFF — best friend forever of the cow world! The breed was originally used for dairy production and well known for it's wonderfully fine-grained meat. They were a beautiful red colour and had no horns, so there was no need for the terrible de-horning practices. They were a medium size and they were rare. Perfect! The only issue was where to get them?

I found a farmer a couple hours from me that had a herd of Red Polls. He would allow me to go and pick out whichever cows I wanted from his herd. I picked six. These cows had no barn and only lived outside through the Canadian seasons with no shelter, except some bush for cover. They were hearty, healthy beasts. Apparently of the six I picked out, they were some of the best ones, so they wouldn't let them go. In the end, I got three pregnant cows that gave birth soon after arriving in late September. Although they were range cows and had never been handled, the first calf born was a gem. A beautiful little red heifer, that was the epitome of sweetness. "Leyla" was only just born and was already coming to me! The breed was perfect, just like I had read. I was hooked!

I immediately started calling around to see if I could find breeding stock. Where to find rare cows? The few herds I saw in Ontario were fairly scary specimens! I wanted to start with stock that was good and unrelated to the stock that I had seen. Ideally, I wanted to find good old lines, milking bloodlines. The Canadian market had mostly gone just towards being a beef breed, losing the extra bonus of the mother having a copious amount of milk for her calves. I found some out east in Nova Scotia, but could not find transportation for them.

I managed to locate a breeder way up the Alaska Highway in British Columbia. Although not ideal, at least it was a start. I ordered six heifers and an unrelated bull from the available choices. They arrived in November, after they had been weaned.

Just prior to their arrival, I felt blessed to have found another breeder of Red Polls, a veterinarian, located in North Carolina, United States. He was totally dedicated to saving the breed, bringing in great genetics from all over the world, had cows with more milk, more meat, good genetics and temperament. I wanted to cancel my order from British Columbia but it was too late - they were already coming.

Leyla had been born first, as the perfect calf. Had she been born second, my life may have turned out differently. If I had met the second Red Poll calf first, before Leyla, I likely would not have even gone into Red Polls! Heather was a wild little thing; the complete opposite of Leyla. I remember walking up to Heather when suddenly in terror, she jumped high into the sky and landed squarely inside the metal sheep feeder. I required help to get her out. Sigh. It would be a year before she was even reasonable to be around.

Oh well, from North Carolina, I ordered seven top quality Red Poll cows, all bred with A.I. with a variety of different genetics. Dr. Wilkins wanted to sell me a bull as well. Now keep in mind, I had just purchased a young bull from British Columbia and although the one he was offering was better, I had to pass. I didn't have enough cows for two bulls and the one was already en route.

By November 8th, Brandy started nesting, and I knew another long night was ahead. I sent Jules a message asking her to check in on Brandy. She had told me, "Puppy number seven is going to be special to you." I pondered that through the night while I stayed awake by Brandy's side. Her water finally broke at 4:25 AM. I gave her homeopathic Caulophyllum 30x, every half an hour for five or six doses. By 6:20 AM, female number one had arrived! Weighing in at 16 oz, she was half a pound smaller than the first puppy from Litter C. This was good news since it was Brandy's first litter. With Éowyn, the puppies were usually very spread apart, so I was a little surprised at how quickly the next puppies arrived! Female number two was born only fifteen minutes later! The homeopathic remedies for uterine inertia had really worked! Another twenty minutes and I'd already met female number three!

Luckily, I had a little breather while the boys were lining up to take a turn at entering the world! It was just after 8 AM when the first male made his appearance; followed quite quickly by male number two, twenty minutes later! Wow, what progress!

It was almost two hours before number three made his entry, but I welcomed the reprieve as I had the first batch of puppies to take care of! The special puppy Jules had mentioned turned out to be female number four. She did not waste any time entering the world, only a few minutes after her brother got out of the way.

I had always picked the names of the puppies based on characters from J.R.R. Tolkien's works. Of all the "D" names I had picked out, this one seemed the best for her – Donnamira Brandybuck. I liked the thought of partially naming her after my friend Donna, from Millar Brooke Farm, who had died a few years earlier. This puppy did seem special, although I couldn't quite put my finger on it just yet.

About forty-five minutes later, we were introduced to male number four – but he wasn't so sure that he was ready to be in this world. He would not breathe and was as lifeless as the stillbirths I had encountered in other litters. Before, I would have cast him to the side and continued on with those that are living, saving the tears until later; but not that day - I had tools. I had an intention and a commitment to 100% turnout. I would find a way; he would live.

One resuscitation tip that I'd been told of was to put a thin needle in the point above the lip, below the nose. Apparently, by putting the needle in and spinning it – it causes a reset – like jumper cables on the system. I had a needle handy in case it had been needed. I felt uncomfortable sticking the needle into the baby's face. What if I wasn't doing it right? No one had actually showed me this method on a puppy! Well, I figured he couldn't be worse than dead so I took a deep breath and pressed the needle into the soft skin. When it was in place, I spun the needle. It didn't take long and the little body shook.

He took a deep breath.

He was alive! I did it! Thank God.

I had a little break after that, the next puppy, male number five arrived almost an hour later. Not to be outdone, male number six was quickly to follow a few minutes later. They were followed closely by male number seven at 1:30 PM! I could hardly believe how fast they were coming this time!

At this point I already had eleven puppies and they'd been arriving quite regularly for seven hours. Within another hour, the eighth male arrived, followed close behind by the ninth male! I'd reached the maximum number of puppies that I'd ever had previously, but this time, they were all alive and well! I was so pleased!

Thinking that she was done, I was quite surprised when an hour later, female number five arrived at 3:55 PM! Wow! Fourteen puppies! It was amazing to have such a big litter of healthy puppies. I was having a bit of supper, when all of a sudden, we heard the sound of Brandy licking at something. Oh my goodness! Another one? It was 8:20 PM! Male number ten was not in good shape; he had been waiting in line far too long. Oh no, no, no!! He could not die. I would not let him!

100% turnout!! Please God, help me!!

I called out to my husband to bring the oxygen tank. We set up a little tent and got him breathing. He was at least alive, but was crying out in pain. What could I do? I needed a miracle; I called Tanny. She said that he is filled up with air and that I had to get it out. But how?

She said, "Do you have a vibrator?"

"Pardon??" I said. "You are on speaker phone!"

It was hardly the time or place for such talk and children were present!

She said, "A vibrator… you know, like a massager?" Oh.

Clayton ran to the bathroom and got the hand-held electric vibrating massager. Tanny said to vibrate it on the puppy's nose! Clayton gently put it on the little nose and AH-CCHOO! went the little puppy. Clayton did it again and then again. Sneeze and sneeze and sneeze.

Okay "STOP!" I told him! That was enough! It worked! He had blown out the air and was able to be more comfortable. We kept him on oxygen for a while longer, until we thought he was out of the woods. What a triumph! *Fifteen* puppies! Oh my goodness! What a long day! How had she fit so many puppies in there on her first time!?

I fussed and stewed after the puppies for the remainder of the evening. I thought that perhaps I'd take the opportunity to have a little break and maybe get cleaned up in the bath, while my husband was still up to look after the puppies. I knew I would be up all night again with them, might as well be clean! I was starting to undress and still had my turtleneck on when I was alerted by a sound coming from the whelping box. I walked out of the bathroom to see something hanging out of Brandy! What could this be? Oh no. This is not something dead, something leftover inside!? Is Brandy okay? What is that dark thing? What in the world is going on!?

At 12:50 AM on November 10, female number six, puppy number sixteen, literally ran out of the womb and into the whelping box. I say ran because she literally did. She should have been dead by all stretches of the imagination. She arrived exactly four and a half hours after her last sibling, eighteen and a half hours after the first puppy had been born. She exited the womb, without slowing down and practically ran all the way to get a drink! She must have been very thirsty! I have never seen a newborn with a purpose like that one! She was determined to live and she arrived in style. She came so fast I didn't even have time to intervene! I stood in the middle of the kitchen, half naked, crying out with joy and astonishment! The Miracle sixteen! 100% turnout!! Wow!

Nothing could have prepared me for the amount of work required to hand rear sixteen, giant sized puppies. Brandy was a little overwhelmed with her brood and although contributed to feeding and cleaning the puppies – most of the work fell to me. I didn't know if she was able to make enough milk to feed so many and I didn't think she should have to. Brandy's hip seemed to be out of place and I contacted Dr. Jodi, the chiropractor to see if she could come to help her. It would be one week before she could travel out to the farm for a house call. I could not take Brandy or the time away from her puppies to take her in. What I didn't realize at the time was that Brandy was only laying on one side to nurse the puppies. Because she moved around, I figured she was changing sides. It wasn't until the chiropractor came and we were looking at her closely, standing, that I realized that she only had milk on one side! Only four teats were working of eight because of her hip and not rotating her teats!

Crap! Now I really had to keep up the feedings! I had no one to help me, so I fed the sixteen puppies, every two hours – but it took one and a half hours to feed them, because there were so many! I couldn't just start over so I fed them every two hours, after I finished feeding the last puppy. Then I also had to bath them once a day, since they were not staying clean and Brandy couldn't keep up. Very young puppies have to be licked by their mothers to stimulate their excretion to help them to pee and poop. I had to complete baths daily and wipe them with a warm wash cloth in case Brandy missed anyone.

Between feedings and bathing there wasn't much time left for anything else. When Brandy went in the box, I had to ensure that all sixteen puppies were safely out of the way, each time she laid down.

Litter D in a sleigh on a day trip to the barn, although not all are visible

I also had to ensure that everyone got a turn on the four teats. It was a constant process – hour after hour, day after day.

If you recall, I mentioned that our house was small, so when my husband had realized we were having a large litter, he went ahead and built an 8x12 foot building for the puppies to stay in. He made it out of six inch thick, metal covered, Styrofoam insulation. He put it on wheels so that it could be considered temporary and put it on the front lawn, next to the porch. He ought to have known that I don't leave the puppies unattended when he created the building and it was coming into a Canadian winter. I couldn't imagine sitting outside in the snow with the puppies, but what could I say. If they wouldn't fit in the whelping box, then they had to go in that building.

A couple days after he put that building up, a complaint was made to the town council. There is an apparent law about having a building in front of a house – so even though it was less than 10x10, mobile and temporary on wheels, it was illegal. The person complaining made another comment to the county as well; "and they have too many dogs – more than twenty!"

Well, yes, if you included sixteen newborn puppies, that would be true! All of my dogs were legally licensed and it was not illegal to have puppies. Apparently though, it was illegal to breed! That was news to me. Everyone up and down the road had a litter of puppies from time to time. The people we bought the farm from had litters regularly before moving next door after we bought the property; they continued to breed their farm dog there. I always claimed my puppies as income for the farm, charged HST and sold the puppies under strict contracts with a clause that the puppies must be returned; never to be rehomed or sent to a shelter.

When the county showed up to tell us about the complaint with the building, I showed the by-law officer the puppies! I was so proud to have sixteen live ones. I had no idea that it was illegal! Not allowed to sell, advertise, raise or even show dogs apparently! Who knew? How is it okay for everyone else and not me? They said it was complaint driven. They were only allowed to stop breeding where there was a complaint, due to manpower issues. We moved the makeshift house on wheels and it was never even used, not ever.

It was the beginning of December and I had been mostly awake for over three weeks. In each twenty-four-hour period, I got zero to a maximum of four hours of sleep.

Litter D in the whelping box

If I rested at all, it was on a cot next to the whelping box on a mattress we'd gotten out of an old camper. Clayton called it the "Poof bed." Why? Because as soon as I laid down on it, "Poof" I was asleep. I woke up for every little noise the puppies made – I had to make sure that they were all okay.

When my Basque Shepherd pup Argibel was ten weeks old, she shipped out from Spain to join our family. She had the most beautiful red coat and striking yellow eyes. She arrived on December 10, when my Miracle sixteen litter was only four weeks old. I did not have a moment to spare. I did manage to get someone to look after the puppies while Clayton and I went to Toronto to pick the little thing up. She was so wonderful and smart; I just wish I'd had the time to spend with her. She spent a lot of time in the whelping box playing with the puppies. She would go in the whelping box to pee. I didn't have a good schedule to try and house train her. Eventually she started going in the litter box like the puppies were trained to do. I literally did not have time for her.

When the puppies reached nine weeks of age, the first ones started to leave the nest. Only one was going to be placed very local, to live with the people that had Thorin; she left the first day she was old enough to, on January 11. Most of the others were being shipped and needed to be ten weeks of age, before heading off on their new adventures. Two would have to wait until early March when they were sixteen weeks of age as they were going overseas to Sweden! They needed to have thirty days past their rabies shot in order to be able to travel.

I was excited to meet my new Red Poll cows that arrived the next day. The seven cows had travelled all the way from North Carolina on a transport truck and my herd was finally complete, or so I thought.

Although I had a lot of wonderful irons in the fire, so to speak, I felt like something was still missing. I went to the library and borrowed some audiobooks. The main ones were *The Secret*, *The Power* and *The Hero*. It had been several years since I had bought the books and I had no time to read them. It made sense to get the audiobooks, so that I didn't have to take time out from working to get the information. I was always the sort of person that worked until the job was done. I never went to bed until everyone, people and animals were looked after. Everyone but me. It was time to get back to creating. I started manifesting some great stuff – putting my long-forgotten talents to good use.

THE EAGLES ARRIVE

It was a cold afternoon in early February, when I was sitting in front of my computer in the office, while having a conversation with my friend Karin. She and I were both breeders of the Pyrenean Mastiff. It was from her that I had purchased both Gandalf and Éowyn. We'd become fast friends and were having a conversation about my current problem of no longer being allowed to breed dogs on the property. I wanted to move away from the complaining neighbours that watched, took pictures and videotaped our every move. I was also fed up with the county and their crazy laws that could only be enforced if someone complained. Some days it felt like the laws applied only to us. It was about who you knew, not what you did that mattered. Karin and I were discussing whether I should give up my dreams of breeding or what to do next?

We were typing back and forth when a black figure caught my attention outside of the window, directly over top of the computer screen, which faces the backyard. The windows in the office were on the corner, facing in each direction. I saw the figure move over to the right. I looked up and into the top of the spruce tree next to the house and there was a beautiful big, Bald Eagle! Oh my goodness! And what happened next? Another Bald Eagle dropped from the sky – right on the top of the head of the Eagle in the tree! What? Two Bald Eagles outside of my office window!

Obviously, the second Eagle could not perch on top of the other Eagle's head for long, so it flew away. I had my camera in the office and started snapping pictures through the screen. I could hardly believe it! I had only seen one Eagle in my whole life and there it was, plain as day, just outside my house – barely twenty feet away! I attempted to go outside to see if I could get a better picture, but the Eagle flew away. I did not realize it at the time, but my life was about to change in a big way.

On the day of writing this, I am sitting out in the pasture field … three times so far this afternoon, an Eagle has graced me with its presence. Thank you Eagle. Although high in the sky, I can tell that it is you, because of the long stretched black wings and the glimmer of white, not seen against the clouds, but since no head or tail can be distinguished from the white clouds, it can only be you. Climbing higher and higher to the heavens, on the winds of a thermal.

The puppies that had been waiting to travel abroad were shipped off to their new homes in Texas, California and Colorado. We had to get the puppies to the United States in order to put them on planes with direct flights. If we'd shipped from Canada, the puppies would have an overnight layover and I didn't think that was a good idea. But we'd run into some trouble getting the second batch of puppies across the border. In order to get their puppy, the people that lived in Virginia and New York had to drive over the border into Canada, where I was waiting with their new family member.

It was around that time, when I posted a favourite quote by Stephen Hawkings, which read:

"However difficult life may seem, there is always something you can do and succeed at, it matters that you don't just give up!"

I had no idea at that time, how important this idea would become to me.

Mid-February brought the first calf from our new Registered, Red Poll Cattle, a nice little heifer. Later in the day, I was at my computer in the office when out of the corner of my eye and through the window, I again caught a black figure.

The Eagle in my treetop next to my house

It was almost a repeat performance of the last sighting. A huge, Bald Eagle landed on the top of the very same tree. This time I was quicker grabbing for the camera and out the front door! I stood on the lawn and took pictures of the Eagle in my tree! I stood in amazement and wonder. I hoped the Eagle would stay, but I also wanted it to fly, so I could get some more interesting pictures! I couldn't just be present with it though, I had to be ready to take a picture!

One puppy, Drogo, was supposed to fly to his new home in Alberta, but at the vet check it was noticed that he had abnormal toes. They weren't likely to affect him and he might grow out of it – but we could not say for sure. The man who had picked him originally, no longer wanted him. He decided to trade him for Dudo – even though he was missing half of his tail from a little accident with his Mama soon after birth. A Great Pyrenees rescue in South Carolina, wanted to have a puppy – they'd never owned a puppy before, as they had only seniors. They had ended up with a Pyrenean Mastiff at one point and had fallen in love with the breed, which is not a hard feat! Drogo might become special needs at some point or he might be fine; these folks were willing to take a chance on him. They had a lady that drove a rescue van and was going to be coming close to the border and could meet me, to pick him up. Only thing was, she couldn't come over to Canada – I had to get him across the border on my own.

One morning in early March, I was gearing myself up to leave. I had packed *The Power* audiobook that I had picked up from the library to take along. I could not allow a negative thought to enter my mind – I just visualized Drogo with his people. I was standing in front of the kitchen and dining room table and glanced out the window. I saw something fly into the field across the road. I stepped out the door onto the front porch for a better look. They flew from the left to the right, then turned directly towards me – flying over the road – low enough to be under the power lines. I stood in awe as not one, not two, but three Bald Eagles zoomed directly over my head, barely high enough to make it over the house. Three Eagles! Who sees three Eagles? I knew I would make it across the border that day; I just knew it.

That entire trip, I listened to *The Power* audiobook and practiced gratitude. Although I had read the book years ago, this was my first time listening to it. As I was approaching the border, getting in the lineup, I started to get a little stressed. What would I say to the border guard? How shall I act? What shall I do?

The Eagle launched off the tree, flying over my house

A part in the book started talking about negative feelings being like riding a horse. If you climb on an angry horse, you can get off it again. If you get angry when someone else is angry, then you just climbed on that angry horse with them. I got a picture in my mind of someone climbing on a cranky horse and it struck me as hilarious. I started laughing so hard that by the time I was talking to the guard my vibration was really high. I didn't say I was a breeder, I just focused on poor Drogo's curled up feet. I demonstrated dramatically to the border guard with my fingers, of how the feet were shaped; why he was being sent to a rescue in the US and that I just *had* to meet the rescue truck. I offered to show him the puppy's feet, but there was no need. He allowed me passage, as I knew the Eagles' appearance had told me quite clearly that morning. Thankfully

Drogo made it to the van and now has a wonderful life in South Carolina.

The Eagles started to come by more frequently after that. I thought maybe we should build them a nest - although after doing a little research – they have really big nests and need quite a bit of engineering, so I let that project go.

I remember sitting on top of the hill in our pasture field, on the old metal park bench and seeing the Eagles sitting on the treetops along the west fence line. I saw them there several times; often because they were flanked by noisy crows, letting everyone know of the predators in their area.

Another time I was on the bench, talking on the phone to my old friend Daryl from the US, when the Eagles flew directly overhead. I'd met Daryl in the early 2000s during one of my spiritual growth and development courses. He's one of those people that you meet and feel like you've always known them. Although we don't talk often, when we do, he's always had an uncanny ability to see right through my stuff and help me get to the point. Where I can't see the solution, he will hold my hand and lead me to it. This time the Eagles were acknowledging the shift that his super-powered friendship often propelled.

Once, while I was driving home through the town of Caledonia, an Eagle flew low over the bridge, just as I crossed it. Each of these Eagle sightings surprised and fascinated me!

I felt privileged and blessed to have every encounter. After waiting my whole life to see Eagles – they had finally come!

THE RED POLLS OF NORTH CAROLINA

D r. Jefferson Wilkins, whom I had bought the bred Red Poll cows from, finally persuaded me that I should buy his bull. I'd convinced myself that the bull that I had from B.C. was okay, as I had just figured I would use him for a couple years and then get a better one. Dr. Wilkins educated me, that it was better to start with quality right away, than to try and fix problems later, over time. I knew he was right.

There was one puppy by the name of Doderick that had already been returned, because he had gotten too big to carry; the owners lived in a house with many steps. Thankfully, Doderick found a new home, but it was in West Virginia and I had to get him there. Since I was going to North Carolina anyway, it seemed like a good idea to kill two birds with one stone, so to speak. I could deliver the puppy and pick up the bull on the way back.

A few days before I was to leave on my trip, I was inspired to take a copy of *The Secret* book along – to give away. I didn't know why, but it seemed like a reasonable thing to comply with. I was driving out of the feed store parking lot when a sign caught my attention; it was for a little Salvation Army Thrift Store. I thought to myself, '*The Secret* book is going to be there'. I waltzed over to the bookshelves and searched through them all, as they didn't really have that many. It wasn't on the shelf. I felt that it had to be somewhere in that building! Perhaps on a display in a different part of the store? It was not a very big store, so it would not take too long to check. I could not find it anywhere else. I thought I didn't see that sign and come in for nothing. I *just knew* that it was there! I went back to the shelf with the books and had one last look. Plain as day – there it was. I purchased the book for two dollars, no tax. I packed it away in my suitcase when I got home, happy to be a compliant member of the universe!

Later on in March, I borrowed a big aluminum livestock trailer from a well-to-do neighbor that I didn't know very well at all. I'd asked to borrow the trailer for a few days, not mentioning that I was going to be driving 2500 km *and* over the border. Our trailer would *never* have made it, but I believed theirs would.

I was bringing Spotty along as my traveling buddy, in addition to the puppy Doderick. I felt I needed some companionship and possibly protection. Spotty, although not quite a year old, would suffice for both. Just prior to leaving, I tripped, stubbed my foot and developed a terrible pain in my upper leg. Regardless, we departed for our journey south.

The next hurdle was the border. Jules had discussed with me, prior to going, that what I will bring *my* attention to, is likely what the border guard will focus *their* attention on. All the way to the border I maintained positive vibes. When I arrived, apparently, I ended up in the wrong lane.

"Where are you going?" I was asked.

"I am going to pick up a bull in North Carolina," I replied calmly.

"What's in the trailer?" he asked.

"Nothing, it's empty," I replied.

"Do you have the registration for the trailer?" He queried.

"No, I borrowed the trailer from my neighbour and he was away at a cattle show when I picked it up. Do you want to see the paperwork for the bull?" I asked him.

"No, not necessary. Go ahead," the guard instructed.

Some of my Red Poll Cattle

I drove into the United States of America, with Spotty and Doderick, quietly unseen in the back seat!

Since I had left late, I had no choice but to drive almost non-stop for the entire day and late into the evening. Apart from potty breaks for us all from time to time – we just drove. I met Doderick's new family in West Virginia, before stopping at an AirBnb for the night. It was an unremarkable night, but I got some much-needed sleep. The next morning, I was up and on the road with Spotty in good time, because we had an appointment to see Dr. Wilkins and his cattle operation.

On previous trips in the US, I had always been uptight and scared, afraid to talk to people. 'America is dangerous' is the word on the street! On this trip, that was proven incorrect. I met kind and wonderful people all along at the stops that we made and was pleasantly surprised.

To be fair though, I did send positive energy and an energetic abundance of money to each   person I saw and every car that I drove past! I also listened to *The Secret, The Power and The Hero* the entire way – to ensure that there were no breaks where negative thoughts could come. That leg cramp stayed with me and kept me present, the entire trip – I would rate it at 8.5 out of 10 for pain. I certainly wasn't feeling peace in my body, but wasn't giving myself time to sort that out.

I had a wonderful time talking about cows with Dr. Wilkins. He told me that he would take me out for dinner and we could talk some more about Red Polls, so that was nice.

After supper, I drove to my accommodation for the night, an Airbnb in the nearby town. It was a large, beautiful, stately home - like the Governor's house or something. They had a very large fenced-in backyard where Spotty could walk around freely. The room was located upstairs. Hmm. This was Spotty's first attempt at going up stairs; luckily the Pyrenean Mastiff as a breed, generally take everything in stride and she lived up to her heritage beautifully.

The room was perfect. I had my own washroom with bathtub and living area as well. The living room had what I have always dreamed about, a great big massage chair! I think I spent an entire hour in there, since I was so sore from sitting for two full days. After the electric chair, I went and had a hot bath. I took in a small notebook and a pen in the tub with me and started to write. I began writing a list of people that I was grateful for. Then I added to the list the animals I was grateful for. Then I wrote things from the trip, home and anything I could think of, that I was grateful for. I wrote and wrote and wrote - one thing after the next, until I had a huge gratitude list! I finally stopped after I felt the shift – from negativity to peace.

I slept peacefully during the night.

The next morning, I got up early and went back to Dr. Wilkins' place to load up our young new bull, Kingsley. With the new bull safely loaded in the trailer behind us, Spotty and I set off on our journey home. Apparently, a blizzard was coming across the middle of the country, so we were told to get going and not to dilly-dally.

As I write this, my Eagle is flying in the distance...

All the way to North Carolina and a lot of the way back, I had two bird totems for the trip. Close-up it was crows. They would fly just a short way ahead of my truck from right to left – almost continually flying across my path! Every few minutes down the road – a couple more, then a couple more. Off in the distance, there were turkey vultures continually in my view. Going round and round in the sky. If I caught up with those, there were more waiting down the way. On and on, the whole way – crows and turkey vultures! I hadn't realized it at the time, but the turkey vultures were likely migrating north as it was springtime. Their companionship only ceased when the blizzard hit. I soon realized that there were no birds, because of the snow. The birds of the south are not used to weather like this – neither were the people!

I felt like I was alone in the world for a lot of the trip home! In West Virginia, my truck was practically the only vehicle around. The roads had not been cleared, because they apparently didn't even *have* snow ploughs! I was blazing a new trail across the snow-covered highways and byways.

All this talk about snow storms, had me hankering for a Blizzard from Dairy Queen! After so many hours of driving alone in the snow, my GPS said there was a Dairy Queen only thirty miles ahead! My mouth watered as I drove the distance and got off the highway at the town where it was located. It was no longer snowing, but there was about four or five inches on the ground. It was three in the afternoon and I'd been driving all day. I went into the restaurant and found a guy was sweeping the floor. We were completely alone.

He said, "We are closed."

What? Why?

"Because of the snow storm."

What? It wasn't even snowing! He said he was the only employee that could make it in because of the snow; he couldn't do everything alone, so he was closing. I told him that I just drove for hours to have a Blizzard – could he not just make me one quick? No. I asked to use the washroom and he at least allowed that. I continued on my journey, a little bit disappointed, but with no room for negativity, I travelled on.

At last, I arrived at my Pennsylvania AirBnB. The owner had cleaned the lane for us, so we could get in and park. He offered that I unload my bull into his barn for the night, because they had no other animals. It might have been good for Kingsley, but with the weather the way it was, I wanted to make sure that I didn't lose any time in the morning, in case we had trouble getting him back in the trailer! I parked the trailer right next to the shed, so he was out of the wind. After I had fed and watered Kingsley, I ensured he had enough bedding to keep him clean and warm for the night, before taking Spotty for a little walk. She had been an absolutely perfect travel partner, hadn't made a step out of line – or at least, hadn't yet...

I was invited to a delectable and delicious dinner by the hostess, that had been hired to manage the facility. It was a birder's paradise, which was one of the reasons that I was attracted to it. The hostess and I hit it off; she was only twenty-three, but had accomplished a great many things. We were kindred spirits. We talked late into the night about everything including her love of sweet potatoes, food, environmental conservation, vision boards and many other topics. The most surprising thing that she had done for a job, was being an egg donor! She was paid well for the harvest of her eggs – and no she was not a chicken! She was young, in perfect health and beautiful! She has several children out there in the world. She was giving of herself, so that others could have their dream of having children. It was a noble sentiment that I had never thought of before.

It was the last night of my trip – she had not heard of *The Secret* – even though her boyfriend out west had vision boards, she didn't know why. I went to my room – which had a duck motif – and reached into my bag for the little book that had travelled a long way to get there. I went back downstairs and gave her *The Secret*.

In the morning, the hostess got up very early and took Spotty for a long walk with her in the frozen wetlands. Little did I know that Spotty had put the Pyrenean Mastiff spell on her, like they often do when meeting new people. Just like I had seen that first day with my own father, she was in love with the breed. This turned out to be a good thing, because when I went to collect Spotty from the garage and storage area where she had spent the night – I found that she had chewed up the hand carved boot puller, that the owner had made himself. Oops! I have no idea why she did that – perhaps it was her way of communicating that she did not appreciate being away from me, especially in a strange environment. They had a rule that no dogs could go on the floors, because they had just been re-done. Perhaps they didn't know that Pyrenean Mastiffs have retractable claws like cats and do not scratch the floors like other dogs! Luckily the people took it all in stride. The long lane was cleared to ensure our safe passage out to the road and back to the highway. I gave Kingsley some fresh water and hay before starting off on our long trip back home.

Spotty and I drove all day, although the snow and the after effects certainly slowed us down. I made sure to keep in contact with the border as the day progressed, to let them know I was coming. I had to be there at a certain time or else the vet would be gone and I would have to wait until morning for them to come back. I stopped for gas before the border and called the vet to let her know that I wasn't far – just had to get across the city. She said she would wait - if I would hurry. I sailed in and parked. I ran up the stairs to the vet's office and she greeted me, ready to be going home, but fine with the fact that she waited. She came in the trailer and checked Kingsley over, went through the reams of paperwork and everything had been in order. Dr. Wilkins had insured from his end that we had everything we needed for smooth sailing across the border.

Fifteen minutes later she said: "You are good to go. You just need to give your customs paperwork in at the counter and you can be on your way."

Huh? Customs paperwork?

I thought there was no duty or anything on livestock? I had checked!! She said she didn't know and sent me downstairs to that department. I waited in line.

They asked: "Where is your paperwork?" I handed them the big wad.

They inquired further: "This is for the vet, where is your customs paperwork??"

I did not have any.

"Well, you need to get that before you can go across."

What?? It was getting late in the day, I didn't even know what to do!

I ended up calling the trucking company that had brought my cows to me in January. It was owned by my friend Michelle's father. One fellow had been extremely helpful before and I called him in desperation for advice.

"Help! What can I do to get across the border?"

He informed me that I'd need a broker. He said that there was Purolator there – he would call ahead and get it sorted out. I needed to go to that department and talk to them; I found the place and went in. It would be a while until they got it all together, but they would do it for $85, I just had to wait three more hours. I was getting upset; I was so tired and just wanted to go home. Finally, I received the paperwork, went to the customs office and got to go!

As it turned out, home was not a welcoming place. In the days after my spectacular trip, despite my deteriorating marriage, I managed to keep myself "up." I was starting to take charge and even make a few decisions on my own. I was beginning to stand on my own two feet. A new me was emerging, a person that could actually even smile!

I was still able to manifest stuff, almost instantly at times! I was on a roll – or so I thought. I did not realize that it was downhill. I was beginning to fear the negative. I lived with a person that pushed my buttons, but I was determined to stuff all negative feelings away. Get them away! If I was so quick to manifest good stuff, I became quite worried that it might be way too easy to manifest the bad, just as quickly. I *had* to stay positive. I *had* to keep that smile on my face!! I finally talked to Jules about it and she said that I *had* to balance the darkness and the light – but I didn't know how!

One afternoon in early April, I watched a Bald Eagle hang in the clouds like it was attached with invisible strings. I could almost feel the freedom that it felt when flying. I knew my life was not as it should be - something had to change. Little did I know then, that four days later my life would be changed forever.

A LIGHT IN MY DARK WORLD

That first night in ICU was a long one. I stayed still for the entire night, laid out like I was in a coffin, arms folded across my chest. I was frozen with fear – not really understanding what was going on. I had no phone, no personal item of any kind. I had an I.V. and catheter so there was really no reason anyone had to even talk to me.

Friday morning, at 8 AM, Joe, the man from the store across the road, fitted me with a hard plastic, "Miami J" cervical neck collar. At that time, I had no idea that I would have to wear that collar 24 hours a day, seven days a week, for the next six months.

Saturday in ICU was very long. I had no visitors at all, and still no personal items. No one spoke to me. There was no clock. There were no windows. No way to gauge day and night. I was completely alone. I did hear some nurses talking about an ice storm and how things were sort of shut down – but that was all.

By Saturday night, I got moved into the Step-Down Unit. At least there was a digital clock on the wall. It had little red lights on a black background. It was high on the top of the wall so I could see it from my vantage point. I could watch the hour, the minute as well as the seconds, tick by.

By early Sunday morning, I faked a panic attack, heart attack or whatever they thought it was. I didn't care. I got every machine that was attached to me, to beep and buzz. I needed some attention and didn't know how else to get it!

By five o'clock in the morning, the nice lady doctor was called in to check on me. I asked her, "What is wrong with me?" I'd been in the hospital for a few days already and I still didn't know!! She took out her phone and pulled up a picture of a skeleton hanging by a rope around its neck. Nice.

She said, "You have a hangman's fracture of your C2 vertebrae." She showed me on the picture how the C2 bone was broken in two places by the rope. It's caused when your neck goes all the way forward and then all the way back.

"You also have a fractured lateral malleolus of your right leg." I knew my leg was broken because it was in an air boot and it hurt to walk.

The doctor asked if I wanted someone to talk to? She was acting a little weird and I think she was trying to quietly suggest that I needed a shrink, like there is a stigma attached to that.

I replied, "I would talk to Santa Claus, if I thought he would listen!"

I asked if there was a phone I could use? I felt so alone there. There was one cordless phone for the entire ward. She said that they would let me use it that day. I called my husband and said, "You can't just abandon me here." Then I asked for him to bring me some personal items; he did.

I finally had a book, but when I tried to read, my eyes didn't work. I couldn't make sense of the words. I was unable to change the audio CDs without help and the radio did not work where it was, because of poor reception. Although a bit helpful, I still would rather have had company.

When I had use of the phone, I also made a call to my dear friend, Rachel. Although it was an ice storm and the roads were bad, she was going to make the trip to visit me, if I wanted, that afternoon. A visitor!? Wow! Someone did care that I didn't die!! She was coming from Kitchener-Waterloo to Hamilton and she had to drive carefully, because of the weather. I counted the minutes and seconds until she arrived. Thank God she was safe and was there with me. A friend – a true friend.

I don't remember much about her visit, other than she was there; that I had company; that she cared. It truly made it a day worth living. She was a wonderful distraction. I think Rachel really understood how important her visit was, because she told me that she would return with her housemate to visit the next evening, after work. At last, I had something to look forward to! I was also able to get a cell phone, so that I could finally have contact with the outside world. That evening, they moved me into a room, with three other people. Then, I was all alone in a crowded room.

Monday brought the hustle and bustle of a hospital alive, after a weekend with reduced staff due to the ice storm. The doctors, psychologists and physiotherapists all wanted to speak with me. I basically hadn't slept since Wednesday night, because I was suffering horrifically with PTSD. I didn't even know what that was, but I will explain to you what was happening. Every time I closed my eyes, I would be in a new situation. Each time it was completely different - but it always ended the same way. I was in the desert, or in the jungle hanging upside down from a vine, or any of a thousand other situations and positions. At the end of each long scene, I would slam my right foot down and my neck would snap. Over and over and over. I was extremely tired, but I could not sleep.

I was so grateful that Jules fit me in for a telephone appointment on Monday, thank God. When the phone rang, I was in my semi-sleep state; I was riding on a hospital bed and it hit the wall with speed! I slammed my right foot down and snapped my neck – I was awake. Jules found a re-circulating energy pattern and got it flowing. After the appointment was complete and I hung up the phone, I felt a sense of relief. Someone cared – I finally had some support that I understood and cherished. With the PTSD somewhat gone, at the next opportunity, I finally fell into a deep sleep.

Rachel and her friend went to the hospital cafeteria and picked up some food before coming to my room. I had coverage for a private or semi-private room, but there had been none available. As soon as they'd laid out the buffet, a nurse came in and said that I was being transferred to another room. They packed everything up again, grabbed my stuff and followed to my new room, where the food was again laid out. I was used to eating whole, organic foods, mostly grown myself and although this was from the cafeteria, it was still way better than the hospital food. I still didn't have much of an appetite though.

For some reason, five days after the accident, my teeth started hurting – a lot. My face felt like it had been smashed into something. I imagine that my teeth had been rearranged after hitting the airbag. It was interesting that it took five whole days for that particular pain to emerge, but it was probably good, no point in being overloaded all at once.

On Tuesday, a physiotherapist that I had met the previous day came to teach me some more skills. I had to be able to get out of bed from a lying position, on my own, climb stairs and walk with a cane, before they could discharge me.

Wednesday, the physiotherapist came back and said that the hospital had decided that they needed my bed and I was to go home. Home wasn't ready? Too bad – I could go to a hotel or whatever, I just couldn't stay. She laid me flat in the bed and instructed me to get up. I couldn't! I was in so much pain!! At her forced prompting, I finally grabbed my hair with one hand and reefed myself out of the bed, screaming in pain, tears streaming down my face.

Then, I was supposed to lay perfectly still while the collar was removed for the first time since it had been installed, the week earlier. First the front panel was removed and the old pads taken out and the new ones put in place, although they just put the old ones back in this time, as it was for learning purposes. Then the front was again placed over the neck and the back plate was removed. It was imperative that I do not move. From that date forward I did have a fear of sneezing whenever the collar was not connected for even a few seconds. I could break my neck with the force – it was a real fear.

I had to learn the skills before I could go home, so she insisted that I go climb some stairs and walk there with a cane. Luckily, due to the kind of fracture, I had the air boot so I was able to put some weight on my broken ankle.

That afternoon, a rental hospital bed was delivered to my home and set up. I was placed on the stretcher and wheeled out to the parking lot. I rode home in an ambulance.

The rented electric hospital bed, which was to become my new home inside of my house, was placed in the only available spot – where the whelping box usually went! The bed had been positioned in the main walkway, right in the dining room, next to the front door, the kitchen table in close proximity to the bathroom and the hall, that led to the bedrooms and office. I no longer had any privacy, no peace. I became a fixture in my own home.

After a few days, I convinced someone to adjust the angle of the bed, so that I could see the birds at the feeder out the window. For the first while, I was only able to look at the ceiling or at a plastic shelving unit that was filled with clutter. My brain had wanted to explode.

The first night I was in the hospital, someone had come onto our farm property after dark, turned off the breaker in the pump house and cut the wires to the well pump. What would possess someone to do that? Why would they do it on the same night as my accident? The only people we could figure was our neighbour across the road – they didn't like us, but why hurt the animals? This was the first, but wouldn't be the last time that some unknown person would put the animals in danger.

My state of mind was not good, after learning about the attack on our water, on my first night back home. I had taken my air boot off for the night, for a break. I was alone in my bed in the dining room, when there was a loud bang on the front door! My eyes were wide with fear; I felt like a sitting duck. I could not get out of bed without help or at least a light. I laid still, frozen with fear. After a while I did manage to get up, get my boot on and I did not take it off again, other than to bathe or exercise for the next six weeks. I believe now, that the original bang on the door in the night was Éowyn wanting in, but I was sufficiently scared for many months after that. I did not feel safe in my own home.

ALIVE? YES. LIVING? NO

After coming home from the hospital, I was pretty much on my own. At the beginning, I was fairly optimistic that I could think my way to a faster healing. I have read countless stories about people that had a horrific injury or illness and brought themselves back from it by believing they could.

At first, I wanted to keep doing some of my usual activities. I am a person that can't sit still, doesn't slow down or stop for anything. I always used to have a relaxing bath each night, as the one gift to myself. It was an opportunity to stop, get quiet, read a book or farm magazine, before going to sleep. At this point, I couldn't read and could no longer even have a bath; I literally had nothing to do.

Towards the end of April I felt the dogs were not being looked after properly and I couldn't just lie there and not do something about it. There was no one around, so for whatever reason, I was carrying a chicken carcass in one hand, while using my cane with the other. I opened the door to the porch and put the foot of my cane on the edge of the door, instead of on the porch. It slipped off and the cane dropped heavily, almost six inches, to the porch floor. I jammed myself in the process and was sorely wishing I had better ideas.

I did have another X-ray of my neck that afternoon and luckily it hadn't changed. After that, I was sternly warned by three people; my Craniosacral energy healer Tanny, my in-home physiotherapist, and the neurosurgeon. They all basically said the same thing: "Lay down and give up because if you don't, you could become paraplegic or worse."

The dogs were no longer allowed in the house and I was not supposed to go out to see them. As a coping mechanism for myself, I turned my emotions off and became dead inside. My only glimmer of hope in the day was watching the birds at the feeder. Due to the brain injury, I couldn't read or really even watch TV. I mostly just observed the birds. There were lots of days that I wished I hadn't survived the crash. To hear folks say, "Oh, you are so lucky to have survived!" Really? I couldn't see it. Why *had* I survived? Was I a bad person? Was it karma? Was I supposed to burn in a living hell for some reason? Had I manifested the crash? Was it my fault somehow??

My sister Sue and niece Christine, brought my mother for a visit once, towards the end of April. It was good to have some visitors, but my mother, who at the time was beginning to suffer from dementia, had trouble grasping the situation. She only latched onto that something bad had happened. It was hard, because I wasn't able to see her again for many, many months.

After the accident, my husband had taken a few weeks off work, but needed to return to his job. He asked a lady we knew, if she would do my chores for him in the mornings on days when he had to go to work. She agreed, although I wasn't consulted on this. She took her orders from him, who didn't know how to look after animals. It was only because I had previously taken the trip to pick up the bull, that any of the chores were even written down.

One morning, soon after the lady-helper had arrived, I looked out the dining room window to see Araglas on top of his sister Spotty, trying to breed her! I freaked out and called to this woman to get him off of her!! She told me to "Just relax!"

Brother and sister are breeding on the lawn and you want me to just relax? I yelled, "Get him off of her!!"

She went out, but was unfamiliar with dogs and wasn't comfortable with trying to separate them. I was inside and unable to do anything about it whereas another time I would have tackled him myself. I finally called Spotty and brought her inside the house, while the lady got Araglas into the "bus." A friend of my vet friend Angela, the one who actually had ended up with Araglas' brother through some back door means, had offered to help, in any way she could. I contacted her and asked if she would look after him for me, because I was not able to keep the dogs separate. Usually, I would have taken turns with putting Araglas in or the girl that was in heat into the house, but in this case, a large storage bus was the only option and I had no one to let him in or out. He would have to be in there too long and too much, it wasn't fair to him – especially as all the girls were likely to follow Spotty and come into heat. The woman came to pick him up a day or two later. I had never met her before and my baby was heading off to live with her for an unspecified period of time. I was sad and relieved. Heat time can be stressful enough without everything else that was going on.

I knew, from the beginning, that the neck brace I was wearing wasn't on correctly – but no one would listen to me. I was in pain every minute and it was because my neck wasn't properly supported. *I* didn't feel supported either. I tried to go to church soon after coming from the hospital, but I felt so nauseous and uncomfortable, that I couldn't stay in the service too long. I desperately wanted life to get back to normal quickly, but it wasn't happening. After church we went to the truck dealership in town, so we could look around. It was a FORD dealership so I wasn't really that interested, but my poor truck had died saving us and I was looking forward to finding something new. As my husband was driving across the parking lot, his foot slipped off the brake onto the accelerator and I had nothing behind my head to support it and my head flew back. I was in excruciating pain and after we got home, I didn't leave the property for months, except to go to very necessary doctor appointments.

By early May, the vomiting got worse. My family doctor, whom I had only been talking to on the phone, because of the 1.5-hour distance between us, told me to get checked out at the hospital. I had called her in the morning and told her that I had vomited ten times on the previous day. While waiting in the emergency room for three hours, I remembered that the collar had originally come from "Joe – the guy across the road." I asked my husband, if he would be willing to go and see if he could find "Joe." He shortly returned to get me. I was reacquainted with Joe and he showed us how the collar was fitted incorrectly and finally demonstrated how to fit it properly. That was a game changer for me. After a whole month of wearing the neck brace incorrectly, my neck was finally supported. It had cost me a lot of healing time. To have the fractures always moving, they hadn't begun to heal, but at least I had gotten over the vomiting stage. It was good to leave that episode behind.

I was dealing with more challenges than just broken bones and a brain injury. In addition to the nausea, I was plagued with headaches, balance and dizziness issues – a falling sensation every time I closed my eyes, except while laying down. I felt light-headed, extremely sensitive to smells or noise, sometimes sad, irritable, nervous or anxious, experienced difficulties with memory, concentration, vision and reading issues. My son Clayton and I had both needed reading glasses after the accident as well.

I used to be a certified side-sleeper, but now all I could do was sleep in one position on my back – like I was in a coffin. Never moving. If I had to adjust my clothes at all, I had to use the electric bed and get completely out and try again. I had never appreciated being able to roll over before – now it was all I could think about when I laid on my back! All that and I still had no one to talk to.

No friend or family member by my side, except Clayton of course. Eventually I got a Personal Support Worker (PSW) and they were helpful in keeping the household running to some degree. After a few different tries, I would eventually get one named Loretta, who was very supportive and we are still friends to this day. In the middle of May, I ordered *The Power* and *The Hero*, audiobooks by Rhonda Byrne; It was time to start having some faith again.

One evening around five, we let the cattle out on the pasture in the front field next to the road. Early the next morning, I awoke to someone yelling outside the window. I maneuvered my way out of bed and stepped onto the porch, while Clayton was asleep inside. There were people yelling and some of my cattle were on the road. I got Clayton up and he promptly went out. I woke up our neighbour John with a phone call and he came over to help put the cattle back in. Again, I felt helpless. How could this have happened?

I sent Clayton to walk the fence line and examine where the problem was. He found an area in our new page wire fence that had been cut straight down, yet hidden behind some bushes. Who would have done this? Why? The only people we could figure again were the "neighbours" across the road. They were the only ones that seemed to have issues with dogs and animals being in their view. Why would this have made them feel better? To put people and animals at risk? I'll never know.

DONNAMIRA'S DEVASTATION

On a beautiful morning in late May, I was enjoying the fresh air from my chair on the porch, when my 87 pound, six and a half month-old, beautiful puppy Donnamira came to visit me. If you will recall, she was the special puppy number seven, that Jules had told me about. I had realized soon after Donnamira's birth, why I had loved her so much, from the moment I had set my eyes on her. She was that special one that I had been waiting on for more than ten years! Donnamira was my Ivy reincarnate; a kindred spirit; my soulmate, so to speak. I watched with concern when she abruptly sat down and started to chew on herself. Upon rising, I noticed that she sported a small hot spot at the base of her tail.

Since the dogs were no longer allowed in the house, she was placed in a cage in the dog room attached to the house, as I'd made it clear that she needed to be inside and wear a cone. I called Dr. Rasa and under the circumstances, requested antibiotics. I could not take her for walks or get her out of that jail cell, so I hired a neighbour girl to walk her, but Donnamira wasn't feeling well and didn't want to go.

Overnight, two days later, Donnamira got the cone off and by morning she looked like a burn victim – with a soccer ball sized hot spot on her back! After that, I informed my husband that she must be brought into the house and wouldn't take no for an answer. There was a space big enough for a cage in the back office.

I stayed with Donnamira in the office all morning and she started vomiting. I called Dr. Rasa who stated clearly, that she must be seen immediately. In desperation, I made a post on my page, asking if anyone could drive Donnamira to the vet. A person I'd met once in a homeschool group, offered to clear her schedule and make the long drive. I let Dr. Rasa know that I'd found someone, but then she said it was unnecessary – they'd sorted out a ride for her! Dr. Victor happened to be doing a clinic in the area and would pick her up around 5 PM.

In the evening, after we'd had a surprise birthday party for my son Clayton, I could not hold off any longer and called the clinic. There was no answer. I called Dr. Victor's cell phone and he said to keep calling the clinic, and that they were busy trying to save Donnamira. What? I called the clinic repeatedly until they finally answered. Nothing could have prepared me for what they were about to say.

I listened in shock and horror as Dr. Dawn explained Donnamira's grave condition. Hidden amongst the fur on her back, they'd discovered deep holes - filled with hundreds of thousands of fly maggots - eating her alive. The largest hole was five inches long and over an inch deep. There was no skin with which to stitch them closed. She also explained that due to the toxins created by the maggots, she did not know if Donnamira would survive the night. She promised to do everything they could to save her.

As I hung up the phone, I started crying uncontrollably. It was the first time that I had shed a tear, since they'd cut my sweater off at the side of the road. I had made a promise to Donnamira when she was born, that I would give her extra attention after her fifteen siblings went to their new homes. I'd barely had two weeks between the last puppy and the accident! Now she could die? By 10:30 PM, Clayton fell sick and stayed in bed for several days. He was always very attuned to me and loved Donnamira too. I would not give up on her…

My beautiful Donnamira

I would have camped out with her at the vets, if I'd have been able…but I wasn't able, that is why she was in this situation. If you remember, my sister Sue had made me that good luck charm Grumpy Bear, which I have slumbered with since I was nine years old. I pretended that Grumpy was Donnamira and held him next to my heart all night long. Between the fits of sleep that I had, I played the image of Donnamira and I winning Best in Show together – the both of us - fully recovered! I used my energy imagining what I most wanted and spent no time thinking the unthinkable.

The next morning, Dr. Dawn explained that the road to recovery would be a long one. The fact that Donnamira was alive was all that mattered to me at that moment! About an hour later, Dr. Rasa called to tell me that Dr. Carol Graham, the owner of the clinic, was on her way to my house and was donating her time on a Sunday, to drive the

200 km round trip to make sure my other dogs were okay. No one wanted to see a repeat of the horror cast on my sweet Donnamira.

Upon arrival, Dr. Graham thoroughly examined each dog and began grooming some of them. She found Dirk had diarrhea, making him a candidate for maggots too. She told my husband that all the dogs needed grooming, but that Dirk needed immediate attention. I put a post out, requesting help to get the dogs to the groomers and help came. Even an old friend I hadn't seen in twenty years, since my University of Guelph days, came out to help.

Meanwhile, our new cattle were having their own challenges with the flies. One of the British Columbia heifers had contracted a case of pink eye. Natural treatments usually have to be done right away, in order to work well. I wasn't going out to the barn yet at this point and was not able to diagnose or treat the animals like I would have, if times were normal, which they were not. I did not realize the gravity of the situation, when the lady doing chores called me and said that the heifer had a scratch on her nose. They brought the heifer in for the natural pink eye treatment and put her in a box stall in the barn. I told her what to spray on the so-called scratch. Later, my new PSW, Loretta needed something from the freezer to thaw for supper, but didn't know how to locate the freezer in the barn! I was overjoyed at the thought of getting out of the house, and offered to go outside to show her.

As we walked past the first box stall, I noticed the heifer. It was the sorriest looking creature I had ever had in my care. Both eyes were completely white, there were streams of mucous coming out of both nostrils, her skin was sloughing off her face. Her breath was laboured as if she had pneumonia! I cried out in anger and disgust! I could not believe the condition of this poor creature!

I called the vet, who upon seeing the heifer, offered right away to end the misery and euthanize her! I was heartbroken! My beloved heifer, just barely a year old – she didn't deserve a fate like this! How could this have happened? How could life be allowing these animals to suffer? How can *I* let them suffer? She should have had help much earlier. This was just the beginning of a very bad epidemic of pink eye in our area.

I didn't know until later, but around the time that Donnamira got sick, Araglas was in a similar situation. He was always the perfect dog; he never did anything wrong and always did everything right. I was very surprised to find out that for some reason, Araglas had eaten four dozen eggs that the woman had collected and left in a pail! Why he did that I will never know, but he did manage to get diarrhea. I guess for whatever reason, he started dragging his bum across the gravel and when she had a closer look, she discovered that Araglas had maggots too! She took him to our vet friend Angela, who put him on a lot of medication. I only found this out much later and wasn't consulted about anything. They had thought I had enough on my plate already.

Eight days after she had gone into the vet hospital, I got the wonderful news that Donnamira was finally out of the woods! She was going to recover!!

By the middle of June, a lady from the church came and planted some veggies for me in front of the porch, where I sat in my chair. My friend Simone also came and planted a larger garden, down in front of the barn. I felt better having growing plants to look forward to. The fracture in my ankle had finally healed and I got to take the air cast boot off. But, most importantly, I was finally allowed to, and even supposed to, walk outside by myself! Freedom!!

For sixteen days and nights, I kept good luck Grumpy Bear close to me, envisioning Donnamira and I in the winner's circle. I even put our money down and signed us up for a dog show at the end of September!! I had to have faith and a reason to live; Clayton and Donnamira gave me that. In order for her to come home, I needed to hire help. My rental hospital bed was moved from the dining area to the living room to make space for the exercise pen, where Donnamira would be staying when she returned.

In mid-June , my little girl was finally ready to come home! Dr. Jodi, my chiropractor friend, who had helped Éowyn after her accident, offered to drive to GAH and pick her up. It was raining when they arrived home, but that was okay by me. My face was wet with tears of joy anyway!

I was really unprepared for what she looked like and the constant care that she needed to have. I had put an ad up on classified online advertising Kijiji, and had been able to hire some help, morning and evening to do the chores in addition to help with Donnamira's care. My friend Simone graciously came over on several occasions to bath Donnamira and help keep the wounds clean and on the mend.

Even though her boss said she wasn't supposed to, my PSW Loretta helped with Donnamira, took her out to pee and for little walks during the day, while she was supposed to be inside doing domestic stuff. It was more helpful to me to have her help Donnamira, than to wash my bed blankets yet another time!

I found it disarming when someone pointed out that Donnamira and I were both stuck inside, unable to take our neck collars off – for the foreseeable future. I was very sorry that she had to go through this ordeal, yet I needed her with me so much, that I really felt like it was divine intervention. It was the only way that she could become a permanent resident in the house – with me. Neither of us were living our own life anymore, but we were together and that was all that mattered at the time. The joy I felt from her return was overpowering. When I got the $5000 bill, which was very low for the care that she received, I was surprised but also grateful.

Donnamira was always very clear about what she needed or wanted. Every morning at 7:30, she would put her face on my bed and stare at me. If I didn't take notice, she would go and jump on her large toy snake that contained seven squeakers. She would jump on that snake until my electric bed would start to whir, like I was getting up. Then I would say, "What?" and she would look at her "dress." She had a women's nightie that she had to wear in order to go outside. For a very long time, she didn't have any hair, or even skin for that matter, on most of her back. Since I have only had dogs that lived in the country, I have never personally had the entertainment of watching a dog react to seeing a leash, knowing she is to go on a walk. Donnamira would look at this nightie, look at me, look back at the nightie and then jump up and down on the snake! It was an incredibly cute gesture, in my very bleak world.

Donnamira was my constant companion after that, for the next five months until her hair started to grow back in. Neither of us were in any shape to go to a dog show by the end of September like I had originally planned, but we both gave it the good old college try! We would have our day, but we had to save that joy for another year.

"ONE SIDE IS GOOD ENOUGH FOR ME!"

At some point, we ended up hiring a tutor for Clayton. He was very far behind in Grade 3 and he needed to be caught up. The lady we hired, although she came with a degree, didn't follow the homeschool curriculum. She had her own ideas. To be honest, for the rest of his grade 3, I had just wanted it done. I could not think and was unable to help him. I looked forward to the two hours of peace and quiet that I had each day, in order to have a nap. Clayton's behaviour had been questionable at times since the accident, but he had so much to deal with. He and I had been inseparable before, but after the accident and my slow recovery, he just got to do nothing by himself. He started to hate school and what it represented, it was no longer fun.

The tutor continued with Grade 4 in the fall. I thought she would have been halfway done by Christmas time, but she'd barely done anything with him. It was difficult for me to take over, but we could not afford to keep paying her a high price for not much, except friendship for him. I still could hardly understand the things that I was supposed to be teaching to Clayton. I couldn't comprehend the words I was reading, let alone teach the concepts. We muddled through and Clayton started teaching himself. The curriculum starts to be written to the student directly by that time, so it wasn't too bad, except that he now hated school. My boy that had been an absolute joy to be around before the accident – who had loved people immensely – was withdrawing into himself.

In early July I was truly distressed that I was still having so many problems with my brain! Due to the concussion, unless I was lying flat on my back in bed, I couldn't even close my eyes for a minute, or even for a moment. I could not rest my eyes or my brain like I had been instructed to. As soon as I'd close my eyes, I felt like I was falling a very long way with no end in sight. My brain would get so overloaded, it would go into the danger zone. I still couldn't even read at this point. I was very frustrated.

One day, I had to go out to the barn to give instructions to the girl doing the chores. I took the opportunity to visit and finally see my horse Digger, who I hadn't seen in months. I went right in the pen, but he was afraid of me! I didn't know if it was the collar or the cane, but I couldn't understand why after twenty-five years of knowing me, he was running away?

I wasn't the same person he knew though. By this time, I had started watching *Heartland* on DVD. I saw Victor tell Amy that Spartan wasn't the problem, it was her. I began to understand that I was the one with the problem, not Digger. I had a few things to sort out.

In mid-July, as my husband was driving me to my appointment with the neurosurgeon at the hospital, I could see in the distance, off to my right, two beautiful Bald Eagles, soaring free. Due to the concussion, I was wearing these big dark green glasses at the time and had to remove them, to get a better look. I was barely alive inside, but I felt the Eagle's freedom as it climbed to new heights, and it filled me with hope.

When we got to the hospital, the neurosurgeon ordered me to get three X-rays taken. We waited for my turn and when I went in the X-ray room, I was instructed to remove my collar. That was very scary for me. I had been in that thing non-stop for thirteen weeks at that point! I had to lift my chin up for one picture; down for the next and open my mouth straight on, for the third. Oh my goodness, did that ever hurt! I could hardly move my neck at all, so the tech tried to force me! Suffering in pain, I went back to the office to await the results.

What the neurosurgeon reported after looking at the slides made my heart ache. He said, "Looking between the X-rays, I saw movement. The breaks are not yet holding."

He then ordered me to get another CT scan. I had been complaining to him about headaches and memory problems and he said, "I told you before to go see a neurologist!" If he had said so, I hadn't remembered. He finally said he would make a referral to the Concussion Clinic.

At the end of July, it was recommended that we shave Donnamira's remaining hair from her back. She had such a strange pattern of thick fluffy fur scattered amongst the parts that were damaged. The thinking was, that it would be better if it was even and could grow in all at once, but interestingly enough, it didn't grow back! After she was shaved, I wasn't so sure about the idea at all — her whole body looked like she wore pig skin. But the good news was, that she finally got her cone off! We both had been wearing our "cones" for a long time at that point, - at least she got some relief!

Donnamira's hair finally started to grow back at the end of August. It didn't grow at all, until her body had finished its hard work of closing in the giant holes on her back. The hair was fully in by November except for the large scars, which she will have for the rest of her life; but at least she has a life!

In early August, I received some good and bad news from the neurosurgeon. Of the two breaks in the C2 vertebrae, one side was healing, but not the other. I was obviously a bit surprised to hear his remarks, "One side is good enough for me!" He then informed me that I would not have to have surgery on my neck, but that I would have to endure four to six more weeks in the collar!

A couple weeks later, Loretta took me to the Concussion Clinic, where I finally got to see a Neurologist and a Neuropsychologist. A med student asked me a lot of questions and then relayed the information to the doctors, when they came in the room. They heard about the various medications I was on and were giving each other weird looks. Apparently, my family doctor had me hooked on strong opioids - the ones that are given right after an accident. They are supposed to be changed after a few weeks, a month or two at the most. I had tried to wean myself to lower doses several times, but had such severe headaches, the family doctor had recommended that I just stay on them.

There I was with these two doctors and they couldn't tell if my symptoms were concussion caused, or if I had opioid side-effects. They left the room for a few minutes, since the neurologist wanted to consult with the pain specialist. He was usually booked up for four months in advance, but they thought they would ask for a little extra consideration, because I was a difficult case.

We were back in the room and the Neurologist was trying to figure out a plan to help me decrease the opioids, when Dr. Eldon Tunks came right in and unexpectedly took over the appointment. He told me exactly what I needed to do, what medication he was switching me to, and why he was doing it. I was on quite a few drugs that were very hard on me and not even working. He addressed each problem as it was listed. He gave me his phone number and also told me to call him to update him. I believe he called me every day while I was going through withdrawal, or at least returned my call every time I called in. He was aware that while I was going to be suffering through withdrawal on a week-end, I might need a medicine change! He said not to use his cell number if I didn't have to, but didn't want to leave me without a way to contact him. He listened to my issues and was the first person since my accident to hear what I was saying. His care and concern made all the difference to me; someone was finally listening. I had found my Santa Claus.

Almost every night while I had been sleeping, I was waking up hearing heavy metal music playing on an alarm clock radio. I would move my electric bed so that I could get up and then I would search the house for the alarm clock. It must be around there somewhere, I'd think. Why couldn't I find it to turn it off? I would also hear ring tones playing, when there were none. People thought I could use my phone as my memory and have a ring tone go off, to remind me what to do when. It was haunting me in my sleep. On September 6, Dr. Tunks diagnosed me with musical tinnitus. I had never heard of such a thing before. He said that it would go away when I got my neck collar off, after I started to move my neck. He offered to put blocks in my neck, so I wouldn't be in so much pain. He stuck needles in my back and neck and froze everything, saying it would last for several weeks. I think it did eventually help with the musical tinnitus. I had just thought that it was another case of me going insane. He froze my neck a few more times, until it actually hurt more to put the needles in, than it was helping. He taught my chiropractor friend Jodi, how to do a special kind of acupuncture, that really helped to release the solid mass of muscles across the top of my back. They were rocklike from holding my neck up for so very long.

By early September, five months in, the concussion continued causing me problems. I still could not tolerate any noise. I could not listen to the radio, but one day I turned it on and heard just one song.

It was Martina McBride's song *"Anyway,"* and it gave me hope.

"God is great, but sometimes life ain't good

When I pray it doesn't always turn out like I think it should

But I do it anyway…"

I clung to even brief moments of hope.

In October, Araglas returned from his adventure with his brother at "Summer Camp". Apparently there had been some trouble between Araglas and one of the owner's male dogs. Araglas had been very tolerant of the younger dog badgering him, but he did have a breaking point. One day a truck had come in their lane and the owner had quickly shoved the dogs in a containment area. Araglas could not get away from this deer hound's badgering, when he had enough. He put the deer hound into the hospital.

After that, the owner had been trying to cope, not having the two dogs loose at the same time, but they were going on vacation and it was time for Araglas to come home. He had stayed away all that time, because I was waiting for the girls to all come in heat. Not one did, until Araglas had been set to come home, that triggered them all. Argibel was in standing heat just prior to his arrival.

Only three days after Araglas came home, something was wrong. His front leg swelled up the size of a football. We couldn't figure out what was wrong, but Jules had suggested that he may have been poked by something. I thought maybe it was related to coming home. He'd been unceremoniously ripped away from his brother and brought home again without explanation, just after he'd finally gotten settled there. Then all the girls were in heat too. It was a mess. He was placed on a concoction of medication including Clindamycin, which I believe, caused him to become constipated.

He had been my shadow for his whole life and I think he took it extra hard, to be with me, in my condition. His leg did heal, but he didn't really get better. He was good enough to fake it most of the time and keep the straining to go poop mostly hidden.

At the end of October, we were on our way to church, I was sitting in the front seat, with Clayton behind me in the rear passenger seat. The river was on our side and I managed to steal a glance over to the water. A giant black figure came down from the heavens and made a splash on the top of the water. No sooner had it touched down; it was lifting back up again. A beautiful Bald Eagle had just caught its breakfast! A big fish hung down as it flew up into the sky. The Eagles were back! It was the first Eagle that I had seen since the accident on April 12. They used to come much closer, but afterwards, they were always flying high. I began to realize that the Eagles usually showed up around a certain subject, and this time, it was concerning the future of my marriage.

WRITING THE ROAD TO RECOVERY

It took until the beginning of November, to be able to listen and hear *The Power* again and be able to give gratitude a try. I really had struggled with being grateful for being alive after the crash. I really wasn't. I was certainly extremely grateful that Clayton was alive, but not so much me. I was mostly in survival mode, or so I have been told.

By late November, I was still requiring a daily two-hour nap. I was on a lot of medications; anti-nausea, opioids and an anti-convulsant for headaches. One day, I suddenly felt the urge to write. I found a notebook that I had been saving for years and had never written a word in it. It had polar bears on the cover and I hadn't wanted to ruin it by writing in it. That day I needed the strength of the bear to write.

I sat in my office, took out a gel pen and wrote a good-bye and thank you letter to my old truck. I'd had that truck since it was new and we'd been together for one day shy of eleven years. It had been a shock and extremely hard on me, to have her just disappear after saving our lives. I had created that truck with my first vision board and the manner with which she left was still so hard to comprehend. I hadn't given up when they'd originally said I couldn't get her and that truck didn't give up on me, when we needed her the most. That truck saved our lives. I wrote about a five page long letter to my truck and felt complete when I was done.

The amazing thing was that something shifted for me after that. I ended up writing once more in that book. I started one night about midnight and wrote until 3:30 in the morning, without stopping for air. Thirty pages! I have no idea why and had no intention to send it, but I wrote it in letter form to Tanny. I expressed everything that happened prior to the accident, and I stopped the moment that I got to day one at the hospital. I couldn't write anymore. I couldn't go there, but I had gone far enough! The shift I noticed the most, was that I no longer needed to have the two-hour nap! Sure, I still needed a rest, but not a full two-hours of sleeping, just to get through the day! I also decreased the meds quite a bit and no longer took the anti-nausea drug. In addition, I was able to cut back on the opioids and anti-convulsant as well. I was beginning to understand, that the power of the word is strong.

Now that I had let go of my old truck, perhaps it was time to start driving again. I was terrified of being in the car. I felt completely sick and thought that every other vehicle was going to come in our lane. I signed up for an expensive driver desensitization course. After the initial assessment, I was assigned to Tim Danter. Apparently, he was a famous person! I didn't know, because I don't watch TV and hadn't for many years. Tim Danter was allegedly the head coach for the show, *Canada's Worst Driver*. Upon our first meeting, he was quick to give me his credentials, which included that he and his wife had started the very successful business, *Young Drivers of Canada*. Although he had since sold that business, he wanted to be very clear that he was not there to teach me how to drive. I had been driving for twenty-eight years before the accident, so I didn't need driver training – I needed desensitization – which he was also very good at.

It was the middle of December, when I took the dogs past the pasture fence for the first time. I had not left the pasture on my walks since before the accident. I felt I needed a change. I took my three sticky dogs; Araglas, Spotty and Argibel, went out into the hay field and walked into the forest. I knew that they would stay with me. With my two hiking poles, I walked carefully and cautiously, but was so extremely happy to have been on at least a little adventure. Life had become much like being in a jail cell; it was good to experience even a little taste of freedom!

After several sessions with Tim driving me around – I was finally ready to give it a go. On December 14, eight months after losing the ability to drive, I did it; I drove. It was so incredibly scary. I was to "glance" at the oncoming cars, but I was staring them down! What if they come over? What can I do?

"Look at the tires," he would say.

That was the best advice that he gave me, in addition to use my horn and look way ahead.

"If you are looking way ahead, you can see what is coming. If someone ahead is stopping, or turning; if someone is leaving a parking lot and entering the street; if you see them ahead of time, then there is no surprise! If they pull out in front of you, it's okay, you know they are there in advance and are already prepared! If you watch the tires – they will tell you what the vehicle is going to do. They are either rolling or stopped, turned or straight – that's it!"

The oncoming traffic was still an issue for me. How could I control what the other drivers were going to do? Tim also taught me a head-on collision avoidance technique. It was basically driving half on the shoulder, to get over, and let someone get back on their side. I was glad to have learned it for mostly one reason. I could see for myself that had I have known that skill prior to the accident – it wouldn't have made a hill of beans of difference. The shoulder had been small and the other driver was completely in our lane by the time he hit us. The only thing that I might have been able to do differently was to blow the horn, but I do not know if it would have been heard in time, with the extreme speed that the fellow was traveling at; I'll never know.

In mid-December, I got a call from the Ministry of Agriculture and Rural Affairs. She told us that the neighbour across the road was again complaining about our dogs, the manure pile and whatever else they could drum up. We were not doing anything illegal. They wanted us to remove the dogs from the front portion of our farm, so that they did not have to see or hear them. They thought that the dogs should have to be kept behind the barn with the front fenced off. The front *was* fenced off – to keep the dogs on our property, but that wasn't good enough, they wanted us to put up more fences. Apparently, the dogs shouldn't even be allowed to sit on our porch and definitely not allowed to bark at them when they got their mail twenty-five meters away! We offered to fence them away from the field in front of their place, but that was no good. It was all or nothing with these folks. They liked to complain each year around Christmastime. Merry Christmas, your neighbours hate you. We had already adjusted so many practices and the complaints still rolled on. They would never be happy.

We had one sheep that used to frequent that front field in front of the neighbour's house. 3Bs was our resident "Nomad" sheep. She was really old and had no need to be with the rest of the flock. She wandered around the property, doing whatever a sheep would want to do. I didn't want to get her bred, so she had to stay away from the ram, who was in the main group. When with the others, she sometimes got beat up or knocked around and it was not good for an old lady. She was from a long line of very important sheep. She was the fifth generation to my very first sheep, Georgian, that I got in 1985, as a gift from Brenda and Shane. Georgian had a daughter named Adelida, a pretty little Cajun queen who had a daughter named Belle. Belle, as you might remember, was a very significant member of my family too. She had a daughter named BB

Baby Belle whose daughter had been 3Bs – Baby, Baby Belle. 3Bs was the last of a long line of named sheep. She had a remarkable personality and deserved every bit of kindness shown to her during retirement. I believe she was about thirteen years old at the time.

3Bs passed away in December, a few days before Christmas and it was a great loss to me. I loved her so deeply and she had been with me since before I had gotten married. On her last day, Clayton and I spent much time with her in the barn stall where she was separated from the others. We wanted her to know that she was loved and to support her in her time of need, like she had done for us over the years. She was very stoic even at the end. Clayton and I went in the house for a bite to eat and when we returned, we found she had gone. A legacy was ended and she would be missed.

THE LIFE I'D KNOWN WAS OVER

It was a new year and it was time for a new me. After the most extremely stressful New Year's Eve ever, I made the decision to end my marriage, although I didn't know when or how. My sister Sue, although she personally didn't want to hear about my problems, suggested that I call the local women's shelter for support. She gave me their number and I became a regular to the crisis line. I couldn't get in to see a counselor until I had an intake appointment. Pat, a kind lady from my church, offered to drive me there in secret. It would be six more months before I could get in to see a counselor, but at least I was on the list and had the crisis line when I needed it.

It was the middle of January when I drove for the first time by myself. It was only 2 km down the road to get my hair cut, not a long distance, but I did it! I felt a huge sense of accomplishment! At least if I could drive, I had a better chance of some day driving away to somewhere safe.

Araglas had been sick off and on since his foray into summer camp the previous year. He was often straining to poop, but he'd been doing okay. I asked my helper to look under his tail, to see if he had diarrhea or not. She dutifully complied and reefed up his tail while he laid on the kitchen floor.

That was a mistake that could have been fatal! My gentle giant turned his face towards her so fast we didn't even see it. The roar was like nothing I had ever heard from a dog; It is a sound that can still be heard in my memory. His face was reminiscent of a huge

Tibetian Mastiff I once saw on YouTube - fierce and roaring in a fight. Araglas' mouth was open wide as he curled his body around to hurl himself at her. She felt his breath as his teeth touched the skin around her arm. She sat still in shock and I stood watching on in horror.

It was all over as quickly as it had begun. There was not a hair out of place on the young woman, except it was maybe all standing on end in fright. She was not a happy camper, but was not hurt in any way. Araglas was a good boy, but it was apparent that he was not feeling well. He did have diarrhea and showed me this by relieving himself on the living room floor. I called the vets office, after hours or on the week-end and they said I should give him a medication for diarrhea. It did not help, because it actually wasn't diarrhea.

He was still hungry and eating, so that night he ate four pounds of raw pork riblets with the bones. The next day he was in rough shape. I still didn't have a vehicle and my husband was not on board with us spending more money for the vet. I asked Pat's husband Rod from church to take us. We made the 200 km round trip trek to GAH with him.

When we arrived, Dr. Rasa took care of Araglas. They X-rayed his insides to see if he was impacted. The picture showed that he was chock-full of food for a couple feet, with the four pounds of undigested sharp bones coming in last. She said they didn't know if he was going to survive. They would have to keep him and would do everything they could. I didn't want to leave him, but I could not stay – it was my longest journey away from home and I was a passenger – Rod had to get home.

Araglas was in the hospital for a few days and the staff worked very hard to help him. Finally, he was given relief when their many efforts paid off. He was able to have a large bowel movement and they said he could come home. That was great, but I wanted to know why this had happened? Why was this happening to him?

Dr. Rasa did not know, but figured that he had an enlarged prostate so he was given medication to that end. They suggested that he should be neutered, but he wasn't well enough at the time. When I got a ride back to GAH, I was so happy to see Araglas and to get my shadow home, where he belonged.

The first time I drove with Clayton in the car was at the end of February in 2019. We both were a little nervous, but we were not going too far. As we drove out of the driveway and started down the road – at exactly the same time – we both let out a huge sigh. I guess we had both been holding our breath. We had a little conversation about how we felt and were off to the races.

Part of my secret planning to exit my marriage had been to ask my old friend Ohmer, if he had any rental places available. He had said he had none, but gave me a call in March to say he'd thought of one. He had a little 800 sq. ft. apartment that Clayton and I could move into. It was built onto his sheep shed. I could bring my sheep, chickens, cats, dogs, Digger and even my entire herd of beef cattle! I was so excited even though it wouldn't be ready for a while. I finally had a plan; a place to go.

In early April, I had my very last driving session with Tim. I was no longer afraid to drive – my knuckles weren't white while I held onto the steering wheel. He said that I was ready and I had done well. He was a very good coach and I was blessed to have him there beside me for those ten hours of driving. Originally huddled in the passenger seat, afraid for him to back out of the lane… to at last being ready to purchase my own vehicle! I was ready for some freedom!

It was on this same day, that my husband and I also became legally separated. If I thought life was rough at that point, it would continue to go downhill for the rest of the year, before making a slow curve upwards.

I had not been having much luck locating a good used truck to purchase. Ohmer had heard of an estate sale in my area, and let me know that there was going to be a truck auctioned off. The deceased owner had a tow truck company and was mechanically inclined, so I figured that it would be a good truck. I didn't get to see it until auction day, after a neighbour had driven me to the sale. I met up there with Ohmer and was determined to get this vehicle.

When I finally viewed the truck, it wasn't exactly as advertised and was a year older. The auctioneer had said there was a little part that had been repainted several times, but the paint didn't match up properly. It turned out it was the entire driver's side box! The man had repossessed a car of someone that wasn't happy about it and they had entered the shed where it was housed and apparently set it aflame. This truck was nearby and it had melted the paint – such that it looked like alligator skin and yellowish. The rest of the truck was pearl white. They forgot to mention the two-foot crease on the passenger side box as well – but I didn't care. I needed a reliable truck and hoped this was it. Most importantly, it had a backup camera, which was going to make a huge difference for me, because I still could not turn my head. It was a Chevy Silverado with a crew cab pick-up. Going once, going twice... SOLD to the lady by the truck!

I was grateful that Ohmer was still watching out for me. I finally had wheels under me again. I was back in the driver's seat exactly one year after I got out of the hospital.

Only two weeks later, my well-laid plans were dashed. One week before I'd planned to move into Ohmer's apartment, the deal had fallen through. I was back to scratch. We could not find anywhere to go; we were stuck living in a very uncomfortable situation.

We got the farm ready for sale and it was sold by auction in early July. The farm had been in such disarray that we hadn't wanted to do showings and opted for an auction. In some ways, that was a poor choice. With soaring real estate prices, we thought we would do quite well. In the end, with only one serious bidder, the property sold for barely more than we had bought it for, five years earlier.

The potential buyer had promised that Clayton and I could stay in the house and rent the barn and pasture for a few years, giving us time to regroup and heal. We were in a private conference with the buyer and the auctioneer, faced with one question: With such a low price, do we let it go?

At that exact moment, something high above me caught my attention. I looked up and saw a beautiful Bald Eagle flying North West, low and directly over top of our ongoing negotiations. I knew without a shadow of a doubt, that it was time to let the farm go.

I had no choice but to sell off my beautiful Red Poll herd, because I was unable to look after them myself and could not afford to keep qualified help. I did not know if or when I was going to recover, so had to let them go. By the end of July, all the Red Poll Cattle had new homes, except for Leyla. They were top quality, rare breed cows that I had worked so hard to have. One of the best herds in the country – dispersed. Thankfully, I managed to find good caretakers, who would appreciate the rare genetics.

IN THE FOG WITH THORIN

In the fall of 2018, I had received notification from Thorin's new family — that they were moving far away. When we had originally agreed to let them provide him with a home for us, they had promised that they would never move. One year later, they told us that they were moving to Sault Ste. Marie — about an eighteen hour round trip by car , if you didn't stop anywhere. I had still been in the neck brace at the time and there had been no way that we could have demanded him to be returned. They promised to continue to feed him raw, take care of him and make him available for breeding when needed.

Barely a year later, in August of 2019, I got word that Thorin was not being taken care of properly. A lady with a littermate of Spotty, had driven a long way to breed her dog with Thorin. Not being there, I couldn't assess the situation or help much with the breeding. I'd advised her, if she was concerned about Thorin not making a tie at the right time, she should call a local vet for help with a side-by-side.

I did not hear from her for a day and a half. I had hoped that all was going well — that no news was good news. When I finally received a call from her, I was astonished and alarmed at what had been taking place there!

My suggestion had been that the lady could take Thorin to a vet for the side by side, collection from him, and insertion into her female. This woman decided, without my knowledge, to take matters into her own hands — literally. I would never have even guessed that she would do that! She apparently had been taught by a breeder-friend a few days earlier, how to collect semen and inseminate her own dog! She had never mentioned that option to me. You'd think she might have even asked, before doing such a procedure on someone else's dog!

When she finally did tell me about this, I found out that there was something wrong with Thorin…that he wasn't as "into it" as he should have been. My own thought was maybe she had hurt him!! She apparently collected him and inseminated her dog, two days in a row! She told me he had diarrhea and also a very bad ear infection. The contents of the ear were gray and bloody.

These folks that had Thorin, also had Donnamira's sister. They had spayed her at nine months of age, even though they had signed a contract to say, that they would not spay until she was at least two years of age. It had been a convenience thing for them they'd said, because they had Thorin. They apparently let her eat all she wanted, and had changed their food from raw to kibble. I saw some pictures of her. She was a very large bodied, overweight little girl, with a small head. Almost grotesque.

On her last night there, this woman proceeded to tell me, that she had taken Thorin out for a half a kilometer walk and had to practically drag him back. When she had arrived, he had collapsed on the garage floor and wouldn't get up. She said he didn't even get up to pee, just continued to lay there with a puddle forming around him.

This was not the dog that I remembered. Something was terribly wrong. What was going on there?

One morning in late August, the woman said she was going home, because there was no more breeding to be had if Thorin was sick. I begged her to take him along with her to Quebec. I would find a way to get him from her, but at least he would be safe. The lady waited to tell me she had left, until they were too far away to go back. She said it would be too crowded in her car and didn't want to inconvenience herself with another dog.

The people where Thorin lived were planning to go away on a trip and leave the dogs in a kennel for two weeks. I did not figure that was a reasonable thing to do, if he had such a bad ear infection and possibly other problems. They said they would take him to the vet before they left. I called their vet and sent them a copy of the contract that indicated I was to be involved in all medical decisions, and asked if perhaps they could have the consultation over the phone while they were there. I called in at the scheduled time and apparently the vet clinic canceled the appointment with them at the last minute. They said that they would wait for me to be able to come in at the same time. It would take over eighteen hours of driving and I was not planning on going there!! It took great convincing, but I got the people to drive Thorin to Manitoulin Island before they went away on their trip, instead of taking him to the kennel.

I told them I need to have him checked out by my vet, for breeding purposes. I hired a guy to drive us in my truck for the 640 km round trip to Tobermory. In addition, we had to get the ferry across to Manitoulin Island. Luckily, they were there as promised, as there was only a twenty-five-minute window before the ferry made the return trip back to the mainland.

I exited the MS Chi-Cheemaun and went to meet with the people and Thorin.

Thorin barely even noticed me, his eyes were staring straight ahead. I took the leash from their hand. I said, "Let's go" and walked him away from the people he had been with for two years. He never looked back. He walked straight into a small elevator and up to the top deck of the ferry. After we showed him around a little bit, he laid down and did not get up for the rest of the almost two-hour ferry ride.

When the boat docked, Thorin would not get up. The man that was with us, had to lift him up. He cried some on the way home, but mostly stayed in the truck for the four-hour drive.

I took him for a little walk the next day. The dogs went at their normal pace and he barely dragged himself along. After the short walk, he was out in the barn stall, where I had put him, while Araglas was outside. He was still panting heavily an hour and a half later! I thought; "He must be *really* out of shape!"

Thorin was in poor condition when I got him home. Why had they stopped taking care of him? I guess because they had stopped taking care of themselves. What else could it be?

He smelled worse and was dirtier than my seven farm dogs put together! He hadn't been brushed or bathed and his nails were so long that they were curled around his toes! His anus had a five-inch circle that had no hair, from diarrhea scalding! He had a hitch in his step and had a hard time rising.

I called GAH, but my good reproductive vet Dr.Rasa was on vacation and wouldn't be back for a week. I thought it would give me some time to get him acclimatized to being home, before rushing him off again. Twice during that week, he passed out after some brief exertion. I could hardly wait for the appointment.

In early September, when we arrived, Dr. Rasa looked him over and then ultra-sounded his belly. She said, this was not a reproduction issue, and transferred us over to Dr. Denise for X-rays.

We went to the X-ray room and they got him on the table. He almost coded right then and there! I was watching in shock as they were saying things like: "Hurry take the picture or he's not going to make it! "

"What?"

When they put him back on the floor and then looked at the X-rays. I said to the doctor, "Oh, he also has an ear infection, and a hitch in his step." She said, "None of that matters."

Clayton hugging Thorin, November 2019

What?

She said, "Look here," while pointing to something on the screen. "It's enlarged... his heart..."

I said, "He's a big dog and has a big heart!"

She said, "No. Look here..." and she pointed to his chest X-rays and showed that they were filled with fluid. They did an EKG and tested his heart rate. His heart was beating at over 300 beats per minute! She said that he could be referred to a cardio specialist or they could send the info to a cardiologist for their take – it would be about an hour wait. I said that is fine, I'd wait.

When she came back with the results, she said, "He has left sided heart failure, which has caused fluid buildup in his lungs, he has an arrhythmia and something else, which I promptly forgot when she said the next bit. The part I remember clearly was when she said, "He has two weeks to six months to live!"

What?!

My champion breeding dog from the Czech Republic not even six years old, is so sick that he is going to die!? How could this be?

We will never know for sure, but it is thought that the high protein, no grain dog food kibble that they had put him on after taking him off of the good raw diet, may have been one of the culprits. Apparently grain free kibble can cause severe heart problems, if not treated right away. He had not been well treated, that is for sure.

When his people had moved up north, they'd left their one-story bungalow for a two-story home. They lived in the upstairs with the other two dogs, but Thorin hadn't been able to climb the steep stairs. He stayed in the basement or in the backyard all of the time, mostly alone. I still believe his heart was broken. I had not been able to support him, like I had before the accident; before they moved away. I put him on every drug or therapy the vet suggested – the drugs alone were over $400 a month. I had to save him if I could; I owed him that much.

One day as I was walking to the barn from the house, I was almost across the barnyard when I looked up and saw an Eagle flying so close, I could see the expression on its face. It wasn't long before it was gone over the roof of the barn. I marveled in wonder for just a moment, then quickly got back to my chores. There was always much to be done and everything took so much longer than it did before.

That night I took out my pastels and drawing book. I sat for a moment and thought about what to draw? I knew I had some stuff to work out, but wasn't sure what. I picked up the black pastel and viciously coloured the entire paper. I sat for a moment and looked at it. Yup. That is where I had been. I turned over the next page. I picked up the dark gray pastel and vigorously coloured the entire paper gray. That was the end of the drawing. It laid open on the table like that for two days. That was my world; I lived in a fog.

Clayton had just started to visit his dad every other weekend, so this was my first opportunity to have some time to myself. I went for a walk in the field with the dogs, like I often did. I stood at the back fence and pretended that the man who drove head long into us, was standing in the hay field. I yelled everything I could think of at the guy. I sang, I screamed – whatever came to mind. I stayed out there until I had nothing left to say about the matter; then I forgave him.

When I went back to the house, I sat down in front of the gray paper. I turned the page; I was able to move forward. Then I drew a new picture with just a glimmer of light seeping in; the next page had more. I then drew the last moment before impact – what Clayton and I had seen, with the car directly in front of us. I drew the impact and whatever else I needed to – rushed and crudely – but got it out and onto the paper. I drew page after page until the scenes became serene. I drew my way out of the darkness. On the last page I wrote, "Life is simple and easy." I was finally out of the gray.

IT WAS THE BEST AND WORST OF TIMES

Early one morning in late September, I got up earlier than usual and went out to the field. During my walk with the dogs, it was the first time that I was able to experience the feeling of gratitude, since before the accident. I felt a new aliveness in me.

The next evening at 9:30 PM, I got an email from my landlord, Joe. It said very plainly that he wanted us to vacate the property by mid-December, so he could spruce up the house before listing it with a Realtor!

I was in shock! Hadn't he promised me that we could stay for a couple years? The very next week the For-Sale sign went up! He had got it so cheap that he was flipping the property and had it listed for $300,000 more than he paid for it!

Our first dog show in two years was coming up on the week-end. I was not going to let a little thing like eviction ruin our time there; I had waited too long for this moment. I could worry about whatever I wanted to after the week-end, but this was Argibel and Donnamira's first time showing; Clayton and I needed all the confidence we could muster. He was going to do the showing, as I didn't really think I was ready to do the running around bit. I remained positive and upbeat all the way to the show with only one goal in mind! Best in Show baby!! I had two beautiful girls along to compete for it, perhaps there would be a tie!

Argibel was the first-ever Basque Shepherd to be shown in Canada, possibly in all of North America. The judges hardly knew what to make of her, with her red hair and shocking yellow eyes!

There was also one little detail that I hadn't considered fully in regards to Argibel. She is a one-person dog and *I* am her one person. The breed itself is very one person-ish. Argibel follows me unequivocally and would walk through fire with me, but it was to be Clayton that would have to show her – away from me! Yeah, that did not go as well as hoped; she had to be looking at me at all times. Although Clayton and Argibel tried their best, they struggled.

There were two shows happening at the same time. Clayton had run Argibel in one ring and Donnamira in the other. He hadn't shown a dog in years and these two hadn't really been anywhere in their lives; most certainly not to a dog show! I really, really wanted to show Donnamira and as it turned out, Clayton was showing Argibel in the other ring when the time came. It was really important to me that Donnamira was showed to her best ability. It was *my* dream after all to show my baby, the culmination of all my years of dog breeding. I let Clayton know that I was going to show Donnamira this one time. Other breeders and the President of the dog show were asking if I needed any help; if I thought I should do this? I had to.

It was explained to the judge that I might not be as graceful as the next competitor, but that I would do my best. He said that he would not make me run the full distance. When he had seen all he needed to see, he would let me stop. I thanked him profusely. He remarked that there is often a lot of unnecessary running around and it wasn't needed.

I jogged where I needed to and Donnamira was in fine form. She did everything I asked of her and looked beautiful doing it. If I thought I was overjoyed when we won first place in the working group, I have no words to describe my feelings about what happened next! Donnamira did it!! *We* did it! She won BEST IN SHOW!!

I was so happy that I was bawling my eyes out.

Donnamira Best in Show, September 2019

After everything that we had been through in the previous year and a half together, to win this honour was more than a dream come true!! I was over the moon! Folks were yelling their congratulations, but I was looking down and just trying to get back to the truck. I had hardly shed a tear since the accident and buckets and buckets were coming out now. I cursorily waved at the people as I went past in response to the cheer. It was unfortunate that at the time I could not say thank you to everyone for their support, but I was temporarily out of order! I was so happy and proud that I could not stop crying.

A week later, I wrote a letter to the people of the dog show. It contained pictures from my accident, me in a neck collar, Donnamira with no hair and covered in scars. I had felt very badly about not acknowledging the congratulations, especially with such a huge accomplishment as Best in Show. I had only won this title twice before in all my years of showing. My wonderful Araglas had been Best in Show when he was only eight months old and did it again at eighteen months of age. This was my first girl to win and she was Araglas's niece. It was the triumph after our tragedies that meant the most to me though. We both could have died; succumbed to our injuries, but we didn't give up! I wanted the folks to know that I really appreciated their support, but at that moment I had been too overwhelmed to respond in an appropriate manner. Everyone understood how sweet my victory was. It might be the last show we ever went to, but it was a good one and well worth it!

The end of September brought surgery for my Border Collie, Dirk. He had been having bloody mucous coming from his left nostril for a few weeks, at that point. Dr. Dawn had said that he had a broken, rotting canine, perhaps it was causing an infection. He'd been on medication, but if they removed the tooth, the hope was that it would remove the problem.

But that was not the case. After the $1000 surgery, Dr. Dawn thought that it had not been successful at eliminating the problem. An X-ray of Dirk's head showed an air obstruction on the one side, so something not visible was causing an issue. If I thought things couldn't get any worse, this was just the tip of the iceberg.

October 4, is a day that I'll never forget. I left Thorin in the house to rest, while I took the other seven dogs for a walk. I was talking on the phone to the mother of my childhood friend. It was our second conversation and she had been supporting me with my separation and the likes. It was a nice evening and I thought I would go beyond the fences and have a longer walk in the hayfield. It would be a nice change and although we had walked out there many times in that summer, I never would have done it in previous years; when my thinking was more alert.

I opened the gate and the dogs rushed through, a little quicker than usual. I turned my back to them and closed the gate behind me. When I spun around the dogs had scattered over about ten acres of the hay field! What was going on? I guess I hadn't been paying close enough attention, because I had been talking on the phone. Dusk was rapidly approaching as it was already early Fall. I hadn't expected it to be getting dark so quickly. Another thing that surprised me was, that we weren't alone out there.

We were surrounded by a pack of wild coyotes!! I screamed for the dogs to come back to me!! I had to get them back into the fenced pasture, but they were all over the place!

Upon seeing the coyotes, the three oldest Pyrenean Mastiffs did what they were bred to do and were going to protect me at all costs. Éowyn, Brandy and Araglas took off after the now fleeing coyotes! I screamed for the dogs to come and the rest did. Spotty, Donnamira, Dirk and Argibel came to protect me. I ran to the gate and returned them to the safety of the pasture. Argibel came right back through the fence, as though she was water. I couldn't make her stay and I really had to go. Darkness had quickly fallen and I didn't even have a flashlight! I charged into the darkness screaming in vain for the three missing dogs the whole way. The poor woman stayed on the line, in bewilderment, listening to the goings on from her home in Toronto.

When I would yell, the coyotes would yowl back. I was so afraid. Where were the dogs?? Oh God – please bring them home safely. Please!!

When I got two-thirds of the way down the hayfield, I could just make out Brandy's shape in the neighbour's field, through the bushes in the fence row. She was acting very strangely and would not come when I called out to her. I ran further down to where there was a break in the fence row. She was showing me something.

What was that out in the field? A plastic bag? A feed bag perhaps? That it was white was all I could catch in the dim moonlight. As I got closer, I could not believe my eyes. I didn't want to believe them. What the hell? Dear God!? How can this be??

Into the darkness I screamed in horror at the top of my lungs and I fell in a heap onto the ground. The coyotes, so close in the bush answered back.

As I looked up from my writing just now, I see an Eagle not far from me, flying by, understanding my pain, I guess.

I looked at the lifeless body of my selfless protector. Araglas lay still, eyes glazed. My shadow; my friend. How could a 160-pound dog that never leaves my side – who would run into the back of my leg if I stop suddenly - have run away and died like this??

I hoarsely sobbed into the phone to the poor woman still waiting on the line, "Araglas is dead. How can this be? Where is Éowyn? Did the coyotes get her too?? I have to go," I said and hung up the phone. I couldn't help myself and let out one more earth-shattering scream. The coyotes yelped and howled back.

I have to say that the coyotes sounded a whole lot like Argibel, if I thought about it. Where was she anyway?? I called to her and she came quickly into view – thank God! What about Brandy now? Still here. But Éowyn? But Araglas. What of them?

I was very frightened and wrought with pain and guilt over Araglas' death. Why had I come outside the fence that night? Why was I out there so close to dusk? I realized I had to at least get Brandy and Argibel to safety; I couldn't risk losing anyone else and I was terrified for myself at this point. Anything that could take Araglas down must be scary! I couldn't fathom it. And why was there no blood?

I screamed one more time for Éowyn. Thank God she came into view. I had to go. I had to leave Araglas where he lay, and get my girls back to safety.

Araglas' body was lying flat on his left side. No signs of trauma. He was facing in the direction he had been going – it was like he just fell over – dead!

Clayton was away visiting his father for the second time, so thankfully he was safe. I was so alone and frightened. When I got the three dogs safely over to the other side of the gate, I called my neighbour John and asked him for help. I told him that we'd been ambushed by coyotes and I needed help to bring Araglas' body back home.

By the time I returned to the house, John had come over with his son-in-law. We put my large snowmobile sled in the back of the truck and headed out to the hayfield. They lifted the lifeless body of my beloved friend and dropped him unceremoniously in the sled which was hooked up to the hitch, and dragged across the grass. Upon arriving I didn't know what to do with him, so we left him in the sled, parked by the barn and I thanked them for their help.

I let Thorin out of the house. He went over and started to bark at Araglas. His arch nemesis lay dead and he couldn't understand why he wouldn't get up and fight. He barked and barked at him.

How could this be? Only thirty days earlier, Thorin had been given two weeks to six months to live and there he was, barking at Araglas who was suddenly dead? I had to quickly return Thorin to the house. I think we were all still in shock.

After a fitful sleep, the next morning, I had the unenviable task of having to deal with Araglas' remains. I went out and had a good look over his entire body. No signs of distress. The coyotes could not have done this. There was no way he would have gone down without a fight and besides, the girls wouldn't have let him! I called

GAH and asked about getting an autopsy. I was a breeder of these dogs and he was only five years old, how could he be dead!?

GAH said that they were not allowed to do autopsies. Only OVC at Guelph was licensed to do it! I did not want to go there again, not after what had happened to Éowyn! Being given only one option, I had very few choices to make. Either do it and know, or don't do it and forever wonder. I had to do it. I figured at least they couldn't hurt him more; he was already dead.

Right about then, the photographers from the Realty that was listing the farm for my landlord Joe, showed up. They were going to be taking outdoor pictures with a drone. Araglas was still laying in the snowmobile sled, so I covered him with a white tarp. He ended up in many photos, but only *I* knew what laid under the tarp – a large piece of my heart.

I called my neighbour John and asked for his assistance once again, this time for getting the body into the back of my truck. He brought his tractor over and Araglas was unceremoniously dumped from the sled, into the truck bed. I used the tarp to cover him one last time.

I called Frienda. She had just put her cat Gus to sleep that morning, but she was willing to go with me to OVC, if I came with her to say good-bye to Gus at her vet clinic. What a pair we were with neither of us quite able to deal with the shock of our own loss, let alone to support our friend in *their* loss.

Before leaving for Guelph, using a satellite photo, I measured the distance from where the dogs were, to the precise location where I found Araglas' body. He had done a 750-metre dash. He was a porch dog that got very little exercise – especially since Thorin had been home. He was often in the house with me, while Thorin was outside. I still could not fathom how one of my so-called "sticky" dogs, could have been that far away from me. I realize he was protecting me, but usually he would run *towards* me in danger, never away.

That evening, I was doing the dishes and working in the kitchen. Something in the dining room caught my attention. It was a bubble.

Where did it come from??

It was about one inch in diameter, just floating around.

I tried to ignore it, as I was sure it would quickly disappear, but it followed me around! I stopped what I was doing and gave my full attention to it. It floated around in front of me.

How could this bubble just be here, at random, in my house? I realized at some point, that it wasn't random. I wondered out loud, if it might be Araglas, trying to get my attention!? Why did I even think that? It was a bubble, for goodness' sake!!

The bubble, with no known origin, did not go away. When I acknowledged that it might be Araglas, it came closer... right up to my face. I took the opportunity to say what I needed to, as if it *was* Araglas. I wanted him to know that I loved him very much! I had been overwhelmed, by having the two males to contend with, but I certainly hadn't wanted him to die!! I missed him so much already!

With that, the bubble came right up to my chin and gently touched it – without breaking!! Araglas always used to kiss me on the chin; it was his thing. I was certain that the bubble had just kissed me!! I knew that he was saying good-bye. I also felt that even though I didn't understand it then, he was giving a gift to me and the others that were left behind. The bubble lingered a moment more and then went off into the dining room and disappeared. I fell to the floor and wept.

When I got the results from the autopsy, I was surprised to find out that it was his heart. Araglas had a big heart no doubt and he gave everything he had to save me. I was shocked to find that my precious boy's heart had been damaged on one side, by two adult heartworms. The thought was that he had one big arrhythmia and probably keeled over dead. There was nothing else wrong with him.

Heartworm was not something I was expecting. We lived in one of the worst areas for heartworm, but I had always prevented it with a homeopathic as well as other natural practices – at least that was before the accident. With everything that had gone on, I had not remembered to give it to them. That coupled with the dogs having to remain outdoors all summer in 2018 and again in 2019, they'd been left out, unprotected. All of them. Oh no!

In early October, I knew that a shift was coming, when I saw an Eagle on two separate occasions on the same day. They were flying so effortlessly with the wind in the clouds. I hadn't seen even one Eagle in quite a while, and now I saw two.

In mid-October, I was bringing Dirk for more tests at GAH, so I brought Argibel, Brandy and Spotty along, to be heartworm tested that day. Thorin still had to go for a re-check another day and Donnamira was booked in for a breeding health check with X-rays for hips, elbows and knees scheduled in a few weeks. These are big dogs and there was only so much room in my truck!

Éowyn had been suffering from a strange lameness all summer and I'd had her in for a check-up earlier at one of Thorin's appointments, where she had been tested for Lyme disease, which had been in the same test as heartworm. Thankfully, she had been clear.

After they had pulled the blood samples, the senior tech had come in and said that I needed to wait for the doctor to come and talk to me. They'd found heartworm. My heart sank.

I had three sticky dogs; those that were with me all the time; Araglas, Argibel and Spotty. Araglas was gone. Argibel was clear, thankfully and I am sure she probably moved too fast to be bit by a mosquito anyway. Brandy clear. Dirk clear. Oh no... it was Spotty!

They took another blood sample from Spotty and sent it away for further testing. Apparently, they would be able to tell, if she was contagious or not. I asked what the treatment was for heartworm? They explained that there was only one treatment and it cost more than $2000. They said she might die a painful death from the treatment and she'd have to stay in a cage for ten weeks to try and avoid sudden death. Was there no other way?? Depending on what the next test said, well, we would talk again.

I left the vet clinic in shock.

I still had to go about half an hour north to pick up GMO-Free feed for the chickens, before returning home. I called Frienda as I drove out of the little town and told her the bad news.

It became quite apparent very quickly to both of us, that I should not be driving right then. I began to sob uncontrollably and had to pull over to the shoulder of the road.

What the hell was going on with my life!? I felt like I was in some kind of nightmare that just didn't stop. I needed a sign that there was still hope!! That sign was delivered right then, in a big way.

Through my tears, something caught my eye outside of the front and side of the truck. I was safely parked on the shoulder of a blacktop road in the country, surrounded by farm fields and some agricultural buildings in the distance. I used my sleeve to wipe the tears and my nose while I was at it. I looked straight ahead first and then to the side; first in wonder and then in awe.

There were black birds flying from somewhere behind and to the right of me. One by one and by the dozens it was like they were being ejected from an imaginary tennis ball thrower. From my vantage point I could watch the wave of black fly ahead and off into the distance. They were crows. Wow! How many I wondered? There must have been at least thirty or forty! When they were almost gone from my view, the next wave came. One bunch after the next, waves and waves of black crows! I had no idea we even had that many crows in Ontario, let alone to see them all at once! I sat in amazement for a long time and literally saw seemingly thousands of crows appear magically from an unknown point above and behind my vehicle. As I often do when there is a sign from the universe – I pulled out my trusty little book by Ted Andrews and read about the crow.

Crow: Magical help
"Unexpected help with problems and obstacles is at hand to bring relief. Your magic is calling and will be answered."

I wasn't going to give up on Spotty. *As I wrote this, an Eagle was flying in the distance.*

Later in October, I was reminded of one of my favourite quotes from the movie *The Secret*:
"You can start with nothing.
And out of nothing and out of no way, a way will be made."
~ Michael Bernard Beckwith

One morning in early November, I woke up with a start as my beloved Dirk blew his nose in an effort to clear it. There were large blood clots on the floor and wall. Dirk was having a hard time and I felt that this might be his last day. I called Claudia Hehr, the animal communicator, and she spoke with Dirk telepathically. He was having trouble breathing and was afraid of dying by suffocation. Dirk and I were on the same page – neither of us wanted him to leave, but also didn't want him to suffer. The arrangements were made that the next morning would be his last, but that night we would have a celebration of Dirk's life – a grand party. He wanted to eat ice cream – it was his parting wish.

That afternoon Clayton and I drove to town, where we bought ice cream and party supplies; and Dirk had his last ride in the truck.

We had a wonderful evening together. Dirk even got a new toy for a present, although he didn't much feel like playing with it, so Argibel played with it for him. The night was too short as Dirk laid sleeping beside my bed, like always, since like forever.

The next morning, the vet was scheduled to come at 11 AM. Claudia had told Dirk ahead of time and we were all ready. We were as ready as anyone can be to say good-bye to your best friend. Dirk and Clayton had been best adventure buddies for all of Clayton's life. What would he do without him?

Clayton and I sat on the dining room floor with Dirk, our arms surrounding him as the vet explained the procedure and injected the life-taking fluid into his veins. We felt his body collapse and the weight of him fall onto us. In just a moment, he was gone. A bright light in the world had been snuffed out and darkness fell.

The following week I took Thorin to GAH for his check-up and Donnamira for her health clearance X-rays. They were the last two to be tested for heartworm. I prayed every day that Donnamira was clear and thank God she was!! Thorin on the other hand, was not. When I had gotten Spotty re-tested, the results had been that she had only a small number of adult female heartworms – no babies. When I had Thorin re-tested that was not the case. Thorin had 1356 immature heartworm (microfilaria) per millilitre of blood tested!! The vet said that this was not at all normal for Ontario; it was more like south Florida numbers!!

While I was writing this, an Eagle flew from behind me in such a way, that I didn't see it until it was ahead and flying away.

It was not the same as Spotty; Thorin would be contagious. On a good note, he would not be contagious, until the mosquitoes returned in the Spring. On a bad note, he was not a candidate for treatment; he would not survive it.

I knew there had to be a natural solution, there always is. Frienda found an article from *Dogs Naturally* magazine that spoke of a few natural things that could be done. One was of a combination homeopathic that contained eighteen remedies in small potencies. I called Bio-Ag to get them to make it for me. For about $100 they ended up putting twenty remedies in by mistake, but I hoped the more the merrier. The downside was, I had to give the remedy for three to five months, but could start re-testing after two months to see if it worked. I started all of the dogs on it, just in case – I knew it couldn't hurt, but it might possibly help. Twice every day I would give each some in their mouth for the next three and a half months. I would not give up on Spotty.

THE SEASON OF DARKNESS

After the accident, Clayton was always panicked about my whereabouts, wondering if I had fallen and broken my neck or was otherwise in pain and suffering. Even if I called out his name from a distance or he heard a noise – he would arrive in panic, grief stricken, wondering about my ill fate. Clayton now hated school so much that even hearing the word, caused a triggering of great pain and emotion, followed by falling on the floor in a pile of tears. He was really struggling and we were making no progress with Grade 5. Where we were supposed to get through one lesson a week, it was more like one lesson a month. We were having trouble coping.

On December 10, Thorin was acting unusual. He had been keeping to himself and was not laying in his regular spot. When I located him, I brought him into the house. He seemed to be panting a lot. I took out my stethoscope and listened to his heart, counting 250 beats per minute. I called Dr. Denise, thinking that maybe he needed a medication change and she said that he might be going into heart failure. I didn't like the thought of that. I still had high hopes for the miracle that he so deserved.

He was uncomfortable and seemed too hot in the house, so I let him outside. That evening, I went out to check on him regularly. Where was he anyway? He had been on the driveway for a while. I asked Clayton if he wanted to say good-bye to Thorin before going to bed. He replied, "I will see him in the morning." I hoped that would be the case, but we were not so lucky.

I went back out looking again and found him in the front bushes, laying in Araglas' favourite spot. He looked like he was sleeping, but he was not. Ninety-seven days after Thorin's original diagnosis, he was gone.

Let me sum this up for you, so that you are clear with the amount of loss, suffered by one little boy and his mama. Thirty days after Thorin's diagnosis, with a two week to six-month life expectancy, Araglas suddenly drops dead at five years of age. Thirty-four days later we had Dirk euthanized, after almost thirteen years of having him in our life every day. Thirty-three days later, Thorin dies at age six. In a sixty-four-day period, we had lost all three of our boys. Although Dirk was not big in size and weighted only fifty pounds, his loss was felt just as deeply as the giant 165-pound boys, that were now gone. The only difference was that we had a chance to say good-bye to Dirk.

Both Clayton and I continued to wonder what we were living for... What could be the purpose for us to be suffering with one challenge compounding right after the next in seemingly endless supply? We struggled to find answers.

December 16 brought more sadness and mixed feelings. I sold all of my adult sheep and my last heifer, Leyla. I was unable to take care of them very well and needed to get a handle on what I could and could not do. I literally could not handle them; they were too big. We kept only five ewe lambs that were born in the fall, and five that were born during the winter lambing.

Clayton had been with me for Christmas and I'd cooked a small eleven-pound turkey that we had grown. It was too heavy and awkward for me to lift it out of the oven, but I did it anyway, and regretted it. On Boxing Day he had gone to his dad's and I was home alone and went to bed around midnight, like usual. I wasn't able to sleep too well, as I seemed to have a bit of a cold or something that had come on that day.

At 4 AM, I woke up with terrible chest pain and couldn't breathe. I was all alone and didn't know what to do! I looked up the contact info for Telehealth Ontario and dialed the number. After being on hold for a number of minutes, I had the very real thought that I was going to die right there on hold, to be found days later when Clayton came home. Did I want that to be how my story ended? I hung up and called 911. I squawked almost inaudible into the phone to the operator… "I can't breathe and my chest hurts."

I managed to tell them that I had dogs and the 911 operator instructed me that I must lock them away. I put them all in the dog room before the ambulance arrived. At least it kept me busy and my mind off the fact, that I was not able to breathe!

They put me in the ambulance and then I sent one of the attendants back in to get my special pillow. I couldn't lay properly without it. It is filled with the perfect amount of air to support my head and neck. While he was getting that, the female attendant took my blood pressure and heart rate. It was 250 beats per minute, the same as I had counted on Thorin, just before he died.

I spent eight hours in the emergency room while they took blood numerous times and did multiple tests. At 10 o'clock, I realized that the dogs were still locked up and called John and Lois. John went over and let them out.

When it was time for me to be released, I called Lois again to let her know that I was going to be coming home. She asked how? I guessed a cab? She dismissed that idea, and came to pick me up; it was wonderful to have support.

I was diagnosed with rib muscle strain. They had also seen "fluff" in my lungs right where the pain was and they figured it was the start of pneumonia. The trouble breathing had been my first full on panic attack. I was pretty sick when Clayton was dropped off a few days later. I hardly got out of bed and was unable to do my chores, so John had been helping until Clayton got home. We also had a young girl helper, Charlotte, who was called in to assist. At least there weren't so many animals to take care of at that point.

To top it off, I got laryngitis and was unable to speak. Maybe that was for the better? Clayton left for his dad's on New Year's Eve Day. I was still sick, alone and silent. I wondered to myself, "How much more could I take?"

It was late in the evening and I was scrolling through Facebook before heading to bed when an ad caught my attention.

Mike Dooley... wasn't he in the movie *The Secret*? The ad was for a course by Mike Dooley called *Love Your Life in 30-days Project*. I clicked the link and stared at the screen in wonder.

The course started the next day, on January 1.

What is this course? Does it really matter?

I gave myself two options at that moment – either love life or leave it. I would not give up, so I got out my credit card and chose life.

IT WAS THE SPRING OF HOPE

In 2020, when the whole world was starting to fall apart, I was doing the opposite; I was putting myself back together.

It took me five months to complete that 30-day course, but during that time I sorted a few things out. I started to meditate in the bathtub at night and focus on what I wanted to create in my future. It had been fourteen years since I had completed my first and only vision board and as part of the course, I created some new ones. Most importantly, I became aware that I was finally going to write a book. After a break during January, I resumed my search for a new place for us to live.

I found a 50-acre farm near my sister Brenda's place, but although I put an offer in, it wasn't accepted. They took a much lower offer, but with no conditions. Although for the next few weeks, I would be down in the dumps, living in a dark hole about not being able to find and secure housing for us, I knew that somehow, something would change. I knew this because on the way home from seeing the property, an Eagle swooped across the road in front of the truck. The Eagles always gave me hope of better things to come.

Although I'd been packing for a long time already, I'd decided it was about time to start "acting" like I was moving... to help the universe know that I was serious! I put all non-essential items up for sale in preparation for our move. I also decided to stop telling every person I met the reasons why my life felt so miserable; because I had a broken neck, brain injury, and so on. For a while I even chose to stop fretting about the absence of somewhere to go!

Instead, I chose to be calm and peaceful while speaking with people that were buying my farm items. I refrained from saying much, if anything, about the accident. I made only one reference that I didn't currently have a milk cow, because the milker was too heavy for me, but I didn't elaborate further. I began to notice how a lot of the folks that came to my place to purchase the farm supplies, left with more knowledge than they came with. I inadvertently got to impart to them some of my great wisdom of over thirty years of farming. I began to realize that perhaps I had a lot to offer the farming community, even though I was not physically able to do much farming myself anymore.

In alignment with creating a new me, I had been contemplating a name change for over a year at this point.

I have had a long-standing affiliation with the name George, right since I was five years old. My grandfather was named George, and my Dad as well as my brother, both have George as middle names. I found out, after I had picked the name, that my great-grandparents were actually named George and Elizabeth Barg!

I guess it was meant to be, that my name would one day become Georgia Elizabeth Barg. I now had hope for my new future, a new me.

All that I had been focusing on for the previous year was finding a safe and peaceful place to live with my son and animals. I hadn't even been taking any time to relax and heal, because there was so much to do. You can imagine my excitement and renewal of hope, when on a cold day at the end of March, my Eagle flew towards me, low overhead, close over the barn. It was so near I could again see the expression on its face. I knew a shift was coming, I just didn't know when.

In early April, I started writing in a daily gratitude journal. I wrote three things I was grateful for in the morning, while the three things at night had a different topic, that changed daily over the course of a couple of weeks. I really found it very helpful, to begin and end my day with gratitude. Some days it was more difficult to come up with something to be grateful for, but it got easier as time went on. I stopped for about a month at one point and noticed a huge difference in my life, so I have continued on with it and haven't missed a day since.

At the beginning of May, I was astonished to find that I no longer felt guilty for taking a walk with my dogs. I was surprised that I could allow myself the time, that I didn't have to rush to get back to work, and felt I didn't owe anyone anything; I was just walking. I could stop to breathe, collect myself, enjoy my surroundings, look at the birds and even take the time to acknowledge the dogs that were right there with me!

When I'd had the opportunity to, I always walked the same path at the edge of the field; around and back. I usually took that opportunity to call a friend on the telephone. I always went quickly, so I wouldn't get into too much "trouble." My husband was often displeased when he thought I was wasting time away from him, especially when it had to do with the dogs. By this time, he'd been gone from the property for almost nine months and I was only just starting to feel that it was okay to go for a walk!! I was just starting to sense that *I* was okay.

After that day, I really, really, liked my walks and made sure to go every morning and evening, rain or shine! Each time I got to the end of the pasture field, I would stop and hold up my arms wide and declare: "I am open to receive all the good and joy in the universe! Thank you life!" It was a different walk to be sure.

Something else I picked up around that time, which I highly recommend; every time I don't know what to do, I declare: "Everything always works out well for me!" And then I just need to have faith that it will!

By early May, when I finally finished the course, I felt that I finally had Peace. Not just calm, but peace. I was no longer worried about where we would go and how we would get there. We started living life where we were at that moment, instead of waiting for life to begin elsewhere in our future. We planted a little garden; I got meat chickens; Clayton got new hen chicks. I was grateful that the landlord took the property off the real estate market for a bit, so we had a break with the showings, which was peaceful as well.

I began to have a little range of motion in my neck. After two years of keeping it pretty much in the same spot following the double break in my C2, I felt that it was an amazing "side-effect" to being in the course. I noticed the first change in mid-January. At some point I even noticed that I could lift my head off the pillow to move my hair out of the way. It might not seem like a big deal to you, but it was to me!!

The relationship between Clayton and I started getting better, lighter and brighter each day. He had not been doing any schoolwork when we started in January, but by May he'd completed almost the whole years curriculum! We'd made a deal that he could substitute cooking class for American History. We bought a DVD Chef Cooking course and he would practically beg me to let him watch it. He went from scarcely wanting to live, to being a top chef! He began making about six suppers a week, from scratch! They were totally delicious meals, made from a variety of beautiful food which we'd photograph before eating. The food was so good we'd lick our plates clean when done. Well, he did... I just ate all my food without the plate licking! He'd finally found something that he loved to do; and something that I loved for him to do as well!

I realized that I did not need the destination to find peace – I could have it right then. I had thought moving was going to make everything better and fix all our problems. I found inner peace and didn't need to go anywhere to get it; the other troubles would handle themselves.

CHANGE OF FORTUNE

As a child, I remember spending time searching the schoolyard for four leaf clovers. My many attempts to find one always left me empty-handed. I recall a few times where I tried to pretend that I had found one by combining two, to make one with four leaves. I'd never felt lucky as a child and I think it had been reinforced by my inability to find such a magical item.

In mid-May, while collecting grass for my chicks just outside of the barn door, I said to myself, "Wouldn't it be nice to find a four-leaf clover!?" I had been looking on and off for forty years and in that moment, I had no attachment to finding one. Now, dear reader, can you hear the trumpets playing right here? Because lo and behold, there it was! My first ever four-leaf clover!! I promptly picked it because I had never met anyone who has ever found one, and I was certain that I would need proof of such a discovery! I had no idea at that time that it marked a new beginning for me. Maybe luck *was* on my side after all.

After finding the clover, I had told Jules about my discovery. She had said, "Now you will be finding them everywhere!" For the next three days, on my walk, I began desperately searching for another. No amount of looking would bring one to me. Perhaps it was a one-off? Perhaps the point was to just be happy with finding one?

I stopped at the end of the pasture one day, closed my eyes and took a few deep breaths. I gave myself permission to look for and find a four-leaf clover if I want, without judgment or attachment. I turned to continue on my walk. I took barely two steps and there, right in front of me, standing a full inch taller than the grass around it, was a huge one! After that, I was on a roll. If I searched, I still couldn't find them, but if I didn't, there they were.

One day I set up a card table on the lawn to do some writing. It wasn't level so I moved it over a bit, right onto a clover patch. I glanced down and there was a four-leaf clover! I knelt down on the grass and picked it, only to notice it was next to another one! And another one... and another one! There were ten altogether in one little patch on the lawn! I yelled to God or the universe or whomever was listening... "I get it!!" Luck was finally on my side!

On that day, I also found three four-leaf clovers on the morning walk and two in the evening. I had decided after finding the patch and having over twenty four-leaf clovers drying in a big book at home, that I no longer needed proof. After that day, I started a picture gallery instead, with all the four-leaf clovers I have found since.

Towards the end of May, I was driving my tractor from the barn to the drive shed thinking about moving, real estate, and so on. To my surprise and delight, I looked up into the clear blue sky and saw the Eagle soaring across the sky. I had not seen one since driving home from seeing that property in early March. If they signify a major shift, I was sure ready for some movement!

Our property had been listed on the Real Estate listings again and the showings had begun once more. At the beginning of June, I'd found a four-leaf clover on the morning walk, before cleaning up for a showing of the property. At 3 o'clock, just as the people were arriving, I was putting the dogs in a barn stall when I saw blood; Spotty was bleeding! She had ripped her nail off of one toe on her front foot! I made an appointment for 6 o'clock and would take her on the long drive up to GAH.

My double four leaf clover

I was still at home when the people looking at the property left; I found another four-leaf clover. I hoped that my luck would hold.

I had given Spotty the combination homeopathic remedy for three-and-a-half months during the winter. I fully expected that she would be free and clear of the heartworm by this point. I told the vet of a new cough that she had and how she drank a lot more water than my other dogs. I asked for the heartworm test and was shocked to hear that she was still positive. I asked; what about the cough, panting and extra water? They said that the heartworm could be getting worse.

A few days later I asked Jules to check in with Spotty, as I was very worried. I needed 'Spotter my daughter' to be alright. She responded with some bad news and explained there is "Energy density accumulating in the thorax." As I read the text message, I muttered to myself, "What the hell does that mean?" but Clayton overheard. I said to him, "Jules says there is energy density accumulating in the thorax."

He fell over laughing.

We didn't even know what a thorax was, but it sure did remind us of a little orange fellow from The Lorax, by Dr. Suess! Instead of being upset, Clayton made little GIFs and videos of each of us having a turn saying the line and then laughing. Even each dog was videotaped and a voice pretending to be the dog, saying: "Energy density accumulating in the thorax." It was extremely funny; we had to send some of these innovative creations to Jules. When she finally did explain what that was, the edge was already off. I was committed to saving Spotty, no matter what. Jules was concerned that I was willing to possibly risk my own wellbeing for her. I was as determined as ever to never give up!

I contacted my natural vet in Pennsylvania, Dr. Deva Khalsa, who had helped us already several times in the past. I had wanted her counsel already in the fall, but had been stretched financially with Thorin's medications and everything else going on. It was only a financial obstacle that kept me from contacting her then, but it wasn't going to stop me this time.

Dr. Khalsa read my story that I wrote to her, about my accident and the situation I was in with Spotty. I had used her combination of homeopathic remedies, and this is why I was surprised they hadn't worked. I scheduled a consultation with her, and she suggested to start Spotty on a product called HWF, right away. It used to be called Heart Worm Free, but the FDA didn't like that. She also advised, "Buy sixteen bottles of the stuff, it's sold by *Dogs Naturally* in Canada." As far as the cough went, I heard Donnamira or Brandy have the same cough a few times, and figured maybe it was something in the air, not in Spotty! I could only hope! It took weeks for the HWF to arrive and by the end of June, I started Spotty on the treatment. Dr. Khalsa had all but guaranteed it to work; I prayed that it would!

THE JUMPING SPIDER

Clayton and I went to an actual appointment with Jules in early July. She'd shocked us when she told us that she was moving to New Brunswick. I knew we could all use some hands-on treatments, so we also brought a few of the dogs along and had an outdoor appointment, in her backyard. I knew that there were big shifts to be had with an outdoor, real-life treatment for me and I wasn't disappointed. She told me that my neck really wanted attention; so that is what she focused on. The next morning when I woke up, I felt different. While I was taking a walk, I surprised myself when something moved over to my left and I turned my head a bit, to see what it was!

I actually turned my head!!

I was so surprised and amazed! I guess I just had to sleep-on-it to get the full effect of the treatment! This is not to say that I could move it a great distance, but I could clearly move past the one inch off center range that I had up to that point! I no longer had to hold my neck static and that meant the constant pain and inflammation could take a breather, and so could I!

I'd found several four-leaf clovers in the following days, each one instilling me with hope for the future. I noticed that Spotty looked and felt different in the past few days, like she was gaining weight. I popped her on the scale and was pleasantly surprised! It was exactly one month since I had started her on that wonder product HWF. She had gained about five pounds! YAY!! It was working! Thanks be to God. Spotter my daughter was going to pull through; I never gave up on her.

This also marked the day that my farm property was sold for the second time. I went out on my walk that evening and an Eagle flew up and over to my right. A few days earlier I had seen it fly to the left. Something was shifting...

Near the end of July, an Eagle flanked by crows, all flying above the hay field, went off to the Northwest. These birds showed up at the moment I was asking the universe for help with my extra sore back.

The next day, an Eagle flew up from the tree by the hay field and I saw it soaring! It showed up three times in that one day!

On July 31, Joe showed up first thing in the morning, with new paperwork. He told me that the property was to close on September 11 and confirmed that October 6 was our move-out date. The new owners were planning to pull the house down; here we go again.

We'd had another failed attempt to find a new home for us near Brenda and Shane's, even though I'd seen a four-leaf clover before we'd gone.   In early August we'd driven to visit my mother in Waterloo. On our way home, I was contemplating this book and the freedom that comes from flight. I was almost home, but was still searching the sky for answers when something caught my eye up ahead.   I could see several turkey vultures soaring around in a thermal over the roadway. My eyes were looking from one to the next, when I noticed that one of these things was not the same.

"EAGLE!" I exclaimed to poor Clayton, who was startled while reading his book.

I pulled over to the side of the road and we jumped out. There it was, going round and round and round. We snapped some pictures with our phones. We watched it in awe as it effortlessly soared around in the sky, hidden amongst the turkey vultures. I know that soaring around is what turkey vultures do, in order to find food. I was pretty clear that the Eagle was there for the pure enjoyment of flying. I know I would, if I could. I realized on this day that I used to fly, with the hang glider as my wings. What if I could have that awesome experience at any time I wanted? What if I could have the freedom of flight in my life right now?

A couple weeks later on my morning walk, I was contemplating this book, and had the realization that it was time to begin to trust myself and my own inner guidance. I was calm and happy while I found another four-leaf clover. A few minutes later, I was thinking about Jules as she was going to be moving to New Brunswick soon and was trying to sell her house. What was I going to do without her? I thought about how it was time to *BE* all that *I* need. She was going away, but I could stand on my own two feet and still be living my own life.

I searched all along on my morning walk, looking for four leaf clovers. I went all the way around the field and up over the hill to the barn. Nothing. I stopped ten feet away from the barn and centered myself, realizing that I had been in searching mode. I took one step forward. As my foot was coming down, I realized I was stepping *on* a four-leaf clover! I took a picture of it and said to myself, "If I can only find one today, let it be for Jules, who was moving that day."

I took one more picture and was astonished that the second picture contained not one, but *two* four leaf clovers! I had instantly manifested the other one! I still can hardly believe it when I look from one picture to the next – the second picture has two and the first only has one!

During August, on several occasions, my writing companion had been a cute little jumping spider. It kept climbing onto my writing table and physically jumping on me. It was sort of freaking me out!

For some strange reason, I am not a big fan of critters on my skin. On this one day, it returned, even more eager to get my attention. When it would jump on me, I would place it on the ground away from me. It wouldn't take long and soon it would be back. It would climb on my computer or sit on my papers with the ultimate goal to be close to me, is all I can figure.

I wrote a text to Frienda asking her for some advice. "What do I do with this jumping spider that wants to be *on* me?"

I had gone inside to get my phone and had put the spider in the grass. It wasn't long and it was back. I took some pictures of it and sent it to Frienda. She took one look at the picture and said, "That's Araglas!" She totally thought the spider had a dog's face!

Then, I couldn't find the spider and I thought it had finally gone. What I didn't realize right away was that it was sitting on my shoulder!! It spent the rest of the afternoon there. When it was time to go in, I actually had to take my shirt off and place it on the table for the spider to get off. I went right down in front of the spider and said, "What do you want to tell me??" At that exact moment, Donnamira came over to be petted as she saw me bending down. Her bushy tail swooped across the table and the spider was gone. Araglas was gone, again.

By the end of August, we thought we'd found our perfect place! It was love at first sight, especially for Clayton! It had a beautiful kitchen and all the fancy appliances were included. It was on forty-five acres, of which thirty-five were of magical trees. That evening I found another four-leaf clover.

A couple days later, we went to see that perfect place. It was not close by, but located in a beautiful, out of the way spot, with only three places on the little gravel road. We loved it. There was even a small barn and six beautiful acres of hay.

One little problem was that someone had gotten there first. It was the same situation all over again, they had a contract on the property, but had to sell their house first. Since it had only been listed for twelve days, we thought we had a pretty good chance to get it.

I found another four-leaf clover before putting the offer in on the magical place. They sent it back, asking for almost the entire original price. They'd taken off my conditions and changed the parameters. We were planning to counter offer, when we found out that it was going to go into competition, if I sent it back and didn't accept it. It was too much money, but how could I not do it? We needed a place to live and it was perfect! I had to have faith that the money would come; so we accepted their offer.

Then, we had to wait forty-eight hours to see if the other party would firm up. When I talked to my bank, they'd said that I could get a co-signer for the extra amount that was over what I was pre-approved for. But after I put the offer in, they had come back and said they had changed their minds. They explained that I had become high risk and they were not going to honour the pre-approval at all! I needed to have a co-signer for the entire amount! What? I would not give up. I called a private lender and also a mortgage broker. I had everything lined up for inspections, as though the place was ours.

I couldn't sleep during the night so I was up with the sun, out walking the dogs, knowing that the place was ours and wondering how it would all work out. I found another four-leaf clover. Only a few hours later, I found out that the other party firmed up. We were back to the drawing board again.

It was again one of the better things that happened, but I didn't realize it at the time. It would be another year before my separation would be completed and I wouldn't give up.

BECOMING GEORGIA

At the beginning of September, during an appointment with Jules, we'd been defining the need to BE the embodiment of Georgia. The next day, I'd been standing out at the end of the pasture field and declaring to the universe: I am Georgia Elizabeth Barg! I *AM* Georgia Elizabeth Barg! Over and over, until I could believe it, all the while watching some blackbirds in the field. I turned around and went about 75 feet back into the pasture, to sit on my favourite rock. As I sat there, I noticed that quite a few blackbirds were descending on my location, to line the fence and land on the ground – exactly at my declaration spot. With the tall grass in the way and the distance, I didn't really notice the *quantity* of birds, but I could hear that there were quite a few. I was surprised that the dogs did not notice them. I had my phone and I was taking a few pictures of the ones lining the fence, as that was all I could see. Then, all of a sudden, Argibel noticed the birds! As she tore down the pasture lane the blackbirds erupted like a giant had thrown a handful of ashes up into the sky. I changed my phone to video and captured the thousands of birds rising from practically right next to me. It was an awesome experience. In that moment, I understood that it was time to let Georgia fly.

A few days later, I was looking for a small four-leaf clover without success. I declared: "I am Georgia Elizabeth Barg!" I looked down and found a large one by the drive shed. The biggest one ever! I didn't even know that they came in that variety! The next afternoon, my friend Allison came over to let Clayton play with her daughter. I see a kindred spirit in Allison and I wanted to show her the big four-leaf clover that I found. It is not often that I can ever find the same one twice, but this one was so close to the drive shed, I could find it easily. I thought it would be neat to share the experience with someone else. Who even finds them??

My great plan was to have her find it herself. I brought her in front of it and said, "It is here! You can find a four-leaf clover!" She believed me, but could not see it. Instead, she reached down about six inches to the right of it and said, "Here it is!"

What? She had found her own!

A couple of days later, I was finishing up my morning walk nearing the pasture gate when I looked down to see a four-leaf clover – right next to three more! My own little patch! "It must mean good luck today," I thought, as the dogs started barking. I looked up and they were running towards the gate by the road, where a red pickup truck had pulled up. Two men had gotten out and I tried calling the dogs, but they would not come. I walked all the way over to the road to get them and asked the people what was up. He said, they're the crew sent there to survey the land for the new owners. I asked if they were planning on pulling the house down? They didn't think so, but said they were building a storage facility behind the drive shed. At my request they connected me to the new owners.

A couple of hours later, the new owner Johnny, pulled into my lane. I told him of my predicament and wondered if he was going to need the house on October 6, which was less than a month away, or if we could stay on a while. He said that I could remain in the house until the end of February, no problem. He also offered that I could pay the same rent and he'd give me a lease, so that I didn't have to worry anymore. I found several four-leaf clovers in the days ahead; my luck was holding.

Later in September I was driving with Clayton and Argibel to Waterloo to visit my mother via Wellesley, where I would be seeing my friend Michelle. On our way, somewhere near Bright, while listening to a Michael Bernard Beckwith audiobook, a huge Eagle flew across the road in front of us! It was so large and its tail was beaming with brightness! It flew from left to right and hovered in the air, not far from the road. I have no idea what it was overtop of, because I was so busy yelling to Clayton "Eagle, Eagle, Eagle!" I fumbled for my phone to take a picture, as I stopped abruptly at the side of the road. I managed to take a picture of the clouds, the inside of the truck and even myself, but none of that Eagle! It eventually flew back across the road and soared away into the sky... while I was still fumbling around with the phone. My takeaway was perhaps to just be present with the Eagle! I had thought that my next Eagle encounter would be the end of my book! I wanted to capture it for posterity. In the end, I didn't get a picture and I also was not present with the gift that I'd just been given.

It was so cute, on my birthday, September 20, Clayton made me a double layer cake. On it was one candle in the shape of a one.

I said, "Why one candle?"

He said, "Because it is Georgia's first birthday!"

I love that child. I gave him a hug; he understood me.

A few days later, Clayton was going to be away for five days and I planned to have a Spiritual Writing Retreat stay-cation. If possible, no phone or internet – just to BE – and write. The weather co-operated with a beautiful 25°C each day, which couldn't have been more perfect for that time of year.

The first day I spent half the time setting up my table and chair way out in the field, next to my special rock. A few days later I received, what I literally called a three-Eagle day! They were seen at different times, all flying very high, yet perfectly visible from my chair. You might wonder how I got any writing done at all, with my head in the clouds!?

The next day, I wrote for a while in the morning and had my camera along. I saw an Eagle flying in the distance and tried to take a picture. I'd found a four-leaf clover in the morning so on my way out of town, I thought I'd try my luck and buy my first lottery ticket!

A few days later, I had decided to take the day off of writing, as I had been pushing myself and needed a break. All morning, I was out in the field, knowing that I needed to pick up Clayton after lunch and I wanted to just spend some time relaxing, before he came back.

I spent the longest time ever with my eyes closed, in a meditation. I did whatever felt right to me in the moment, and had the whole morning to just BE. I had not even been able to close my eyes for ten minutes before, so being out there and letting myself BE was a big stretch for me. I had to give up the thought that I was going to miss something. What if my Eagle flies by, while I have my eyes closed? What if …?

I spent quite a long time in a process that I hadn't intended. One at a time, I thought about each member of my family and the different people in my life, that I had perceived had "done me wrong" in some way. I pictured the person, thought of the worst thing that I could think of, where I had felt wronged or damaged by their actions. I only thought of the negative action long enough to acknowledge it, and then I let it go. I forgave that person for what they had done and then replaced the negative thought with a good one. Whether it was something good they had done or a positive wish for them, if nothing else good could be conjured up. Starting with each parent and sibling, to friends, neighbours and others – one by one – I let all those hurts go and let love fill my heart. I had watched the movie, *The Power of the Heart* during the week that

Clayton was away. It was the perfect complement to me actually opening my heart to life and letting love in. It had been closed for a very long time.

I stayed out there on my rock for the entire morning. I was also contemplating my inevitable lottery win. I had the winning ticket – didn't I? What would I do with all that money? Would it change me? Would I be able to finish my book in the way that I wanted? Would I be respected for my personal changes to freedom or would it be clouded by the fact that I had won so much money. Was that the ending of my book? After all that had happened? Would I win millions of dollars and live happily ever after? Was I ready to be rich? Was I ready to live?

Time was up. I had to go back to the house and get ready to pick up Clayton after my five-day stay-cation. I was walking out of the back pasture, looking for my signature clover sign. I went to the left instead of out the gate, along the middle pasture fence for about ten metres in my search. I turned toward the back of the farm, outstretched my arms and declared, "I am ready!"

"I AM READY!" I yelled to the sky.

At that moment, a large red-tailed hawk happened upon the wind. I continued to yell, "I AM READY!" I figured that it would leave, being afraid of someone standing large, arms stretched and yelling; I was wrong.

The hawk came directly in front of me. It hovered there, about three meters out and six meters above. I yelled again as tears streamed down my face. "I AM Georgia Elizabeth Barg! I AM a Peaceful Profitable Author! I AM READY!!"

At that moment, shadows landed on the ground beside me as dark figures came from behind and over my head. Three turkey vultures closely swooped around the hovering hawk. I was clear that had they been Eagles, I likely would have fainted dead away. It was a powerful moment in time.

The birds eventually dissipated and I went back to the house to get ready, but not before I checked my lottery ticket. I had not won. I didn't even have one number right. Then I read about the kind of ticket that I bought, and it was an all or nothing 45-million-dollar ticket! Every number would've had to be correct. I tossed it in the garbage and headed out to my truck.

A few days later in the morning, I saw the bright white of my Eagle's tail in the distance, diving down and out of sight. I decided to go to my declaration corner for a few minutes, before getting back to work.

In a few moments, the Eagle was back, soaring unmistakably above the back drop of the trees in the distance. Round and round in the thermals it flew, higher and higher, seemingly without a care in the world. I called out to the Eagle as I often did, "Come to me! Come by here! I am ready!"

I watched in awe as it soared effortlessly so high in the sky, until it finally disappeared into the clouds. I checked my phone and a full fifteen minutes had passed while that Eagle had stayed in my view. Wow.

I am ready. Ready for what? I pondered to myself.

Am I ready to follow my heart to freedom?

I had been calling to the Eagles "Come to me!" When in fact, it is *I* who must follow them. The freedom of flight is available to anyone who heeds the call. Will *you* come and fly with me?

Two days later, I was in the field writing a very sad tale indeed; Araglas' untimely death. It was the first time that I had actually processed the event and it was very hard on my heart. I glanced up from the screen of my laptop to see a large Eagle close by, in the pasture field, flying towards me low and slow. When I saw the magnitude of the bird that was so close to me, I was startled. The

Eagle turned instantly and went out towards the back of the farm. If I hadn't looked up right then, I wonder how close it would have gotten. I didn't realize it at the time, but I was actually deathly afraid of an Eagle coming close to me, yet it was the thing I wished for all the time!

A few days later, the jumping spider returned to me, but this time I was way out in the field. Then, just as I was writing about Thorin's passing, an Eagle came from behind me and flew over my head.

In an appointment with Jules the next day, I told her how freaked out I would have been, when that hawk was hovering over my head, if the three other birds had also been Eagles. I told her how it would have scared me, if the Eagle that had been coming low across the pasture field at me, had landed on my table. She said, "They are not trying to frighten you!"

We realized during that conversation, that I had some big fears I was not addressing. Although I asked the Eagles to come, it actually terrified me. My biggest goal was having my own property, which was admittedly also my biggest fear. She told me to go within and be with the fear instead of cowering from it.

"Ask it what it wants to show you." So, the next day, I did just that.

I sat on the rock and closed my eyes. I envisioned an Eagle coming down from the sky, talons outstretched – straight towards me. I was afraid, but stood still. I breathed deeply as I allowed the Eagle to tear me apart. It was an interesting sensation. The Eagle sat next to the broken me and I started asking questions. What do you want me to know? Why am I so afraid?

I realized that for most of my life, I had other people to guide me in making decisions. I used to have my parents to guide me, but my father was gone now for six years and my mother's mind is gone with dementia. I always looked to my husband to make my decisions, until the accident. When I think about owning my own property, it is all up to me! What if I screw it up? What if I fail? What if…?

FIRST CHAMPION ARGIBEL

One morning in early October, I woke up with the inclination that I needed to take Argibel to the last dog show of the year. Although we had taken her once the year before, I hadn't given much thought to showing, with all the stuff going on during the summer. I woke Clayton up, then asked him if he wanted to show Argibel in several shows on the upcoming weekend, and go into the Junior handler class at the show. He was game.

The night before the show, we bathed Argibel. I contacted the show coordinator to see if they had the breed standard for the Basque Shepherd – Gorbeikoa variety. Oh yes, they had a standard. I packed one along, just in case.

The next morning, we arrived just as the first show was beginning. I noticed that our breed was not on the board. We asked for it to be put on, but we were still not called. We were not in the book - they didn't even have a standard! I provided my standard and we were soon called to go in the ring, however the judge had not reviewed the standard. They said, "Oh, she is familiar with the breed!"

I thought; not likely. This is not a Nova Scotia Duck Tolling Retriever!!

When we went in the ring, the judge was French and said she had judged a specialty of them once before. I almost started crying with excitement, that she actually knew what she was looking at!! There were a lot of dog breeds in the herding group. It was new for us to be with the herding dogs, as we had always showed the Pyrenean Mastiffs in the Working Group.

Argibel took a major win with a Group First! The judge told me later, that Argibel was "exquisite!" She had even considered her for Best in Show as well! She explained, while we were having our picture taken together, that once while visiting her mother in France, she'd been asked to judge a specialty of Basque Shepherds, so she really did know what she was talking about!

By the end of the week-end, Argibel had done it! She was the first Basque Shepherd to ever be shown in Canada and was a new Canadian Champion.

I went home and sent a message to her breeder, Ixaka, in Spain. I thought he would be as excited as I was; I hadn't realized that he would be even more delighted. He asked if he could chop Argibel out of a picture that I had recently posted of our family.

I said, "Just wait a day or two and I will provide you with the show pictures!"

One afternoon a week later, I got a call that I wasn't expecting from the new owner, Johnny. He said, "I have to put the farm back up for sale."

What? He had only taken ownership thirty-two days earlier! Joe had put the farm up for sale only sixty days after taking over! What was going on here?

By that evening, the show pictures arrived in my inbox. I picked out my favourites and sent them to Ixaka, before going to bed. The next morning, I woke up to a message saying that we were famous! While I had been sleeping, they had been writing an article about us in Spain! Argibel was not only the first Canadian Champion, but also the first Basque Shepherd to win a title outside of the borders of France and Spain; they were oh so excited!!

Our family ~ (from left, clockwise) Argibel, Brandy, Georgia, Donnamira, Clayton, Éowyn and Spotty (centre bottom)

The article was published with the show picture of Clayton and I with Argibel, the new champion. We were famous and it all had started by me following my inner guidance. Perhaps I was finally getting it?

TREK TO THE TREE

There was a lady that used to come weekly to my house from the Acquired Brain Injury Clinic in Hamilton. She assisted me in learning how to set up reminders and schedules, to ensure that tasks got completed in a way that wouldn't overwhelm my brain or body. On this particular morning, in mid-October, she wanted to know if there was such a thing as a gray and brown Eagle? Um, I didn't think so, but why did she ask? When she had gone out to her car to come to my house, she had found one sitting, waiting for her. She showed me the picture of a gray and brown Eagle sitting on top of her car! It was the first time that I had ever seen a blonde Eagle, also known as a Leucistic Eagle! They have the same white head and tail of the Bald Eagle, but the rest of the feathers are much lighter than usual! I hope to someday be so lucky to see such a beautiful bird for myself, but I did find it interesting that she was on her way to see me and had such a rare Eagle encounter!

The farm showings began once more near the end of October. I thought; here we go again! We had to get everything ready and had eight showings in the first three days. I had to show the people around and answer all the questions, as the latest owners hadn't a clue about anything, since they'd only owned it for one month! I was feeling quite depressed and couldn't seem to shake it. Every time I thought we were getting a bit of a reprieve, we were back at it again.

Two days in, Johnny wanted to take an early offer he got on the farm. He said that we would have to be out in thirty days to give vacant possession. That was not going to happen. We didn't even have a clue where we could go and legally, he had to give us at least sixty days. He was still mad about this, when the gas hot water heater in the house decided to quit and he refused to fix it. It was almost two weeks before he finally installed an electric one. We sure appreciated hot water after that!

A few weeks later, I was driving to pick up Clayton when I saw an Eagle flying ahead of me. The road was winding and the Eagle veered off to the right. I tried to follow it, but lost it behind the fire station. I got back on the road and suddenly it was again close in front. To me, it was another clear sign that a shift was coming.

I had been stalled for a couple weeks, rolling around in my quagmire - wondering how I could ever get out. It was the perfect place to be in, I realized. I was pushing the current - trying to be something that I was not. I was attempting to train and become a transformational life coach, write this book, look for a home and hold it all together for my family. None of it was working and my brain was still not interested in retaining new information.

It was through the farm being put up for sale a second time, that I found my calling. During the countless showings, I met so many people that asked me to teach them how to farm! One day, Frienda finally said to me, "Why don't you make a business out of that? You don't even have to think about it – you already *have* all the information!" She was right.

By the middle of November, I finally found clarity. For six years, I had lived on the same farm and for at least five I'd hated it and wanted to leave, more than anything. I even cried every day before we moved there! It wasn't until the year 2020 that I made peace with the property, but now I feared leaving the safety of the familiar.

For the past year I had walked, out to the end of the pasture field to the gate that lead into the hay field. In the warmer months, I enjoyed walking in bare feet. Twice a day, I'd survey my surroundings, look for birds and wildlife and had my meditation rock to sit upon. This one morning, I was looking in the distance and saw a tree, standing head and shoulders above the rest. Weird. I'd never seen it before... how could I have missed it? I took a picture of it from the pasture field and put it in the back of my mind, that the tree wanted my attention. During a meditation class that day, that same tree came into my mind during the grounding exercise. I ground through AIR, I'd recently learned, so in my imagination, there I was, on top of the tree. I didn't get much deeper than that. I really understood that I needed to go and find the tree in order to get the message.

After the online class, I set off on a little hike, but the tree was farther than I thought. It was about a kilometer as the crow flies, but I am not a crow and the walk to the tree was about 1.5 km away. I took my two remaining sticky dogs along. It should have been a nice little walk, but I was terrified to go. It was already 4 PM and would be almost dark in an hour. It was the first time in thirteen months that I'd left the confines of the pasture, since Araglas had died. That day, I needed to see that tree for whatever reason; I was about to find out and went through the gates.

I had brought leashes along and attached them to the collars before we went across the railway tracks, into the bush. The whole way along, I was fearing coyotes as it was getting late in the day. My mind even entertained cougars. I hadn't walked in the bush in years either, not since I had found shotgun shells that didn't belong to us on our own property! The police had said afterwards, "Wear orange!" So I added that to my fears, the fear of being shot, attacked by wild animals, and the likes. We walked across the tracks.

Like I said, the tree was further away than I thought. In the end it wasn't even on the property, it was on John's side, in a deep valley!! Then I struggled with whether to call and ask permission, or just turn back. I could almost see the tree, but was worried about getting in trouble now in addition to being shot or attacked.

I found my courage. I would go to the tree. But there was an obstacle, a very deep creek bed that was mostly dry. I went around the one way expecting to make it to the tree, but it was still in the way. I felt like there were obstacles everywhere.

Inadvertently, we ended up tumbling into the creek bed, which to my surprise was *really* deep and the banks were *really* steep! Hmm... I've come all this way, do I just give up now? I wasn't that far away from the tree, I could have thrown a stone at it. I could at least see it. Was that good enough?

As I searched the bank for a way to get out, I saw a vine. Really? Who finds a big vine right where it needs to be, attached perfectly and seemingly strong enough to hold my weight? Apparently, I do. I climbed up the vine to safety. Argibel, the Basque Shepherd scaled the steep wall with no problems. I looked back and Spotty was still in the creek.

Spotty weighed 130 pounds and had recently pulled the adductor muscles in her rear leg. Now she was struggling to get up. Shit. I hadn't thought about that and I couldn't convince her not to come. She has always been my other shadow. So here I am, hanging onto a vine overtop of the cliff, supporting Spotty to get up. I still had a ten-pound weight lifting limit, so it wasn't exactly the best idea I've ever had; all my limitations from the accident usually kept me from adventure.

There we were, finally standing at the tree that I needed to get to so badly. Oh my, what a very tall tree! No branches at all for at least fifty feet! I put my hands on the tree and closed my eyes. What is the message? Something profound? All that effort, just to get to this tree? Where is the Eagle's nest? Where are the fireworks??

I mostly just saw the tree bark in my mind. Really? That's it? I said, "Tree, I have to go – if you have a message, I'll still be listening but it is going to be dark soon." We left via a different route out of the bush that didn't include any cliffs.

My message suddenly became very clear. It's all about the journey, not so much the destination! Fear. Peril. Adventure. Friendship. Support. I'd even used a vine to climb out and to pull Spotty to safety! I felt like Indiana Georgia!

I also realized the whole point of everything I got, that my book is about... the point is that I found peace here, within and amongst everything that happened and was going on. It's not about the peace that I thought my new property would bring me, it's about the peace that I have now. I had been making myself wrong for not being able to maintain that persistently   How can I write about it in my book and then be rolling around in muck? That day I finally understood, that it's definitely the journey and what you make of it that counts!

I had seen a few snowflakes while I was walking to the tree and back. When I returned home, I checked in with Clayton and immediately went back outside about two minutes later. It was almost dark and it had started snowing so heavily, I could barely see the path to get to the barn! I was grateful for the safe journey.

At the end of the month, I took a long walk with the dogs in the afternoon and watched an Eagle flying high in the sky. It looked so free and I wondered about the power of the wind that keeps such a beautiful creature floating in the sky like that. Later, it was time for a talk with my old friend Daryl. In our two-and-a-half-hour conversation, he helped me see that I can stop beating myself up for all the reasons that I stayed in my marriage for so long. He suggested that I have compassion for myself. What a novel thought! I would have compassion for someone else in my position, but not for myself. Hmm. It was definitely something to consider!

As part of my meditation class, we were to write out a list of our heart's desires, to help bring them into the light. This is what my desires consisted of: to run, jump, wiggle, laugh, and dance with my son. I desired to: ride my horse again; lift a bale of hay; lift anything I want to; feel comfortable in a chair; have my eyesight return to normal; have my brain back in working order; read a book of my choosing; wrestle a sheep; travel with my son, overnight on an adventure away from home and get my book published. I strongly desired having a beautiful, safe, permanent, affordable property of my own, that suits all of my needs for Clayton, myself, and our animals. Last but not least, I had a strong desire to be able to roll over and sleep on my side in bed, at least every once in a while...

TENSIONS WERE RUNNING HIGH

In mid-December, I drove the 200 km round trip to GAH to take Éowyn to the vet, as she had become suddenly very lame. I took Spotty along as well, because she had been limping since the end of September. The Craniosacral and chiropractic treatments she'd received, had not improved her condition. I had been treating Spotty for many months at this point with the HWF and it was finally completed. She looked so good and I was confident that the Heartworm was finally gone! I was so excited to be able to show Dr. Rasa that the natural approach had worked! Upon arrival, I had to wait in the truck, while they took the dogs in one at a time. I waited for hours as they did whatever was needed for t both of them. A vet tech brought them back out to the truck and I was to wait for the results. Before she went back inside, she informed me that Éowyn had CL damage and there was nothing that they could do at her age, except keep her quiet for a few weeks. Spotty too was to be only hand walked for a couple weeks. Oh, and by the way, she was still positive for heartworm!

How could that be? She looked so good!

I was distraught. Just then my counselor called to make an appointment with me. I was sitting in the truck, just starting to talk with her on the phone and WHAM! My truck shook. WTF!?

I told her that I had to go, as I noticed the red car impaled in the side of my truck! The car backed up and pulled into the parking spot beside mine. "Are you okay?" asked the little old lady.

Yes, I was okay. I jumped out to look at the damage. She got out of her car and said she was sorry, but that she was having trouble with depth perception. I snapped back that maybe she should get that checked out! She said it was hard to get into the optometrist lately. I told her to go to Walmart Vision Center, that they were accepting new people. She was worried that her son was going to be very angry with her for damaging the car, as it was barely a year old. She kept saying that he would fix the damage to my truck. I wanted to be mad with her, because she had hit my parked truck and I was already distressed and in a bad mood.

We looked at the truck and her car damage.

She said, "I am here to pick up my dog..." then faltered.

I thought; of course you are lady!

Then she tried again, this time completing her sentence... "I am here to pick up my dog's *ashes.*"

She went on about her dog and then about how her son would be mad. She wasn't worried about what her husband would say, because he was an invalid. I promptly looked in my truck for a towel. I wiped the dirt away to assess the damage and, in the end, I buffed up the lady's car as good as I could, to make it not look so bad to her son. I told her not to worry about my truck, at least she had hit "the bad side."

Moments later, a staff member brought out a little paper bag, containing her dog's ashes. She talked some more about her dog, offered once more to have the truck fixed, then thanked me for my kindness and drove away. I had wanted to be mad at her, but I couldn't. I sat in my truck and drove home.

It would be many weeks before I could get Spotty back onto the HWF treatment. Although it hadn't gotten rid of the heartworms, because apparently it doesn't work for mastiff type breeds... it was still helping. The company said that if it doesn't kill them, HWF at least freezes the worms, so they cannot do anymore damage. When she was not on it, during the following weeks, I noticed her starting to go downhill considerably. I would be happy to continue the product, at whatever the cost. I had no intention of giving up on Spotty, not then and not ever.

That evening, for whatever reason, Argibel knew there was something wrong with Éowyn and attacked her; first in the kitchen and then again out in the field. What was going on?

We were eating supper in the living room when Argibel attacked her for a third time. Clayton and I each had a bowl of hot soup with mine being on a card table. This time, Éowyn was trapped in between the desk and couch, with Argibel going to town on her. It was not long, before the other dogs had to join in the mix. The card table was upset, my favourite bowl with hot soup inside crash landed on the carpet, breaking in half, while my milk spilled onto the floor.

After the food settled alongside the table, I glanced over at Éowyn in horror! There was blood streaming from her eyes!! I believed that Argibel had bitten into her eyeballs and that she was now blinded forever! Her eyes would have to be removed? I had just come back from the vets! It was late, I was tired, how could I possibly drive back *again*? I was *so* angry with Argibel. Clayton says he'd never seen me so mad. I jumped on top of Argibel screaming! How could she have done this!? I did not know what to do with her. What if she attacked Éowyn again? What was going on?

I instructed Clayton to get a cage and set it up. We would have to keep Argibel in there for the time being. As soon as it was erected, I pushed Argibel in and ran to the office for my first aid kit. I grabbed a handful of gauze and ran back to Éowyn. I wiped her eyes down completely and held gauze on them, to try and stop the bleeding. After a time, I had the courage to pull back the gauze and look at the damage.

To my amazement, two beautiful eyes looked back at me! Oh, thank God!! Argibel had thankfully only bitten into her eye lids. Although the blood had been coming out of her eyes, it had not been from the eyeballs. I called Dr. Rasa and she told me what I could put in her eyes to prevent infection. What an ordeal! I eventually let Argibel out of the cage when I thought she had calmed down enough. I still don't know what happened there!

Although I was still tired from the day before, I decided to drive to Ohmer's farm and purchase a couple of bales of hay for my sheep. Clayton came with me for the day trip to Wellesley to get it. The way home was filled with Eagles! I stopped and jumped out of the truck at least seven times trying to get a picture of them! Clayton thought we would never get home.

A few days later, I went and sat on my rock to just BE with my connection to Georgia and Beth. "I AM Georgia Elizabeth". I felt that the connection is like a braided rope… it's three-ply, very strong. I asked what the three represents, when I thought I was only talking about two…

Outer beings: One – Georgia, Two – Beth… then the third is my inner being! Equal in strength, together we are whole and complete and can DO, BE or HAVE anything! I stood at the back pasture fence and declared like I believed it now … I *AM* Georgia Elizabeth!

A little while later, I got another call from Johnny. The farm was sold again which to me immediately represented no more showings! He'd accepted an offer of more than a million dollars for the property! The new closing date was April 6, 2021!

Eowyn on guard, on the hill, in the pasture by the barn in Caledonia

A few days later in the afternoon, a guy from the internet company arrived and was going to install faster, unlimited internet for less money! I was so excited! He called me from the driveway and I went out, only to learn he was sorry to be the bearer of bad news at Christmas, but there was no way that the tower signal was going to reach us. He explained that they were building new towers in the spring, maybe then...

But I wasn't paying too much attention to what he was saying, because an Eagle was flying right up behind him! It was coming from the field across the road and it had my full attention! It flew almost right over us and across the front lawn at the height of the tree tops.

I pointed up and he said, "Is that a Bald Eagle?"

I replied, "Yes, it is indeed!"

In the afternoon on December 24, Clayton called John and Lois to come over and share Christmas dinner with us that night. They are the original owners of the farm and had helped us countless times over the years; anything from borrowing a teaspoon of a spice or a lemon, pulling out stuck calves, removing dead bodies and everything in between! They even let us shower at their house, for the two weeks that we didn't have hot water in November.

Clayton made most of the big Christmas dinner and it was delicious. Clayton and I were going to be eating our dinner alone and we were so glad that we had invited these wonderful friends. It would be the first time in my forty-seven years of life that I was not with my family on Christmas Day.

We were blessed with snow on Christmas Eve and it continued through Christmas and Boxing Day. A few days later, while I was walking from the snow-covered field, thinking about getting my book done, there, peeping out of the snow-covered landscape was a small patch of green – which supported a four-leaf clover!! I would not give up.

ANGELS AMONG US

In early January, I started taking more notice of the time 11:11. I had been noticing that specific time, sometimes even twice a day. I hadn't really thought much of it, because I didn't know that it meant anything. It wasn't until I was in that meditation course and the ladies were talking about angel numbers. 11:11 was about new beginnings. I started to take pictures of the 11:11 with my phone and taking more notice of what was going on at that time.

After I had received the news about the property closing on April 6, I had figured that would be the date that I had to leave the farm. Johnny came by on New Year's to tell me that he still wanted us to vacate the premises by the original date of February 28. I temporarily dropped back into panic and stress mode, because I continuously searched for rentals and places to purchase, but had come up empty handed thus far.

During that winter, I became reacquainted with music and even dancing! Except for two-stepping with a partner to country songs in university I'd barely ever danced much at all. It was great to be listening to music again. One day, before travelling to look at yet another property, an amazing new song came on the radio. I thought it was odd, but I just couldn't help it; I simply had to move my body to the beat! I had never heard of the wonderful Canadian group, Tim & the Glory Boys before, but I immediately loved them! The song was called, *"When You Know You Know."*

On the day I first heard the song, I had hoped it meant that we would be finding that special property... but instead, I was clear after seeing it, it was not the right one. It might have been an affordable price, but oops, the house had fallen off the bluff into Lake Erie, and likely the rest of the property would eventually follow suit too!

After I heard that special song a few more times on the radio, I looked it up online. I listened to it at least once a day, and I would dance my heart out. One day, when Clayton joined in and was dancing with me, he exclaimed that it was the most fun we'd ever had! It was one thing that I could do to experience joy in each day; something that had been sorely missing in my life. There was no way that I could stay still, and remain sad or mad while listening to that song! If I could find Joy even for two minutes and fifty-seconds, it brightened up the rest of my life immeasurably!

In early February, while I was driving home from some appointments in Hamilton, I began to get a little worried that I only had three weeks, before I was to be out on the street. During the course of that day, I saw twenty-five red-tailed hawks! They were not all together in one place, although I did see five soaring in a group on that drive home. I knew that a message of hope must be coming – I prayed it would. All I needed was for an angel to show up and be the messenger of hope.

There were only three days remaining, before I was supposed to leave. I had been selling off many of my belongings, because I didn't have anywhere to take them.

Blain, my neighbour, who bought a large quantity of items, was loading up his wagon when I saw a very large dark coloured bird, flying right behind him. It was huge and flying very low, lower than the roof of the barn or drive shed. I just saw it before it went behind the barn, so I had to run around the end to catch sight of it again before it was gone. I kept running to the next corner to catch another glimpse! The only defining feature that I could make out was a small, thin white line on its tail. I went inside the house and looked it up online, I was wide-eyed in amazement! Wow! It was my first ever Golden Eagle! I hadn't even realized that they were also in Ontario!

Riding high after seeing that magnificent bird, Clayton and I drove to Wellesley to pick up some more hay from Ohmer. On the way home, I got a call from an angel. It was Michelle; she had a big idea. She suggested that they could build an apartment for us on the back of their house, if I loaned them all of the money that I was to receive from the farm sale and divorce. Years earlier, together with her husband Harold, they had bought Ohmer's Home Farm and now ran the dairy there. It was the same house that I had eaten lunch at, each day for most of twelve years, back when I worked for Ohmer.

The next day, I was thinking about Michelle's offer and it sounded really great to me, although I wasn't sure when I would be getting the settlement. It would be good to go back from whence I came; and basically return home. I could be nearer to family and friends and not be alone anymore. Clayton's dad had been pushing for him to enter the public school system; I decided to check out the school that Clayton would be enrolled in, if we moved to Michelle's. There, on the website, I got the sign I needed. Wellesley Public School "Home of the Eagles!"

Our scheduled day for leaving the premises on February 28 arrived in short order. Although I did a lot of research into the apartment idea, it was not going to be built in time, and I still didn't have anywhere to go. I contemplated buying a live-in camper trailer for the summer. I got permission from the township, so figured it was the best idea for the short term. The new buyers of the farm were not taking over until April 6, so I figured I had a bit of time, although the landlord did not to think so.

In the morning, I had an appointment with Dr. Tunks. A certain person had been saying that I should be working full time and I set out to find out from my specialist, if they were right. I compiled a list of things to discuss with him.

I explained to him that I had trouble learning new things. I had been trying to re-train in a new profession, that didn't require physical exertion like farming does. I thought I would try my hand as a transformational life coach, but I couldn't seem to retain any of the information or concentrate on the videos. He declared, "You would not make a very good life coach".

I explained that I planned to start my new business, at *LearnToFarm.ca* and do farm consulting – teaching beginner farmers to farm.

He continued, "Same with life coaching, you cannot expect that you will be able to take in someone else's problems and then formulate answers to those problems, it's just too much".

I further explained that I wrote a 110,000 word manuscript in the fall, but can't read or edit it. He answered, "You shouldn't expect that you could."

I relayed to him that I bought a paperback book, that didn't come in audiobook. I related to him my issues with trying to get through the first chapter and then having no recollection of what I had read only a couple days later. I just couldn't understand or retain stuff!

He affirmed, "You can't expect to read like you used to. You must take it one paragraph at a time, read it through slowly, out loud and then take a few word notes, take a break, come back later and do another paragraph."

I voiced how I used to enjoy reading books in the bathtub.

He responded, "Not anymore".

Then he asserted, "You can't work full time, you can't even work part time. You have no competitive advantage and likely couldn't get a job anyway – and if you did, you likely wouldn't be able to keep it very long, it would be too draining emotionally."

Well, although this kind of final declaration would do me nicely in court, it was not what I expected him to say. I thought he would say, "Yes you should be able to work." I was a little overwhelmed with this information. I did not want to remain disabled; I was not going to give up.

DIGGER, MY BEST MATE

At the beginning of March, I decided to sell most of our stuff. If we were going to be in a camper, then we needed to unload a lot of the baggage that we had. We had been repeatedly packing, unpacking and repacking, for a couple years at this point and I kept letting stuff go each time. A lot of large furniture just had to go. Clayton contemplated selling his fish tank, because we could not take it into a camper.

A few days later, we sold the 8 x 12 foot building that had been originally built for the puppies, the one that had caused so many problems with the county. Clayton had wanted to have it for a chicken coop at the new place, but since we didn't have a proper place it was time to let it go. As the local buyer was tying the flimsy building onto his trailer, I looked up and saw a Bald Eagle flying around and round in a thermal above the barn. I pointed up while running to the house for the camera! I got a great picture of that four-year-old Eagle.

The next day, Donnamira was continuously barking to get my attention. I know better than to ignore her, so I went out to the end of the drive shed, to see what the fuss was about. There was another Eagle, flying low over the pasture field.

To simplify our move and travelling, I sold half of my remaining twelve sheep to Ohmer, and delivered them to him myself. On the way, I talked to the Planning and Building Departments in the township about the apartment, septic, camper, and the likes. When I was with Ohmer that day, telling him of all my plans, he just kept encouraging me by saying, "Anything is possible!"

It was already March 12 and I was running out of time to find a structure for us to live in. In the morning I looked at a forty-foot camper trailer and it reeked so highly of cigarette smoke, that I could not bear it. There was only one other reasonable option and I drove a long way to see it. I had high hopes since it was half the price of the first one and had the model title, "Golden Falcon."

I ended up buying it from a shady character, that didn't seem so at the time. I hadn't been able to find anyone to help me pick it out, but with only one option to choose from, it might not have made any difference.

After a few days I was regretting my decision. I would have lost my $3000 deposit and the trailer, if it were not for my good friends, Christine and her husband Dennis. If you remember, Christine was the friend that stayed over for days when Litter B was being born. Christine told Dennis of my plight and he sprang into action. He had already been coaching me over the phone for a week or two, about what to look for. Now I had a trailer that I couldn't get, was going to lose altogether, as well as my deposit! I was at the end of my rope and thankfully they jumped in to save me.

On March 15, with the help of my neighbour Blain, I managed to get my "pet rock" from the back of the pasture field and loaded onto a skid in the back of my truck. That large boulder was my load to drive to Wellesley. I met Dennis at 8 AM with the rest of the cash to pay for the trailer. Thinking he would be making good time, I drove to Wellesley in the early afternoon with my meditation rock from the pasture field.

When I got there, I asked Michelle if I could use their loader tractor to unload my pet rock. She apologized when she couldn't find it and said it was probably away getting fixed! What to do now? I didn't want to bring it home again; it was way too big to go on the moving truck. So, what to do when I need help? I drove to Ohmer's place as it was only five minutes away.

"Ohmer?" I asked, "Can you please babysit my pet rock for a few weeks until I get moved?"

He made a funny comment and then left to get his loader tractor. I was very grateful that the rock was at least staying in the neighbourhood and I would be able to pick it up again in the near future.

After the rock was taken care of, Ohmer and I went to look at my sheep that I had brought him only the week before. As we stood by the sheep pen, a large black figure caught my attention!

Swoosh!

A huge, low flying Bald Eagle, skimming just over the rooftop of the low sheep shed!

"Did you see that!?" I exclaimed!

"Was that a Bald Eagle?" he asked.

"Yes!"

He remarked, "Well, I guess they are around here".

To me it felt like I had come full circle that day. Many years before, it had been with Ohmer just a short distance down the road, where I had seen my very first wild Eagle. I had no idea of just how complete the circle would get, but I was reminded again to NEVER GIVE UP!

Dennis started the long 600 km round trip from his home in Sarnia, which included getting the money from me, driving to St. Catherine's where he'd spent all day trying to get the trailer out of a backyard, then getting it licensed and then following the tow truck all the way to Wellesley, to get it set up.

It was late in the evening when the trailer finally arrived. Dennis suggested that we cover it with a large tarp, to ensure it wouldn't get wet inside, before he'd have a chance to return and set it up. We had run out of time and if it wasn't for him, we wouldn't have had a place to live. I was extremely grateful.

Two days later, Clayton and I went back to Wellesley to meet up with Dennis. He did a basic set up for us and helped me figure out what I needed to accomplish in the ten days before moving! There was quite a list, but somehow I managed to find the people to get it done! While we were there, a familiar black figure was gracing the sky! Of course, it was! We hadn't given up and it was all coming together! Clayton and I raced across the field, hand in hand, in an attempt to catch up with the high soaring Eagle!

It was already March 19 and I'd been trying for a couple weeks to get a temporary kennel license for my dogs at Michelle's place. I couldn't seem to get a hold of the proper lady and I was getting worried as they said it could take up to six months! I had only one week's time remaining and needed to know! I had left a message with the by-law department at the beginning of the week, but hadn't heard back. A couple of days earlier, I had sent the full payment for getting a new kennel and licenses with an apology letter, since I thought I had dropped the ball. Maybe they weren't getting back to me because I hadn't filled out the proper forms and paid the fees in time!

My phone rang on Friday afternoon. The screen on my phone showed "Wilmot Township By-law" calling... I took a deep breath and answered.

They said, "I am really sorry..."

OH NO!! I almost started to cry, because they were telling me I couldn't get a kennel license – what to do?

She continued, "…for causing you undue stress about the kennel license. We have decided to change the by-law. We are allowing you to have your dogs as livestock protection dogs under the new by-law!"

She said, "We want to keep up with the times and with more coyotes coming to the area, more people are going to be like you and want livestock protection dogs. We will refund your $600 kennel fee and you just need to pay for the license for each dog. Don't worry, it will all work out."

I *did* start crying then – I thanked the woman profusely for making my day! I really needed a win right about then and knowing that my girls would be safe, legal and with me, took a load off. I was flying high until evening when I got a surprise I could hardly bear.

Two days earlier, I'd had a conversation with my dearest, beloved horse Digger. I told him the good news; that we were moving back to Wellesley, since we finally had a place! I explained to him that he, the sheep and Isabella the llama, would be temporarily staying at a friend's place, and that I'd go there to look after them each day. It would only be for a while, until I could put up some fences at the new place. I climbed in the pen and gave him a big hug, assuring him that we were finally going to be good, since moving was not far away.

The next day an older fellow, who had bought some items from me had come back to help out. He'd only been near a horse one time in his life and was terrified. Digger hung his head into the alleyway and although the man was afraid, I got him to pet Digger and feed a little hay for a treat! The man was grateful and said it was an experience he would never forget.

The next morning, he returned to pick up some old wood. He had offered to build a ramp for us and the dogs, free of charge. It would help us get in and out of the new trailer. I handed him an apple and said he could give it to Digger. We went out to the barn, but Digger wasn't there. We looked for and loaded pieces of wood for about three hours. Although I saw Digger out in the pasture, he didn't come in for the apple that day.

In the evening, I fed the sheep and again looked around for Digger. Where was he? He wasn't always there, but he didn't usually miss two meals in one day. I didn't have to look far. I saw his leg sticking out from behind the small red sheep feeder.

No.

This is not happening.

It is not.

I am not sure my feet even hit the ground in the large bound I made from one barn to the other. I ran down the alleyway and sprung through the gate; over to my boy. He was not in his own usual place, but in Isabella's favourite spot. He was lying flat on his right side, stretched out on the straw. My beloved constant companion, adventure buddy and friend of over twenty-seven years lay lifeless before me. I am certain that the sound that came from deep inside me would have frightened any onlookers. I was also sure that my wailing could be heard around the neighbourhood, but I didn't care. The pain that I felt at that moment was so great, I could not keep it in.

I laid my face in his hair and wept uncontrollably for quite a long time. With Digger's passing, my major grounding male influence was gone. The only males left on the property were my son and Red, the Ile De France ram that Clayton had picked out. One phase of life was ending and a new one beginning. I just couldn't see that at the time. My Digger was gone, and I felt so incredibly alone.

My Digger, in February 1994 ~ the day I found him in the field
amongst the two hundred horses

NOT A HAPPY CAMPER

In preparation for our move into the camper trailer, Clayton decided to let his fish go. He really loved his fish, but there was no room for them at the inn, so we placed an ad on Kijiji.

I was contacted by a guy named Scott, who wanted to pick up the fish tank starter package that evening. He got the fish from Clayton and the only other thing I remember saying to him, was that we were moving into a camper and that is why he couldn't keep his fish. Then he left.

That same night while Clayton and I were eating supper, I got a text message from Scott saying something like, "You seem overwhelmed." I thought, um yeah. I replied with the likes of, "Yes, I am." He wrote back that he was a single, retired, gentleman and was offering to help me, realizing I had to move by the week-end. From his observation, I was not ready at all. I needed help so badly, that I barely even had to think about a response. Usually, I would run something like this past Frienda before responding, but in this case I trusted my own self for once. I quickly responded, accepting his help, not having any idea what that would look like.

I had been looking for a cap for my truck for months, maybe years by then. I needed it to transport the girls on moving day and I was clearly running out of time. I had put an ad on Kijiji months before and had reposted again. I hadn't been fussy on colour, really anything would work, except beige. I'd been offered one a couple months earlier for $1200, far away and of course it was beige. Now my time was up and a local man in Caledonia contacted me saying, that he just bought a truck with a cap he didn't need. $700 in good condition; I was very excited! Did he have a picture? Yes. I opened the picture... you guessed it! Beige. Oh well, they say to focus on what you want instead of what you don't want. All I had requested was beige – not! Same thing had happened when I got my truck – anything but white and guess what? Well I got a Pearl truck, but might as well have been white! In the end, the guy delivered and installed the cap as well. I was thrilled to have a safe way to transport my girls!

While they were installing the cap, Scott showed up to help. After the other fellows left, he let me know that he'd been raised on a farm. We walked around, looking at things that still needed to be accomplished. He stayed for five hours that day! He came back the next morning and stayed all day, for eight hours. He was there when the Porch Guy, arrived with the beautiful, newly made ramp from my scrap wood. It was huge and in four large pieces, so that it was possible for the movers to easily put it in their truck. Porch Guy reached into his pocket and found that the apple he'd planned to give Digger the few days earlier was still there. I had to tell him what happened. He threw the apple into the pasture as a last gesture to a great horse.

It was the day before I was moving and Scott, after seeing the porch guy size, suggested that he did not think all my stuff was going to fit into one truck! I called the movers and said, "I think we might have a problem!"

On moving day, I woke up quite early and was planning on taking the dogs on a little walk, one last time. As I came up the path in the pasture field, I saw a figure close by but behind the fence, in the back pasture. I had been talking to my sister Brenda on the phone when I cried out loud, "Coyote!" The Pyrenean Mastiffs ran straight towards it, but the center fence line was in between. I hadn't been planning to go very far for the walk, as it was wet and muddy. I didn't have rubber boots on and didn't want the girls to get all dirty. The big girls had to go to one end or the other to get around the fence, but Argibel went right through.

They chased the coyote across the field. I saw a dark figure booking it from the back corner after it had gone up and over the two-acre treed hill and was out the other side. It was running flat out along the edge of the hay field to the forest beyond. Then, what should I see but a carbon copy of the first, doing exactly the same. There were *two* coyotes! But it was what I saw next that had me running and yelling at the top of my lungs!

Straight in line with the other two, but this time a red streak was chasing after the coyotes! Up and over the end of the hay field and across the tracks into the forest – one, two, three – gone! I put my sister on mute and I yelled as loud as I possibly could, "ARGIBEL!!"

I couldn't believe it. How could she run away on moving day? I was glad I had my sister to talk to that morning, because I was beside myself. It didn't take too long before she decided to come back home, but it was long enough to make me wonder if I had done something bad in a past life. What was going on?!

The movers came about an hour late and Scott had been right, everything did *not* fit on the truck! They eventually left a big pile of stuff that they would pick up the next day – we were leaving for good right then. I loaded up the dogs and Clayton in the truck. I hugged my trusty helper Charlotte tightly, shed a tear and said good-bye. The rain had started and the darkness was falling, by the time the movers arrived at the camper.

Before Clayton and I showed up at Michelle's, the moving truck had gotten stuck three times in the pasture field. As per usual, Ohmer was there to save the day. He came to the rescue and kept pulling them out, ensuring that all was continuing to move forward. After the camper items were unloaded, Ohmer had lifted off the heavy items with the tractor. He went with the movers to show them where to unload the rest of our stuff that would be staying in storage, in the apartment on his property. It was the same apartment that we were supposed to move into the year before, and also where my rock temporarily resided.

The rain did not let up through the next day when the movers came back with the rest of my stuff. It had sat out in the driveway overnight and now the boxes were falling apart; some stuff was wrecked and ruined.

My sister Sue had come by the first morning to help us unpack the kitchen stuff into the camper. We could hardly move around in there. With the five dogs, boxes, dog beds and then people; there was just no room. Rachel came over later in the day, in the pouring rain. She helped me set up some electric flexi-netting for the dogs, to keep them contained. Before that, they'd just been in a small area that we fenced off right in front of the camper. It was dark and raining, but the movers helped with this chore.

A few days later, I was on my way home from doing morning chores where I housed the sheep 11 km away. I stopped at the end of the road, where I had to turn down to go to get to the camper. I was in a hurry to get back, because Scott was coming from an hour and a half away to help, but there was something that I needed to do! Apparently early, he was driving around to check out the neighbourhood and happened upon me, standing in the ditch.

"What are those for?" he inquired, gazing at the row of orange flags I was placing along the roadside at the corner.

"Well, I am trying to make the corner more visible, because I keep driving past it." Trying not to be embarrassed about being caught, I pointed down the road.

"Do you see that farm peeking out behind the hill on the right? I lived in that house for fourteen years and managed the pig barn there. The whole time I lived there, I travelled this route several times a day in order to look after my sheep, which were located 4 km away. I also ate lunch every day except Sunday at the house where the camper is now. Even though I moved away eleven years ago, for some reason, I keep driving back to my old home; I have to turn around and come back. So, there you have it. That is why I am marking the turn - so I notice it! I keep driving there, from whatever direction I come from, I can't seem to help it. When I lived in Caledonia, I couldn't hardly get anywhere without the GPS. Here, I haven't turned it on once, but maybe I should, because my muscle memory always takes me back there. It's the actual house where Clayton was born. It is the house I first moved into as an adult and lived there, almost as long as I lived in my childhood home in Scarborough. It's the only place that ever felt like home to me."

I got into my truck and he followed me back to the camper.

The first week at the camper was kind of chaotic. We were short a few amenities, could barely move around with all the boxes and it was freezing cold. It cost over $200 that first week alone, to heat the camper above 12°C. The propane stove would gas us every time we turned the furnace on, so we had to throw away the stove and cap it off. When it rained, the water leaked into Clayton's bedroom. We couldn't have water hookup, because of the freezing temperatures. It was fine for the first night to use the bathroom in the main house, but after that, they kept locking the door when they went to bed, so we were basically "shit out of luck" quite literally. Oh, and when it was windy, the camper would rock so much, it would make me seasick. To say it plainly, we were not happy campers!

After a few days, my sister Sue offered us a lifesaving device, which we gratefully accepted. Although not fancy, Luggable Loo was a welcomed addition to our family. It was basically a 5-gallon pail with a toilet seat and lid on it. It helped to make life a little more bearable. The ability to go to the bathroom when needed is a luxury I'd never had to worry about before. When we got tired of eating cold food, Scott loaned us his camping stove to cook some hot meals. We had no internet and apparently it was going to be impossible to get it. We were cut off from the world, but at least we had a place to call home!

One week in, my permanent plans started to fall off the rails. I was already getting very tired of having my sheep and llama so far away. With driving back and forth twice a day just to see them and then spending the rest of the day securing our basic needs, there wasn't a lot of time leftover. I didn't realize there was a problem until the day when I asked Michelle about putting up the permanent fence in the pasture. She started to back paddle and my heart sank.

It took weeks for me to find a four-leaf clover in the couple acres of pasture, that I walked every day with the dogs. It gave me hope and I had no idea how much I would need that very shortly.

It had been raining for several days and my favourite, lightweight, old pair of rubber boots that I had walked so many miles in, decided to wear out. The grass in the pasture where we lived, always seemed to be wet, either with dew or rain. I was so tired of having wet feet, especially with no way to bathe or warm them up! I had been unable to find my footwear, it was either completely lost or lost in storage! We had searched through the boxes and bins in storage three times already looking for my work boots, rubber boots and another pair of running shoes. Little did I know that wet feet were the least of my worries!

I had done a few loads of laundry at a place in nearby New Hamburg and had even bathed once, which was as a luxury compared to the cold sponge bath I'd been having. Imagine my surprise the day I got a text message, telling me that with the latest lockdown order, the landowners are no longer going to allow us to come in their house for bathing or laundry. Oh, and the local laundromat burned down, so the closest one is over thirty minutes away. I was already so stressed with all the driving to my sheep, that I knew I just couldn't add that to my list of things to do.

A short time later, Ohmer called to say that the stuff we had in storage would not be accessible for six to seven weeks. A small family was temporarily moving in there *with it* for that time. I was supposed to take out what I needed. Take it out and put it where, I thought. Could this day get any worse? I didn't think so, but I was wrong.

Next, I found out from Michelle that the idea of building the apartment was a flop. She said we could still stay in the camper for the summer, but that we needed to search for a new place to live. I walked out into the pasture field, dumbfounded, curled up on the wet grass and wept.

A short time later, I received a text from Frienda that said, "Do you know what day it is?" I looked at the calendar. Holy crap. This was all happening on the third anniversary of our accident! After three years, how could I be in such a state? Were things ever going to settle down and improve? In those three years, I lost my marriage, my farm, my home, my cows, my horse, my three beloved male dogs Araglas, Dirk and Thorin. And now we were homeless, living with wet feet, wondering where each meal will come from, and where will I wash my hands, my body and my clothes? All the while being completely oblivious to the outside world with no TV or internet.

My beautiful girls were going stir crazy in the camper. The seven of us made it quite crowded in there. The four big girls weighed about 130 pounds each and Argibel was about 45. They were not getting enough exercise and were often muddy and wet after being outside. This made the inside of the camper dirty, smelling like wet dog and created a damp feeling that was hard to shake. Occasionally, the windows would be so wet on the inside with condensation and there was no way to get them dry. The dogs started to fight amongst themselves. At one point, the four of them were in a terrifying kerfuffle and Clayton and I were cast into the back corner by the bathroom, yelling at them and trying to break them up, while barely staying out of the fray. Things were looking bleak.

On the way home from feeding the sheep, I stopped in at the storage at Ohmer's because I needed some Kleenex. I had been crying so much and had grown tired of wiping my nose on my sleeve, especially since I now had no way to do my laundry! I was feeling so incredibly sorry for myself, even sobbing as I drove. How could my life be so messed up? Living in a camper with yet another looming eviction seemed a whole lot more daunting than the other evictions we faced, on the 60-acre farm where all our animals were safely fenced and together with us, in a proper home. What was I going to do? As I pulled in Ohmer's lane, feeling the lowest of the low, I found out once again that hope floats!

There, looming large, right in front of me, swooping right down almost to my windshield was a Bald Eagle! WOOSH! And then up and gone! I continued in the lane, parked back behind the apartment and took a deep breath. That was definitely a sign for me! That low flying Eagle very certainly appeared to tell me to NEVER GIVE UP! I got out of the truck and went into storage, took one more look for my boots, found some Kleenex and drove back to the camper with renewed hope.

A few days later I'd found a couple more four-leaf clovers and with their pictures on my phone, I was able to carry on with my little reminders of hope! I had to resign myself to only driving to look after the sheep, once per day going forward. My brain felt like it was on fire most of the time and the extra drive was just about killing me. My friend Em, who lived at the place where they were staying, said she would keep an eye on them when I wasn't there. I didn't feel very good about not seeing them, but had to take care of myself too, so I gave them extra food and water when I did visit. The water had frozen on a few occasions, so the tap had cracked, making it wet in one part of the pen.

One morning I got a call from Em, saying I'd better come over. When I got there, I was surprised and alarmed to see my sheep knee deep in water! The sheep had apparently turned the tap on during the night and Em had only noticed it when the water started to come out of the barn, running uphill! I used up all of the straw I had, trying to get the pen dry, but to no avail. Eventually I had to let them out on the wet pasture, so that they weren't just standing in the wet pen all the time. Whatever I did, it wasn't enough; the problems were just beginning.

At the end of that month, I had a wonderful long talk with my old friend Daryl. After he had said everything that he needed to say, I gave him a brief synopsis of the previous six weeks. He said, "I don't have time to wait for you to figure this all out... what there is for you to get is, that YOU MATTER!!"

He suggested dealing with each situation starting with: "If I matter, what will I do now? If I matter, what questions will I ask? If I matter, what actions will I take?"

The next day, three out of five lambs were so incredibly lame when I went to do my chores, they could barely hobble into the barn to be fed. Sadly, they all had foot scald which is caused by having wet feet. My own feet also hurt from being wet each day, so I sort of understood how they felt. The problem spread to the other sheep and it would be many months before they would finally be free from it. I told Michelle that I needed to bring the sheep to the camper.   Originally, I was planning to wait until I had put up permanent fencing, but since I wasn't going to be staying long term, I still needed to have them with me. I could not keep doing the drive and now the sheep needed extra attention and a dry place to land, as soon as possible.

At the end of April, I drove all the way to Hamilton for an appointment with Dr. Tunks. I told him about the constant brain fog and how it was worse since moving to the camper; it was like my brain was on fire.   We again discussed decreasing the brain medication.

He repeated what he'd said before, "It's not forever and it's not a cure. You are overloading your brain!"

He then suggested that I do a task for fifteen minutes and then take a break for five minutes; repeat, all day long. The only way that I was going to get my head to cool off, was to stop the fog before it started.   Once the brain was on fire, it was too late. Sometimes it took days to feel any better.

We again discussed my inability to read and edit this book. Last time I was certain he'd said that I could not do it, but this time he made sure that I knew that I could. I needed to re-train my brain to be able to read again. He said to read a few sentences and then make a note of one or two words that would be descriptive of what I had read and write them beside.   He suggested to just take it a few sentences at a time and slowly, my brain would begin to believe that it can understand what I was reading.

We discussed posture as well. He said people that break their neck often walk around like a bird afterwards – with their neck forward. He had me doing exercises to help bring my head back into a good position. Although I still didn't move from my coffin-like position while I slept, I was given renewed hope that I may actually recover someday.

Isabella guarding some lambs at the farm near Flesherton

On the first day in May, Scott and Porch Guy came with me to collect my animals and belongings from Em's place. They had helped make ready an old pen for them that was located only twenty feet away from the camper. I was overjoyed to bring the sheep and Isabella home with us at Michelle's. We might not have been home yet, but at least we were all together again!

Going Home

A few days later, early in the morning, my phone rang. I muttered to myself, "Everything always works out well for me," as I'd grown accustomed to doing before answering the phone. It was Ohmer. He said he had some news; I braced myself...

"The renters at the Hohl Place just gave me notice. Would you be interested in renting it?" he asked.

My mind reeled. "Pardon?" I asked him to repeat himself, because I was sure that I hadn't heard correctly.

He said that in addition to the Hohl house, the rental would include: the old empty pig barn, a chicken coop, Digger's old house, a garden and some grass for pasture. The renters had given short notice, and were leaving in only three weeks after being in the house for six years.

I could hardly believe it!! The Hohl Place was going to be available and we would be returning to the spot that Clayton was literally born in. It was time to start packing again, but this time we were finally going home.

Scott worked with me side-by-side cleaning up the only usable space for the sheep in the old pig barn, while Porch Guy fixed up Digger's house and the chicken coop too. I had to clean my old office out with a shovel! Ohmer could feel my distress about the condition of the property and took the opportunity to use his tractor, to clean up the outside of the barn. He worked on it for about twenty-five tractor hours and it looked much better! Scott and I took a trip to the dump, with 300 kg of garbage from the office and the space where I wanted to keep the sheep. That wasn't including anything that could be sold, salvaged, or was wood or metal! I wasn't sure what had happened to the barn since I'd been manager there, but I was doing what I could, to clean it up a bit.

The following week, Ohmer called and described that there was an Eagle sitting in the field by his place. I asked if it was still there as I would've driven over to see it. He said it was gone, but he wanted to tell me.

I said, "I have only seen a sitting Eagle a few times and the last time was right before my accident!"

The very next day, we headed to the Hohl Place, Porch Guy was following close behind and Scott was in the passenger seat of my truck, when I slammed on the brakes and practically jumped from the vehicle!

"Look at that!" I whipped out my phone to take a picture! There in the field, standing with two turkey vultures was a large Bald Eagle! A sitting Eagle! What must this mean? A shift is coming and I hope it's a good one!

Two days later, I was sitting on my rock outside of the camper when the black dot caught my eye in the sky. I put my glasses on and gazed into the distance. Yes! I ran into the camper and quickly got my camera. There circling around over Michelle's barn was the Eagle... heading towards my new home!

I had been seeing the Angel Numbers 1111 everywhere for a while again. I'd look at the clock or get into the truck at 11:11 or 1:11. When I was putting the dog food on the scale, invariably at times, maybe even every bowl full, it would stop at 1pound 11.1 ounces or 1 pound 1.1 ounces. Every night at 11:11 PM for quite a long time, one of the *Tim and the Glory Boys* songs would come on the radio and I would dance my heart out. In addition to the original *"When you know you know"* song, they had released such a fun tune called *"Man Without A Prayer"*. The hillbilly blue grass beat was so invigorating, it brought my vibration up before bed each night. How in the world, one of those songs managed to encompass 11:11 every night, I'll never know! What it did help me to remember, was that the angels were watching over me…

The people moved out on the May 21 and Clayton and I went to work in the garden on May 24. We were planting together all day, barefoot in the dirt – so happy to be working towards our future instead of pack, pack, unpack and repack like our last few years had been. We stepped on the grass to put our shoes on and right next to my shoe was a four-leaf clover! I found one and then another and another… FIVE in total! Wow! Clayton was very impressed, as he had yet to ever find one. He looked down next to his shoe and there it was! He found another and another! His first ever four-leaf clover turned in to three of them! We looked at each other and burst out laughing! We knew we were finally home!

It was a couple of days later, Clayton and I met with the principal of Wellesley Public School. Clayton had never been in a school before and we thought a tour might help him feel better about having to attend. The strange thing was that it was devoid of people. With everything mostly still locked down, there were no teachers or students to be seen. The hallowed halls were eerily quiet and the lights were run on motion sensors so as we moved into each darkened room, it lit up to its usual brightness. The thing that caught my attention, first on the outdoor sign and again covering an entire wall in the main hall was: "Home of the Eagles."

Without having the school full of people, it was hard for Clayton to get a true understanding of what it would be like. I had mixed feelings about having to send my boy to school after he'd been homeschooled all the time. I had been struggling with helping him since the brain injury and I would welcome a break from having to mark his papers.   His dad had written it into the separation agreement and I had agreed, in order to avoid yet another conflict. Although Clayton wasn't sold on the idea, I did find hope in the tour of the school that day and a their sign. It was literally a giant sign with a cartoon Eagle that gave me hope that this was the best decision!

May 29 was finally moving day.   The same movers went to Ohmer's storage and loaded everything up and brought it directly to the house. After it was unloaded, we went over to the camper to get the rest of the furniture and boxes. I never thought I would be so happy to see my washing machine!! I had been doing my laundry in Michelle's dairy barn, using the washer and clothes rack to hang them dry; all of our clean clothes had smelled like cows!

My first day in the new home that was really our old house, I did eight loads of laundry and hung them on the line. The weather was perfect for drying and I got all caught up in one day! I was noticing also how grateful we were to have a 300 square foot kitchen! We stood there and marveled in awe at all the space. We realized that it was the same size as the entire camper that the seven of us had spent the past nine weeks in!

The dogs had moved with us, but the sheep and Isabella were still back at the camper for a couple more days. I needed to bring my girls home as the picture wasn't complete without them and I didn't want to wait any longer to get help. I borrowed Michelle's trailer and asked her daughter Abby to help. Clayton came along and Ohmer met us there with his tractor and wagon. He once again loaded up my rock, sheep feeder and the other large items on the wagon. Abby and Clayton lifted the multitude of gates onto the hay forks of the loader. I backed up the trailer and opened the door for the sheep. They ran straight into the trailer with no fuss! Even Isabella didn't need any coaxing! I guess they too were ready to go home. We closed the door and headed down the road.

We had a birthday party for Clayton on June 2. Em brought her four children, while Michelle came with her two youngest. Clayton had spent so much time playing with these children ever since we had arrived only nine weeks earlier. It was eleven years to the day that we had moved out, on Clayton's birthday and here we were, back again! The joy of the day was catching, and we all had a good time. What a long time it had been since we'd had any fun, felt calm or settled. Here we were surrounded by friends and laughter; finally, home.

HOME OF THE EAGLES

Clayton had been jumping on the trampoline at Michelle's a few weeks earlier and her eight-year-old son had flown into Clayton's jaw – impacting with his head! Clayton had been very sore in his neck and back. Jules suggested going to a chiropractor. I hadn't found a new one yet and needed to find a good one too. Clayton was deathly afraid of going to the crunching kind and Jules knew this. She said, "You need to find a Network Chiropractor."

I had never heard of such a thing. She suggested Lisa Simpson for Neurospinal Care. I looked up the website and there were so many words on it, all I saw was the word BRAIN everywhere. Brain this and brain that – which was exactly what I needed; not only help with my body, but help with my brain! I made appointments for both of us.

Lisa felt quite certain that she could help me reconnect my brain to my body through my spine. She explained that when the upper neck gets damaged, the body goes into survival mode and she felt I was still in that state. Now that I was finally getting settled in my home, I could begin to heal, especially the inflammation in my brain.

The next morning, while watering the sheep, I was thinking about Digger and how his house was now housing the sheep! I looked at the ground as I climbed over the fence to get the buckets. There was the tallest four-leaf clover I had ever seen! It was much taller than everything else and it most certainly didn't want to be missed! I crouched down beside the tall clover and took a picture, with Digger's house in the background. My special Digger hadn't been able to make the trip back home, but his house was here! It gave me a constant reminder that he is always right here with me, in my heart! That evening I found five more four-leaf clovers.

In early June, Clayton and I had a Thank-You Party for the two random Kijiji guys that turned out to be angel helpers, Scott and the Porch Guy! Clayton cooked up a big dinner with lamb and vegetable kabobs and much more. I had been pretty much living in coveralls for most of Clayton's life. The previous year he'd expressed to me, that he couldn't remember ever seeing me in a dress. Being a farmer and wearing cowboy boots even at my own wedding, except Jules' wedding and the occasional dog show, it was unlikely that I would have been seen wearing a dress! I certainly hadn't felt like there was much to celebrate in the past few years, that would warrant such attire. This was a celebration of gratitude, our appreciation for these two men who made a huge difference for us, while helping us from farm to camper and finally home.

In the afternoon, Porch Guy hung a very important picture for me, at front and center on the kitchen wall. It is a 16 x 20-inch picture that used to hang in my parents' home. It is a picture of Digger – going in two directions at once! His front legs are out to the side one way and his back legs out to the side the other. It wasn't until we unpacked it and hung it on the wall, that I realized it was taken right outside the kitchen window; the yellow bricks of the Hohl house were the back drop! He may not have been able to come full-circle with us, but I did have this wonderful memory of our time here before.

We shared a beautiful and delicious meal together and then played some games. Before dinner, I had asked Scott if he would do me a huge, maybe awkward favour. I needed a witness to my signature on the separation agreement.

At the Hohl Place ~ Clayton holding Digger's picture taken twenty-five years earlier

My husband had actually signed a version of the separation agreement, it wasn't perfect but he actually signed something!! I was so excited I could hardly contain myself and asked if he would be willing to sign it along side of my signature. He agreed and we sat in the living room at a little table and went one more time through the agreement, to make sure there were no details snuck in. I put my signature on the paper and he witnessed it. I was almost free! Funny thing was, I was finally going to get my money! It had been held in trust for two years at 0% interest! How I had longed for that money to help me find a home, then the moment I got the home that I was supposed to have, the money followed, almost instantly. What I had thought was a curse, turned out to be the greatest blessing.

A few days later, Clayton and I were going to pick up meat chicks, hen chicks and ducklings after our weekly chiropractor session. Due to all the lockdowns and regulations, we had not been allowed to see my mother for eight long months. Now, we brought the little birds along with us to see Mom and we were a hit! Clayton said he was a real chick magnet! Mom can't remember much these days, but as she looked past the mask and into my eyes, I knew that my Mama recognized who I was and I felt glad. I was also happy, that I moved only thirty minutes away from her and would be able to visit her more often. That night I found another four-leaf clover.

When I drove Clayton to his dad's for the week-end, he was sitting in the front seat, for the first time since the accident. He said that he could see so much from the front seat! I told him that I look for Eagles while I am driving, but that maybe, that was a better job for *him* since I was actually driving! He did point out an Osprey at one point, so I had faith that he was on the job!

While we were coming up to the main road to turn towards Burford, we were discussing school. I asked him how he was feeling about it by now? He talked a little of his fears and then said, "You just want me to go there because it is the Home of the Eagles!" Yes, I said it is a really good sign from my standpoint! It is a large, small town, country school – where 20% of the children are horse and buggy Mennonites – a low key, down to earth, school where the people care about the individuals. I thought he could give it a go.

Just as we turned the corner, the anthem from my separation came on the radio! *Miss Me More*, by Kelsie Ballerini. Clayton yells out "*It's your song!*" Then he points to the sky and yells "EAGLE!!"

We were chasing the Eagle from the road as it flew ahead and over the trees, again and again. We were trying to get pictures for the entire song! Occasionally, I'd pull over to the side of the road when I would get a good view and then we were off again! Just as it was going out of view for the last time, my new favourite song came on the radio!! We looked at each other and cranked up the tunes! *Me without You*, the third release by *Tim and the Glory Boys* was blaring on the radio as we sang along together, flying on the wind with the Eagle. When the song was over I told him, "I am almost finished with my book!" The next day I found five more four-leaf clovers!

The very next night, I noticed that Isabella was hanging out in Digger's old house and not out with the sheep. I thought maybe she was just resting. In the morning, I went out and she was still in there. I looked closely at her and she looked a bit wet in one spot. I looked closer and I could see something moving. For some reason I stopped to listen. There were actually so many, that I could hear them. She was covered in maggots under her wool!

I called the vet and luckily, in only twenty minutes they were there to help. The vet spent hours shearing, hosing and scrubbing her. We dried her off a bit, she was slathered in a cream, sprayed directly - covered in antibiotic insecticide and then sprayed over with industrial fly spray. She was given Metacam for pain and then penicillin as well. I think it was all a lot for a body to take. The next day, she went downhill quite quickly. She waited until Clayton came home from his dad's place and within a few minutes she was gone. I was with her at the end and I am grateful to have shared in her passing, although I wish that she hadn't had to suffer so.

She was only twelve years old, the last daughter of my first llama, Iris. When Iris had passed away prematurely, she left Isabella's little brother, Irish, an orphan. Isabella nursed him alongside her own little one and raised them both, with a little help from me. She never stepped out of line in her life and always took her job of guarding the sheep very seriously. She was born down the road from her last resting place, but unlike Digger, did make the round trip. I was grateful for all the years we had together. She was the last of a long line of beloved llamas, whose names all started with the letter "I". She will be missed. With her loss, it completed the passing of all my original old animals from my life, before I was married. We were starting here fresh and new. We never gave up.

LEARN TO FARM WITH GEORGIA

As a child I had but one purpose – to be a farmer – with a dream to one day have my very own farm. As I am sure you know by now, I am not one to easily give up. I am sure that you have heard the saying "Where there is a will, there is a way." Although the journey was long and arduous, I kept on trucking down the road with faith and determination. To get to one's destination, there isn't always a map. Sometimes the GPS tells you to make a U-turn. Sometimes, the road has detours or speed bumps. Occasionally, you hit a dead end or "BRIDGE OUT" sign and once in a while, somebody hits you. You never know where the road will lead, until you get there.

My road lead me in a big circle. When my life fell apart, I needed to go back to the beginning – back home. I needed a safe place to land, to get my bearings and get back on my feet. Our fortunate and timely move back into the Hohl Place turned out to be our saving grace. It provided safety and security in a loving and familiar community. We came full circle and although it was the perfect place to repose, thankfully, it was not to be our final resting place!

With the wind at our back, we took the opportunity to be open to finding our perfect home, wherever that may lead. It took us a little farther afield than we had originally ever anticipated, but I am getting a little ahead of myself here. Let me back up.

With finally being settled and Clayton starting school, I was able to focus more on healing and creating our new future.

What could that look like? What am I capable of? What are my dreams?

I got down to business. For starters, I rewrote this book and I enlisted a business coach to help me get *Learn to Farm* off the ground. Working on both of those things took up the majority of the winter. By mid-November, I was blessed with seeing an Eagle and felt that things were starting to shift again. At the beginning of December, I drove to Hamilton, to finally get closure with the accident from years earlier. I was ecstatic to view a huge Eagle as I drove along the water on my way there. That day finally marked the end of the dark night of my soul, or so I thought. Either way, it was time to move on.

I was finally ready to add a Jersey heifer to our family. I wasn't in a rush, but I was open to finding the perfect one for me. I wasn't ready to start milking just yet, but wanted to plan ahead for the future, when I had my own place. I looked on Kijiji, but had seen nothing of interest there, so I gave a friend my specific list of requirements in case she came across such a rare find. Only one hour later, I thought I would have a quick look again at Kijiji – just in case. There were several new listings, all were young heifers from a dairy farm only half an hour away. One picture caught my eye instantly and I opened up the ad.

She was a uniquely spotted Jersey, from old style genetics out of the United States. She had A2/A2 parents and was raised organically on a 100% grass-fed only farm. She was young and small enough to work with being only eight months of age. She even looked like a miniature of my favourite cow Butter that I'd had to let go all those years earlier, but that was not all! My eyes just about popped out of my head when I saw her ear tag number. #1111. Holy crap. There she was. I bought her sight unseen and I was not disappointed. She turned out to be an absolute gem. Since it was close to Christmas when I picked her up, I named her Holiday. During the winter, she lived with the sheep and I was able to halter train her without issue. She is so very quiet and wonderful. Another blessing from the angels!

On New Year's Eve, I was hit with one curveball that I certainly did not see coming. I suddenly lost a close personal friend and trusted advisor. If you remember, it was my friend Karin from *De La Tierra Alta Kennels* in California that I was chatting with, when the Eagles first arrived at my house several years earlier. She was person that I got both Éowyn and Gandalf from in 2012. She was there with me every step of the way, supporting me originally as a breeder and then as a friend. We were at the point in our lives where we communicated in some way, almost on a daily basis. To so suddenly be without her, occurred as a tragic loss. Not only for me personally, but also for our breed. She was the one that originally brought the breed to the United States in 1996 and promoted it with the creation of the Pyrenean Mastiff Club of America. She supported all of her clients and helped to foster new breeders that were committed to quality and health, like she was. At the age of 58, after a very brief illness, she was gone. A shining light was snuffed out, leaving a dark hole in the Pyrenean Mastiff world in North America.

Even though I was no longer breeding, I did happen to be well-trusted in the dog world. Suddenly, people started to flock to me for information. Where to get a puppy? How to find breeding stock? How to be a breeder? So many people were lost, what was I to do?

Since I was already in the development stages of my new business *Learn to Farm*, I decided that I needed to include breeding advice in my new line up. In the same way that I would be consulting with beginner farmers to share the knowledge that I have accumulated, I could also offer to dog owners. Just because I wasn't able to breed them, didn't mean that I couldn't bring value to the breed. This was one way of honouring Karin, by keeping her vision for the breed alive and sharing the knowledge that she bestowed on me during our decade of friendship. No one could ever begin to replace Karin and the wealth of knowledge that she accumulated in her twenty-five years with our breed. I can only hope to foster new interest and a new generation of loving, competent and capable Pyrenean Mastiff breeders, able to serve and preserve these wonderful dogs.

The winter seemed long without my trusted friend to converse with and I threw myself into a new project, spent my days writing and kept myself extra busy for the next few months. With impending food shortages on the horizon, I started long term food preparations by investing in a couple of freeze dryers, which I kept going almost continually until the spring. On February 1, I had my ram "Red" loaded up in the trailer and was on my way to Ohmer's place, when I saw an Eagle on the way. I understood its message when I got home and found my divorce papers finally in the mailbox! I was long ready for that shift!

In March, continuing on my goal to become self-sufficient, Clayton and I decided to take the Firearms Safety Training to get our gun licenses. If we were to get very hungry, we could always hunt for food. After booking the course, I realized if I was getting a gun in order to shoot a rabbit, where would I find a rabbit? I'd been at the Hohl Place for almost a year and seen only one rabbit in that time! We'd all be quite hungry, if it was up to me to find a wild rabbit in order to be able to feed all of us! So, I decided perhaps it was time to start a new enterprise, meat rabbits! At least if I was hungry, I knew where the rabbit would be! On my way to pick up the rabbit cages, I saw an Eagle sitting in a tree by the roadside. It had been almost four years since the last time that had happened! The next day I saw another Eagle and knew I must be on the right track.

I called my old friend Bill, that I had gotten the Lincoln sheep and several pet rabbits from years earlier. I asked if he could fix me up with some top-quality meat rabbits. I like to do things well if I am going to do it at all and Bill has some of the best rabbits in the world. Back in the year 2000, one of his rabbits literally won the title of Best Rabbit in the World! I recently came across the picture of Bill with his winning rabbit and you should see the size of the grin on his face! Bill has had New Zealand white rabbits, longer than anyone else in Canada, so I figured I'd be getting about the best I possibly could!

It was in the spring also, that I realized that Clayton and I had not slept away from home in almost five years! I certainly hadn't since my trip to pick up the bull in North Carolina, other than the week in hospital, after the accident. Maybe it was time to make a big step and plan a vacation! We'd really wanted to go and see Jules in New Brunswick, so we thought we'd arrange a trip. Wow! Wouldn't that be fun?!

It was in a conversation with Jules, when it was mentioned that perhaps I should buy a place near them in New Brunswick! What a funny thought! I opened up the *Realtor.ca* website to look at where she lives, just for interest's sake. I was trying to zoom in on the map and the screen became frozen. All I could see was one road that seemed to go in all directions. Next time I spoke to Jules, she said, "Yes! That is the road that leads to St. Martin's!" Can you guess what number the road was? Highway #111.

It was after that day, that I expanded my search to include New Brunswick. I still looked in Ontario, but there was nothing to see. Not one property. It wasn't too long and I included Nova Scotia in my search as well – why not? My family used to drive to there every second summer to visit my mother's brother and their family. I still have about a dozen cousins there. It seemed strange to be thinking of living away from Ontario, but that is why we were going to at least do a drive through, to make sure we knew what we were getting ourselves into!

For several months, leading up to our trip, I looked at properties online every day. I sort of didn't want to find one before we got there, because then I would have to make the decision about buying it without seeing it, and I didn't like the feeling of that too much. I did have to learn to sleep on a flat bed in order to go, but it was worth it. It opened the world up for me. At the very least, we were going to use the trip to see the different areas and provinces and see how they felt. People suggest going to the area and checking it out, but that is fine if you are moving to a part of a city or a specific place that you want to live in. But a proper farm doesn't come along every day and I wouldn't know where it might show up! We decided to tour across the provinces and figured the right property would turn up, if it was meant to.

On June 27, 2022 we set off on our two-week adventure to the Maritimes. The next day, while driving through Quebec, for a brief moment, the scenery changed from trees to farmland. There were several wonderful farms with silos and we noticed an Eagle flying between them!   Clayton took that as a good sign, that we were on the right track to find our farm. We spent the second night in St. Andrews, New Brunswick and went on a whale watching adventure in the morning. The whales were nice, but I loved the two Eagles that we saw even more! Afterwards we went straight to Jules's place in St. Martin's, on the Bay of Fundy.

The next morning, Jules woke me up early, to go with her for a walk on the beach. I brought along my camera. There was an Eagle sitting on a tall tower. I was graced with the good fortune to be able to take the picture for the back cover of this book! I was able to view and photograph the Eagle and its mate, a few times in the days we spent with them. It was interesting to watch the Eagle in behavior, not often associated with a bird of prey. The bird was always preening itself, it really reminded me of our chickens back home. Different yes, but maybe not as different as I thought. It brought me another view and I felt a closer connection to the Eagles through it all. They were not to be feared or revered; we all have our place; we are all connected.

Later that day, Jules and her family took us on a long walk to a private beach, where people rarely visit. An Eagle was flying along in front of us at the shoreline. When we arrived at the beach, we had to climb down a bit of a cliff to get to it. Clayton put his shirt on a log and I placed our water bottles next to it on the sand and there it was!

I'd wanted to find one forever. Unbelievable! I grabbed it and swung around holding it over my head! "Look at this!"

My first Eagle feather! It was big. I had to be sure, so I looked it up on my phone. It was an all-black primary wing feather! I looked Jules in the eyes and said, "Did you leave that there for me to find?" She said, "No! I didn't walk for an hour and half when you weren't looking, to hide it there!" That was a rare find. It's stayed on the dash board of my truck ever since.

Once we left Jules' place we headed quickly out of New Brunswick. We did not see any area in that province that we would want to live in, and certainly didn't find any places to purchase. Once crossing the border into Nova Scotia, it was like the sun came out and beamed down on us. We were cutting over to the east to go to the beach and met with farm after farm. I felt much better than I did in New Brunswick that offered tree after tree. The following day we went on a sightseeing trip and came across another Eagle. We figured, we were going in the right direction!

On July 4, just after 11 o'clock in the morning, I stepped out of the front door of the hotel to look up and saw an Eagle flying right there in front of me! Wow! What a way to start the day! I walked across the parking lot to the truck and looked at my phone... 11:11 AM! Off to a good start, I thought.

Although we didn't know it at the time, an hour later, we were touring a group of large barns and what would someday become our new home! In that day, I saw three Eagles, or so I thought. It wasn't until later, when I got home and realized that I took a picture of a big black bird, that had flown close beside me at one beach we stopped at. It was also a Bald Eagle, but a juvenile. I had a four-Eagle day! That was a first for me. We toured by Jules' place on the way home to see the Eagles, but I did not see one again. I guess it's like my four-leaf clovers – I can't find them if I am looking!

I made an offer for that property on our way home from the trip. It was accepted and I closed the deal, becoming full owner of my very own, 22-acre farm on August 15, 2022! I thought it would have been the best time of my life, but for many weeks, I thought it might be the worst. I've heard it said that only those who fly high can land on a mountain top. Sometimes you have to circle it for a bit, before you can find the courage to land.

Just prior to the trip, I had a consultation with Dr. Khalsa, once again about Spotty. I feared that the HWF was no longer working. She said, "It's not." And prescribed two months worth of Doxycycline to be given twice daily, along with weekly doses of Injectable Ivermectin, orally. That should just about take care of the heartworm issue, once and for all. Spotty is very much in tune with my emotions and prior to the trip she was a mess. Upon our return, she has been feeling extremely well. I truly believe in my heart that this treatment will finally be the one that clears her of this long-drawn-out disease. If that was not to be the case, you know by now that I will not give up! Not on her, and not on me.

At the end of August, Clayton and I flew back to see our property and fell in love all over again. It's only a forty-five minute drive from the Halifax airport, so it will be easy for people to get there! The local school is fantastic beyond belief and the Atlantic Ocean is likewise only forty-five minutes away. I rented Clayton a surf board and a wetsuit, so he could try out surfing. On the way to and from the beach we finally saw Eagles again. We hadn't seen even one since our four-Eagle day when we found our farm.

For my birthday last year, Michelle had given me a really neat stuffed Eagle, which I had brought with us to the new house. The original owner was visiting and saw it sitting, looking out the master bedroom window. He pointed across the road into the valley and described how there are Eagles that nest in the trees along the river. It was another confirmation that this was the right place for us. Later on, with a little help from Frienda, a name for our new homestead was chosen - *The Sacred Eagle Farm*.

I'm always open to the shifts that the Eagles bring with them... but what I have learned through all this is that life happens in the space "between the Eagles." I am very grateful for the time that we get to spend with my mother this fall, before our move to the new farm.

Last evening, my sister Sue sent me a text message, saying she just drove by Ohmer's place and his sheep were out on the road! I called their farm, Esther answered and I told her about the escapees. She said, "Can you come?" Of course. So, Clayton and I drove over to help. Upon arriving, I noticed that of the sheep that were out, all of them had been mine, at one time or another. I knew their number or name, just by looking at them.

Clayton, Ohmer and I were standing together when a familiar black figure appeared. I pointed to the sky just above the roof of the single-story sheep barn and a slow flying Eagle was making its way along the rooftop.

"Is that a Bald Eagle?" Ohmer inquired. Of course it was. A few minutes later, it made a second appearance. It was flying so slowly, I wondered how it was even staying up! I was clear that this was again a full circle. Ohmer was with me when I saw my first Eagle and now this was the third time that he and I had seen Eagles together. The neat part was that this time, Clayton was there too. It was like my past and my future were being connected together. The circle is now complete and we can move on, to our new adventures in Nova Scotia.

Learn To Farm with the backdrop of *The Sacred Eagle Farm* is the culmination of a lifetime of dreams. I have always been inspired to teach about natural farming, but while I was doing it full-time, all day every day, there weren't a lot of opportunities. Although I have always been shy, I love offering my expertise about what I know, in my own environment. I guess I feel like I have been training for this business my entire life. I am looking forward to being able to share my gifts of knowledge with people young and old.

If someone were to ask me, when did I figure out my life's purpose? I'd have to tell them, "It was after the Eagles came."

The Sacred Eagle Farm in Nova Scotia

ACKNOWLEDGEMENTS

M ost importantly, I want to acknowledge you, the reader for flying with me through the pages of my journey. My desire is that you feel empowered to follow your dreams and find the courage just to take that first step, then the next and the next! The most important thing is to never give up and remember that anything is possible!

I want to acknowledge my son Clayton for being a brilliant young chef, keeping my belly full of his delicious and exquisite culinary creations. This beautiful child of mine, taught me about unconditional love. When he was little, he brought JOY to everyone he met – a stranger was just a friend he was about to meet. We were virtually inseparable for the first eight years of his life and then we were thrust into a role reversal. After the accident, he had to be resilient and resourceful, giving up most of his childhood activities in order to take care of me. Life was difficult for us for many years, but he has not given up. He came through it all with grace and charisma. My heart still melts every time I see his sparkling eyes and charming smile. I am extremely proud of my steadfast, beloved son.

First, I wish to acknowledge Ohmer, for being my friend. He is someone I can count on to tell me the way he sees a situation, but then offers encouragement to enable me to make my own decisions. I have appreciated his help and advice over all the years – whether I wanted it at the time or not. In addition to friendship, he afforded me a home and place for my animals on more than one occasion. For these things and many more, I am forever grateful.

I want to thank Jules Hare for guiding me to healing, for her friendship, and tremendous coaching. Although I still must spread my wings and flap, she provides me with a thermal to fly high. You can find her at www.cranialwaves.com.

I want to acknowledge my friend Daryl Donley for the many years of friendship and coaching. He really "gets" me. He has always known that I am capable of more than I think. He is also the wonderful photographer who captured that beautiful moment with Belle and I.

I am most grateful to Tim & The Glory Boys for giving me the inspiration to hang on while bringing the joy of music and dance into my life. It was a couple years after the accident, when I finally started to be able to listen to music again. They were there when I needed them most and now look forward to turning the radio on... "When You Know You Know!"

I appreciate Rita Grisani for the support at the dog shows over the years and after the accident. She has taken many wonderful show pictures and I am grateful for her permission to use them to show off my beautiful dogs' achievements.

I am grateful to my young friend Charlotte Reisiger for taking the wonderful picture of Clayton, the dogs and I, in October of 2020. Also, I could not have asked for a better person to pack, pack, unpack and repack with!

To my sister Brenda and her husband Shane, I credit them for saving me from the city, guiding me on the long road of natural farming and for helping me discover my love of birds. They gave me the perfect gift for Christmas in 1985, my sheep Georgian. I still have Georgian's relatives to this day and intend to continue, for all the days of my life. I am grateful to have been able to phone Brenda and ask "one quick question" hundreds of times throughout the years, which she always answered graciously before rushing back to work!

I wish to thank my sister Sue for inviting me to live with her family in Wellesley, when I was having a rough time in 1996. Without her generous offer – I would not have worked in the pig barn, may not have met Ohmer and my life would certainly have turned out differently! And I am especially grateful to Sue for making me "Grumpy Bear," my constant stuffed companion of almost forty years, who is still going strong.

I am extremely grateful to Frienda – known to the rest of the world as Brenda Backus. She has been my dearest and truest friend for two decades. She has listened whenever I needed it, offered advice when asked, accompanied me through all aspects of my divorce, every step of the way. I would likely not have made it through without her generous support. She is the most helpful person I know. Brenda has the biggest heart and I am so blessed, to be able to call her my friend and life assistant!

Special thanks to my friend and Realtor, Simone Caprice-Payne for sticking by us through thick and thin, after the accident, with Donnamira, finding a farm and more. I have appreciated her friendship and guidance over the years.

I am so grateful to Christine Hammill for being my wonderful friend and caretaker of one of our Pyrenean Mastiff puppies, Beren! And many thanks to her husband Dennis, for his help to find and set up the camper trailer – I could not have done it without them!

Thanks to Pastor Kara Carter from Wellesley Mennonite church, for permission to use the photo of me with my Border Collies, which was originally published in the church directory. I also appreciated the conversation about the origins of Mennonites.

I am grateful to Lisa Du Fresne, for allowing me to share her amazing conversation with my sheep Belle.

Untold thanks to Murray Bast, founder of Bio-Ag Consultants and Distributors in Wellesley, for being a pioneer of natural farming, healing with nutrition and homeopathics. His vision has helped many farmers get out of the pharmaceutical circus by putting nutrition first – a healthy animal does not require any drugs! If you are interested in Working With Nature ~ Naturally, visit www.Bio-Ag.com. Use the code: EAGLE to let them know I sent you.

I wish to thank Michelle Jantzi, for being a true friend with common sense and a great ability to perceive humour. I very much appreciated her stepping in to keep us from homelessness. I will always cherish our late-night talks in the dairy barn.

I want to thank my beautiful friend Alyssa DeLuna, a fellow author who easily provides me with strong encouragement and leadership. A conversation with Alyssa is like a hot bath with a good book – I always feel better afterwards.

I wish to thank my friend Judy Leon, who first and foremost has been a wonderful caretaker for two of my beloved Pyrenean Mastiff puppies. She was also gracious enough, to take time out of her busy schedule to proofread this book, which I very much appreciated.

And to my wonderful publisher, Sabrina Mesko from Arnica Press – I could not have done this without her. She took my giant manuscript and, after reading it carefully, used her strikeout key to take out that, which did not serve the purpose. She supported me in continuing to write a different story, one that is much more beneficial to my life and the world. For this I will be forever grateful.

I want to extend my heart felt gratitude to my friend and mentor, E.M. for his invaluable support through the years. Even though we've never met, I appreciate how he always makes time to chat when I need him to.

I cherish our dogs, Argibel the Basque Shepherd, Éowyn, Brandy, Spotty and Donnamira – our Pyrenean Mastiff protectors, for their unconditional love and companionship. They brighten each day with their positive outlook on life. And to our angels that have gone before us, may they rest in peace: Our beloved Pyrenean Mastiffs Araglas and Thorin; and our Border Collies: Wyatt, Harley, Ivy, Chakotay and Dirk who loved to work!

And finally, I want to acknowledge my trusted advisor, confidant, and colleague Karin (Haywood) – Graefe from De La Tierra Alta Kennels in California, who was lost without warning, too soon. She was a brilliant woman, whose friendship and guidance were immeasurable as I waded through the joys, trials, and tribulations of being the only Pyrenean Mastiff Breeder in Canada. Karin was a true friend and I miss her every day. May she Rest in Peace.

ABOUT THE AUTHOR

Georgia Barg is a down-to-earth, natural farmer originally from Ontario, Canada. She is the owner of *The Sacred Eagle Farm* in Nova Scotia.

Georgia was educated at Humber College in Equine Studies and holds a diploma in Farm Operations and Management from the University of Guelph. She has extensive experience, spanning over four decades, working with a multitude of species not limited to dogs, cattle, sheep, horses, pigs, llamas, goats, chickens, turkeys, ducks, peafowl, guinea fowl and many more.

Through her website *LearnToFarm.ca* and in person at her *Sacred Eagle Farm*, she shares her unique approach to managing animals naturally, while promoting a healthy environment, optimal care and thriving lifestyle for beginner farmers, homesteaders, ranchers and their animals.

Georgia was the only Pyrenean Mastiff Breeder in Canada, where she bred and showed her rare breed working livestock protection dogs for many years. In addition to beginner farmers, she now enjoys teaching and guiding beginner Pyrenean Mastiff breeders through her consulting business.

Georgia lives in Nova Scotia with her son Clayton, their five working dogs and menagerie of livestock.

Visit author websites:

www.LearnToFarm.ca

www.GeorgiaBarg.com

Made in the USA
Columbia, SC
06 December 2022

72356584R00250